CHRIST IN OUR HOME

VOLUME II

CHRIST IN OUR HOME

VOLUME II

Devotions for
Every Day of the Year

INTRODUCTION BY PETER ROGNESS

Augsburg Fortress
Minneapolis

CHRIST IN OUR HOME, Volume II
Devotions for Every Day of the Year

Editors: Mark A. Hinton, Gloria E. Bengtson, and James Satter
Cover image: PhotoDisc, copyright © 2005
Cover design: Marti Naughton and James Satter
Interior text design: James Satter

ISBN 0-8066-5124-5

The paper used in this publication meets the minimum requirements of American National Standard for Information Sciences—Permanence of Paper for Printed Library Materials, ANSI Z329.48-1984.

Manufactured in the U.S.A.

01   02   03   04   05   1   2   3   4   5   6   7   8   9   10

Contents

Introduction

You have either purchased or received as a gift this devotional book, which has a reading for every day of the year. You intend to regularly spend time turning yourself toward God and have your thoughts guided by some people you probably don't know, but who have written these one-page devotional meditations.

Holy Conversation

❖ *Some people would ask:* Why don't you simply read the Bible itself, and eliminate the middle step?

❖ *The answer is this:* Receiving the truths of Scripture *ought* to be done in conversation with others, not alone!

It started that way. Scholars tell us that the earliest writings now in the New Testament probably weren't actually written down until decades after the death of Jesus. How did these sacred truths survive in the meantime? Read the book of Acts or the New Testament letters, and you can't miss the way the Holy Spirit was lighting fires among the believers to tell the mighty acts of God! These stories were told person-to-person. There was no written Word, yet there was a Living Word. The "Word became flesh" (John 1:14), Jesus Christ, the proclamation of this gospel message, was alive and powerful.

The communication among these early Christians had a power, a holiness, and soon people read these early writings again and again in their gatherings. Some of the writings became our New Testament. But before they were holy writings, they were holy conversations!

This good news that the God of the universe has come to us in Jesus Christ, and comes to us still, has now been recorded in scripture for nearly 2,000 years. For three-fourths of that period, the only Bibles in existence were precious few hand-copied volumes, mostly in monasteries. Nobody simply sat down for morning devotions with their Bible. On a few occasions, they might be privileged to have someone read from an actual copy in special church gatherings. More often, the stories of the Bible were simply told. It was part of the holy conversation among the faithful.

I'm all for people taking time to read the Bible personally. I do, often. It's one of the blessings of our day that we can so easily have our own copies, and other study aids as well. But I'm also aware that the Bible's pages are full of people being drawn together into communities of faith. It's been that way from day one. Paul told Timothy, in one of those holy written conversations that later became part of the Bible, "Reflect on what I am saying, for the Lord will give you insight into all this" (2 Timothy 2:7). The words we speak to each other, even those words from Paul that later became part of our Bible, are human words, but God has always moved through these human words. It's the Holy Spirit's favorite channel of communication!

In this book, you are about to enter into daily conversation with others. Read the suggested Scripture verses. Then read what the writer that day has to offer you around that passage. The holy conversation begins as you are drawn into Scripture and the reflections of a brother or sister saint!

Then let those thoughts travel with you throughout the day, and become woven into your day. More holy conversations take place. Your faith isn't simply a narrow set of times and places when you do the "religious stuff," but becomes the eyes and ears and hands and feet of your entire day. All because your day is anchored in these moments of turning yourself God-ward, and entering into holy conversations.

How to use this book

If you have this book in your hands, chances are this isn't the first daily devotional you've ever used. Even so, let me share a few thoughts about how to use daily devotional times well.

❖ *Read only one at a time.* I know, it's easy to get behind, get out of routine, and then read a bunch to get caught up. Don't. If you do that, the thoughts will probably mush together, and none of it will stay with you for any length of time. Maybe try two distinct times of the day if you're driven to get caught up, but don't get compulsive. These are meant to be a respite from the pressures of our lives, not another pressure themselves!

❖ *Don't rush.* Carve out and protect the time of day you read. It doesn't have to be long. When I'm presiding over synod assemblies, there are a few agenda items that are called "orders of the day"—when we stop whatever else we're doing and turn to that item. Try to let this be one of those times … inviolate, unrushed.

❖ *Do the Bible reading.* At busy times, you may be tempted to take the shortcut of not reading the Bible verses. Don't! Take the time to read the verses for the day.

❖ *Pray!* Take a deep breath and turn yourself God-ward. You needn't feel pressured to compose a letter to God. Just pray. (I like the saying, "Pray constantly—use words if you must.")

❖ *Enter into conversation with the writer.* Add your thoughts to theirs, argue if you want, and take their ideas another mile. Then bring it all with you as you move on with your day.

❖ *Remember this above all*—it isn't just these moments that are your "religious gig" for the day. These moments anchor you. But the rest of your day is God's as well, full of holiness—holy conversations and holy actions. You go to work, care for family, serve the poor, and share your faith in words and in the shape of your life.

In today's harried and fragmented society, even in our often harried and fragmented church, we need more holy conversations together. *Stop, read, reflect, pray.* And God will surely bless your holy conversation, and shape your holy living!

PETER ROGNESS
BISHOP, SAINT PAUL AREA SYNOD
EVANGELICAL LUTHERAN CHURCH IN AMERICA

God's lamp

Your word is a lamp to my feet and a light for
my path. ❖ Psalm 119:105

The old-fashioned lantern is a humble little light. I remember
using it so often as a boy when doing chores on the farm. Its
light seemed so dim and shone such a little way. But one thing
can be said for the old lantern. It gave sufficient light for the
next step! If one carried the lantern while walking, it was
satisfactory because the light moved on a way, always enough
for another step. When one thinks seriously about life, one is
led to ask, "Isn't that all the light one needs—enough for that
next step?" Yes, God cannot reveal our life plans all at once.
We could not bear it if God did. But God reveals as much as
we are capable of receiving.

The Bible does not fall completely open at any single
moment. In fact, the most seasoned student of the Word must
live with its many mysteries still. But the Bible sheds the light
for the next step. Faithful use of the Bible will yield the daily
light of truth and the daily measure of power that you
and I will need. Let us not pout and grumble about mystery.
Let us rather love God's mysteries and follow God even
where we cannot fully see. Let us happily carry the lantern of
God's word!

GERHARD E. FROST

*God in heaven, give us this day the humble trust that is
needed if we are to walk faithfully with you. Amen*

Prayer concern: Teachers

Daily Reflections

Glass grass

[God] sends his word and melts them; he stirs up
his breezes, and the waters flow. ❖ Psalm 147:18

On rare days in the cooler parts of our world, nature puts a
coat of icy glaze on everything from the tallest tree to the
smallest blade of grass. This requires perfect temperatures—
warm enough for rain to fall but cold enough for it to freeze
when it hits a surface. The grass resembles glass and appears
to be hiding itself from the world under the ice. Only a warm
breeze that melts the ice can show us the grass as it is.

We humans are like the grass. We put a protective coating
around ourselves so that no one can see the real us. Because
people tend to relate to the image we show them, very few
people ever get close to us because we come across as rather
cold individuals. For some people a remarkable thing happens. As the Bible says, God sends forth the Word and melts
them; God makes the wind blow and the water flow. One word
from God, through a friend, a book, or a thought, melts the
cold pretending image. Tears of joy begin to flow as one dis-
covers that God is loved for who God is and not for what God
pretends to be. Thank God for warm winds over glass grass.

DENNY J. BRAKE

Warm wind of God, blow over us and melt all insincerity,
that we may love you as we are, and be loved as we are.
Amen

Prayer concern: Those struggling with anxiety

Daily Reflections_____
_____
_____
_____

Running away

> Then the man and his wife heard the sound of the
> LORD God as he was walking in the garden in the
> cool of the day, and they hid from the LORD God
> among the trees of the garden. ❖ Genesis 3:8

Sometimes people say it is hard to find God. For many people,
it is more difficult to lose God. The first people started this
business of running away. They tried to hide, but of course
they fooled only themselves. God's "Where are you?" found
them out. Jacob tried running away. So did Moses, and David,
and Paul. God always found them. How much of today's hustle
and bustle is just a running away from God? How much of the
use of alcohol and drugs is an attempt to get away from
reality, where God must be faced? How much of our criticism
of others is a way of running away from our responsibility
toward them?

Most of us never lose the inclination to "get lost," even
when we have been found by Christ. We hide in the bushes
when we know a clear word for God is needed. We run away
when the time comes to stand and be counted on an important
but unpopular issue. It is a peculiar thing about people.
Although we love to run and hide, like children playing hide
and seek, we are not really happy until we are found.

DAVID W. PREUS

*Save us from the solutions sought by running away from
you, dear God. Amen*

Prayer concern: Those running away from God

Daily Reflections_____

_____

_____

_____

Knowing God's purpose

You are my friends if you do what I command.
❖ John 15:14

There is a story about a foreman who asked his crew to dig a hole at a street corner. But after the workers dug a hole about eight feet deep and six feet square, the foreman told them to fill it back up. Then the foreman asked the crew to dig a hole in another spot, and the same thing happened. After digging a dozen holes in this manner, the workers refused to dig any more. Then the foreman told the workers they had to continue digging because it was very important to locate a certain gas main. The engineer's map showing its location had been lost, and the only way they could find the gas main now was by digging in the area where they thought it was located. After learning the purpose of their work, the crew was ready to return to their task with determination and enthusiasm.

Living a Christian life involves taking part in God's work in the world. To take our part in God's work means we must know God's purpose. The first and crucial step for those who want to develop a plan for their mission as Christians is to agree on a statement of purpose, which might begin, "Our understanding of God's purpose is …" The Bible reading for today should stimulate the discussion.

ARNOLD R. MICKELSON

By your Holy Spirit increase in us true knowledge of you and of your will, and true obedience to your Word. Amen

Prayer concern: Laborers

Daily Reflections_____

_____

_____

_____

Sufficiency and abundance

> The manna stopped the day after they ate this food from the land; there was no longer any manna for the Israelites, but that year they ate of the produce of Canaan. ❖ Joshua 5:12

An old joke tells of a man trapped on the roof of his house during a flood. Praying for help as the waters rise, he refuses the aid of a boat, then refuses the aid of a helicopter. Waiting for help from the Lord, the man remains on the roof until the flood sweeps him away. The punch line comes as the man confronts God with his disappointment, to which God replies, "I sent a boat and a helicopter—what more did you want?"

The children of Israel had learned that divine providence takes many forms. During their long journey in the desert, manna sustained them. There was sufficient food for each day, no more and no less. When they arrived in Canaan, the produce of the land was available. The Lord would provide for them in a different way. Here they could raise crops with God's blessing—even enjoy abundance in their new home.

Many people desire abundance far more than sufficiency. It is easy to consider "just enough" to be a disappointment when our wish is for "too much." Like the people of Israel, we need to learn gratitude for all that God provides—be it ample or sufficient.

DONNA HACKER SMITH

Thank you Lord, for your abundant blessing. Amen

Prayer concern: Those who work to alleviate hunger

Daily Reflections

Lord, teach us too

> My prayer is not for them alone. I pray also
> for those who will believe in me through their
> message. ❖ John 17:20

Jesus believed in prayer, and the disciples urged him to teach them what he knew and did so faithfully. The prayers of Jesus were not selfish but keyed in to the needs of others. John 17 is a beautiful example of the spirit of the Savior's prayers. It can widen the horizon of our own intercessions as well.

The church should be the circle of our concern, but it is so easy to circumscribe the circle to those nearest ourselves. We need to lengthen the radius and enlarge the circumference to embrace the needs of all people. Jesus did this. He prayed not only for those who had come to faith in him but also for those who had not, praying that they might. We are told to enlarge our petitions and intercessions even to include our enemies and to pray for those who abuse us.

What a transformation could and would take place in the church and in the world if we exercised the prayer policy of our Lord and did so at the same level of honesty and sincerity. Then pride and prejudice would be conquered and the barriers to our brothers and sisters of another race or culture would be obliterated.

HERBERT NOTTBOHM

Dear God, grant us the spirit of the Christ and widen the horizon of our intercessions. Amen

Prayer concern: Honesty and sincerity

Daily Reflections

Shame

> In you, O LORD, I have taken refuge; let me never
> be put to shame. ❖ Psalm 71:1

Shame is that dark, desperate place where we land when we lose sight of the fact that we are created in God's image. Shame is the belief that we have no value and have fallen beyond the grace and love of God.

It is understandable for anyone who has experienced shame that this prayer for deliverance asks first for a deliverance from shame. Cruel people, difficult circumstances, or our own mistakes can push us into this abyss. The antidote for shame is found in standing fast on the belief that we are of value to God no matter how deep our transgressions or how extreme life's circumstances may be. The antidote is found in trusting that God will not desert us.

God created us and walks with us from birth to death. Nothing can separate us from the love of God in Christ Jesus. This is the rock of our saving hope and our confidence in life. Let that light drive away all fear and shame.

CAROLYN MOWCHAN

Jesus, deliver me from the grip of self-loathing when I fail. Be a mirror of gentleness and grace. Amen

Prayer concern: Those who cannot see God's goodness in themselves

Daily Reflections_____

_____

_____

_____

What's the Bible for?

So that the man of God may be thoroughly
equipped for every good work. ❖ 2 Timothy 3:17

What's the Bible for? Take a minute to give your answer. Do
you agree with Paul, that it is for teaching, correcting, and
training us in righteousness? But these purposes are to have
another result: to equip us for every good work.

It is easy to get the idea that reading the Bible is an end in
itself. We may persuade ourselves that if we go through a few
verses for daily devotions or sometimes read parts of the
Bible for a class, that we've more than done our duty. Well,
any amount of reading is a start, but it is only the beginning.
And if we don't read with the idea of doing something on
the basis of what we read, it probably isn't a helpful beginning.
We are to read the Bible for a purpose: to learn God's will—
then to do it. We learn of God's love and how to respond.
We read to be equipped.

Equipped to do what? To do what God wants us to do. To
do what we would do—what Jesus did while on earth. To
serve our neighbor. If it doesn't lead to this, something isn't
getting through.

ROLF E. AASENG

*Help us, Lord, to discover your will for us in the Bible.
Amen*

Prayer concern: Bible translators

Daily Reflections_____

_____

_____

_____

Guidance

For with you is the fountain of life; in your light
we see light. ❖ Psalm 36:9

My husband and I were on the last leg of our journey, driving
back to Minnesota from Washington. The weather had been
pleasant and traveling had been fine.

Then, without any warning, an early March snowstorm hit.
The snow that suddenly whipped through the night sky
forced us to slow to a crawl. The snow blinded us. For every
flake removed by the windshield wipers, 20 or more would
seem to appear.

Only one thing gave us direction: the yellow stripe in the
center of the road. The color was bright enough to pierce
through the storm and guide us finally to a place where we
could safely wait it out.

Similarly, by God's light we find guidance for our way
through life. What does life mean? Is life of value? Is there
hope for life to come? The light God gives through the Word
and through his Son pierces our darkness. We see how to live
now, and how to find our way home.

KAREN BATES

Lighten our darkness, Lord. Amen

Prayer concern: Those tempted to lie or cheat

Daily Reflections

Take a stand

But as for me and my household, we will serve
the LORD. ❖ Joshua 24:15

We have a stake in the quality of other people's lives. When
I see others living beyond their pay, it becomes easier for me
to charge items I really cannot afford. When I see others
saying "no" to taking a drink or choosing a walk instead of
a rest on the couch, it is easier for me to make a healthful
choice for myself.

It is the same in our life of faith. People who risk revealing
something of their relationship with God inspire me to risk
that too. People who do not talk in faith language tempt me to
remain silent as well. It is refreshing and yet also challenging
to have a Joshua around who boldly lets it be known where he
stands on an issue of faith.

KATHY M. HAUEISEN

*We confess, Lord, that we are not always comfortable
with people who put their faith on the line. May we be
willing to risk testing whether we are choosing you or
some lesser god this day. Amen*

Prayer concern: Our families

Daily Reflections_____

_____
_____
_____

The Holy Trinity

But when he, the Spirit of truth, comes, he will guide you into all truth. ❖ John 16:13

When we are confronted with the trials and tribulations of life, it is easy to believe several lies. We might begin to think that God does not care, God is too far away to even know about our struggles, or God is powerless to help us. When confronted with our sinfulness, we begin to believe the lies that we are no good, that we are failures, or that we have sinned so greatly that God will never forgive us.

Praise be to God, who has sent the Holy Spirit into our lives! The Holy Spirit proclaims to us that God, the God of creation, is a powerful God. The Spirit reminds us that God, who lived, died, and rose again that we might have a new life, is a loving God. The Spirit makes evident God's presence in our lives and God's forgiveness.

KEVIN E. RUFFCORN

Dear Lord, by the power of the Holy Spirit enable us to stand firm in the truth. Amen

Prayer concern: Christian counselors

Daily Reflections _____

_____

_____

_____

Hearsay or experience?

My ears had heard of you but now my eyes have
seen you. ❖ Job 42:5

The Grand Canyon is one of the world's greatest wonders!
As a young tot I had heard of it, and through the years I read
about that sublime yet awesome chasm in travel literature
and *National Geographic* magazine. But still it was far away
and, in a sense, unreal.

One Tuesday morning found us on Route 64 heading
north from Williams, Arizona. About noon I saw the Grand
Canyon for myself. I walked along the rim and looked with my
own eyes upon those incomparable views from Yavapai, Hopi,
Mohave, and Grandview Points. Here was one of the earth's
outstanding spectacles. Nothing else is quite like it in form,
size, glowing color, and breath-taking grandeur.

What a difference there is between hearing about Grand
Canyon and seeing it for oneself. The Christian faith is like
that. There is a vast and eternally significant difference
between hearing about Jesus and his church and knowing
him and his fellowship through personal experience.

PAUL A. ADAMS

*Lord Jesus, grant that we may know you for ourselves and
not merely hear about you. Help us to love and obey you
and thereby know you well. Amen*

Prayer concern: Christian witnesses

Daily Reflections_____
_____
_____
_____

Sabbath people

> Then [Jesus] said to them, "The Sabbath was made
> for man, not man for the Sabbath." ❖ Mark 2:27

All over the country, congregations are finding opportunities for mission. In one town, the church has opened its doors to people who are mentally ill, seeking to meet their needs for basic human dignity and compassion. Christians respond out of their belief in God as one who stands with all, including those often shunned by society. They offer no magic formulas or extraordinary programs. Their gift is a hand to hold, a song to sing, or a friend with whom to talk.

Our Sabbath, our day of re-creation, is a day for mission. No longer divided by stereotypes and prejudices, we are freed to love our neighbors as ourselves. The Lord of the Sabbath is the Lord of all creation. God calls us forth from the death and decay of self-centeredness to work in the arena of creation in which we live. God has re-created us through the power of the gospel. Creation awaits children of the Sabbath to bring hope, justice, and love.

W. Bruce Wilder Jr.

Lord, may your Spirit free us from fear and prejudice and enable us to love without ceasing. Amen

Prayer concern: People living with mental illnesses

Daily Reflections_____

_____

_____

_____

Storms

> [Jesus] got up, rebuked the wind and said to the waves, "Quiet! Be still!" Then the wind died down and it was completely calm. ❖ Mark 4:39

I often choose to walk to my destinations rather than drive. I concentrate on how long it will take me and sometimes forget about the weather. One night I had walked to a meeting. When leaving, I looked only ahead and did not notice the dark clouds coming from behind. When I was about halfway home, lightning started to flash, and the wind almost pushed me over. I was frightened. What should I do? I decided to keep walking, hoping I'd make it home before the rain started. If the lightning got worse, I would knock on someone's door and ask for shelter. I felt very alone and insignificant.

Today's text reassures us that Jesus has power over all life forces, and God still controls the universe. We do not think about that very often, especially when occupied in day-to-day activities. In fact, it's easy to forget about God's control when we live so immersed in technology. But put us in the middle of a storm, we will call out to God for help.

MARLYS A. KORMAN

Dear God, thanks for the reassurance that you are in control. Amen

Prayer concern: Runaway children

Daily Reflections_____

_____

_____

_____

The heritage of love

As the Father has loved me, so have I loved you.
Now remain in my love. ❖ John 15:9

Our family was pretty poor as far as money was concerned, but we were rich in love. Our economic hardships seemed to pull us closer together, and our love grew even stronger. We claimed one another's love as our heritage.

Is there any better heritage to pass on than love? Love is certainly a learned response, but no textbook teaches love as well as the experience of being loved. When our families and friends love us, we receive a heritage of unfathomable value.

Jesus was a vessel of love. Jesus passed on the love he had received from God to those he called his disciples. The love of Jesus overflowed into the people of the countryside. This love also led Jesus to the cross where he gave himself in the ultimate act of love for you and me that we might have eternal life.

ROD C. BRODING

Thank you, Jesus, for loving us and for showing us what kind of God we have. Amen

Prayer concern: To live in God's love

Daily Reflections_____
_____
_____
_____

My happy home town

They will be called the Holy People, the
Redeemed of the LORD. ❖ Isaiah 62:12

Try to imagine real happiness ... the joy of a Kansas farmer
when hail clouds pass by without unleashing their fury ... the
smile of a Detroit factory worker with a large family, as he
returns to work after a three-month layoff ... the rejoicing of
a Miami couple after the birth of their first child ... the thankfulness of a Seattle family that just made the last payment on
their home ... the joy of a man in Kalamazoo who hears a
woman say "yes" to that important question ... the happy
tears of a Daytonian who was blind and now sees.

These experiences represent happiness in many places.
Now add them up. Then multiply them by the national debt.
The result? All the happiness this world holds is but one
drop in the sea of happiness that is the eternal Jerusalem, the
city of those who have been redeemed by Christ, purchased
by his blood, and won for God. The city described by Isaiah is
not alone the one located at 31 degrees east longitude. It is
not only the city built on the four hills of Acra, Bezetha, Zion,
and Ophel. Isaiah speaks also of the happiest city—the city
we may claim as our hometown. It is eternal and wonderful.
God is there, beckoning to us.

OMAR BONDERUD

*O King of Jerusalem, bless us, our pastors, and our fellow
believers as we await the holy city. Amen*

Prayer concerns: Our cities

Daily Reflections_____

_____

_____

_____

Vengeance

Do not take revenge, my friends, but leave room for
God's wrath, for it is written: "It is mine to avenge;
I will repay," says the Lord. ❖ Romans 12:19

"He hit me first!" is a familiar retort when a parent tries to
intervene in a children's scuffle. Retaliation comes instinctively to us. Satan wants us to strike back, return injury for
injury, and repay evil for evil. Our sinful nature encourages
us to think that revenge is sweet.

Scripture tells us otherwise. Over and over in the New
Testament, we are entreated to turn the other cheek, forgive
seventy times seven, love our enemies, and pray for those
who persecute us. What this really does is remind us that God
is the judge, and that we are not. There is no justice when
individuals seek vengeance. Nor is there justice when a
nation's legal system is subverted to the idea of getting even.

Words are fascinating bits of language to study and think
about. Many words are very apt, sounding like they should
sound for their definition and purpose. So revenge sounds like
the idea it is—harsh, bitter, and unsatisfying.

JULIETTE R. MORTENSON

*Forgiving and loving God, fill our hearts with so much
forgiveness and love that there will no longer be room for
animosity and hate. Amen*

Prayer concern: Those with vengeful hearts

Daily Reflections_____

Telling it like it is

I know your deeds, that you are neither cold
nor hot. I wish you were either one or the other!
❖ Revelation 3:15

How easy it is to be a fence-straddler, to be on two sides at the
same time. We hate to commit ourselves one way or the other,
because either way we disappoint someone. But Jesus tells us
that the person who refuses to take a stand either way is the
person who is hardest to take. To say "no" to Jesus means we
have taken him seriously yet decided to have nothing to do
with him. But to say "maybe" indicates that we'd simply rather
ignore him and go through life with no firm convictions. The
fact is that we can't be on two sides. If we refuse to say "yes"
to Jesus, we are living out a "no," even if we say "maybe."

But Jesus doesn't give up on us. Jesus knows that the
abundant life that we were created for can be known only in
relationship with God, and he continues to offer us the chance
to live in that relationship. "I stand at the door and knock,"
Jesus says. Let's quit playing games with his love and mercy.
Let's throw the door wide open and invite him to come in and
take over the whole works of our life. In that relationship with
Jesus, the abundant life is ours. He still offers us the chance
today to live that kind of life.

PERRY S. HANSON

Lord, come in and take over my life. Amen

Prayer concern: Those struggling to make a decision

Daily Reflections

A father's heartache

Do not be afraid, for I am with you; I will bring
your children from the east and gather you from
the west. ❖ Isaiah 43:5

As I write this late in the summer of 2003, by wife and I are
still awaiting the return of our son from Iraq. He is a U.S.
Marine and has been in the region since January 2003. For
more than 40 days, we did not hear from him or know how he
was. All we knew came from scattered news reports and the
Internet.

These words of Isaiah were a sermon for a people in exile
in that land we now call Iraq. He prophesied to a people who
were frightened by forces that swirled about them like the
fire. On many days during the war, I read aloud Isaiah's poem.
I read it for myself. I read it for my son. I read it for the honor-
able soldiers from both sides who were engaged in the terror
of war. I read it for the innocents. Tears often dropped on the
page as witnesses to a father's heartache.

In such times, there is nothing a parent hopes for more
than the safe return of a child. Like a human parent, God's
heart aches for the safe return of God's own sons and daughters "from the ends of the earth" (v. 6). God will make the
promised homecoming a reality.

THOMAS S. HANSON

Rescue us, Lord, from violence of our age. Amen

Prayer concern: Those who seek peace and justice

Daily Reflections_____

_____

_____

_____

Through wind and snow

Lightning and hail, snow and clouds, stormy
winds that do his bidding. ❖ Psalm 148:8

Drive through the seemingly endless prairies of Alberta and
Saskatchewan in September, and you will behold a beautiful
sight. Fields of wheat and barley as thick as you can imagine,
as far as you can see. Favorable weather in the spring and
summer go a long way to make those crops so rich. But many
people forget that it is the snows of a long, cold winter that
provide the subsoil moisture to make such bounty possible.
The cold, biting winds that bring the heavy snows of January
fulfill God's command to let the earth yield its harvest.

People's lives can be like those fields. Not only the warm
and pleasant days but also the hard and stormy days of life
bring truth from God that can yield fruits of faith. Tough days
are reason to praise God's goodness as much as good days,
even though the harvests of our lives may seem far away. Ask
any farmer and the answer will be the same—winter's winds
and snows make autumn's harvest great.

JON TEMME

*Give us faith, God, to praise you during the snowy and
stormy times of our lives, trusting that in your plans these
difficult days also will yield your love. Amen*

Prayer concern: Those who work in dangerous weather

Daily Reflections_____

_____

_____

_____

Ignorance is bliss

> I have much more to say to you, more than you
> can now bear. ❖ John 16:12

Jesus and his disciples are together in the upper room, and the time for Jesus' arrest is drawing near. Jesus has told the disciples much, but he has not told them everything. A person can almost imagine the disciples pleading with Jesus to tell them more.

Because of his love for the disciples, Jesus does not tell them all that he knows about what is to come. What would he tell them? He could tell them of the despair that they will feel at his death. He could tell them of the hardships they will encounter as they travel to distant cities to spread the gospel. He could tell them of the specific persecutions that await each of them. Instead, Jesus assures the disciples of his love and promises to send them the Holy Spirit.

Often we want to know too much. We want to know what the future holds for us. All we need to know is that God loves us and goes with us.

KEVIN E. RUFFCORN

Lord, take my hand and walk with me. Amen

Prayer concern: People who are new in our lives

Daily Reflections

Grace and blessing

[Anna] gave thanks to God and spoke about the
child to all who were looking forward to the
redemption of Jerusalem. ❖ Luke 2:38

A Christian friend of ours is a photographer for a major newspaper in a large city. Several years ago she became seriously
ill, and the doctors doubted that she would live. When her
health was restored, the thanks and praise she felt toward
God could not be hidden.

When she returned to work, she was even more radiant
than before. Everyone noticed. One person in her office
finally came to her and said, "I have noticed for a long time
that you have always had something that I do not have. What
is it that makes you this way? I want the joy you have." My
friend told her about her faith in Christ.

When we are filled with thanks to God for his blessings to
us, our lives will show it. Telling our faith story can be done
simply. It should follow quite naturally our experiences of
God's grace and blessings.

Anonymous

*Holy God, give us thankful hearts and readiness to tell
others of your amazing love. Amen*

Prayer concern: Your family

Daily Reflections_____

_____

_____

_____

Thank you

> In that day you will say: "Give thanks to the LORD.
> call on his name; make known among the nations
> what he has done, and proclaim that his name is
> exalted." ❖ Isaiah 12:4

You receive a thoughtful, unexpected gift from someone who cares. Not only are you touched, but you also feel an urge to do something in return.

This is also the believer's reaction to God's "indescribable gift" (2 Corinthians 9:15), God's Son and our Savior. Who can match that gift? In response, we can be thankful. We can act. We can and will "make known his deed among nations, proclaim that his name is exalted."

There's an old saying that goes, "It's too good to keep." The good news that "God was reconciling the world to himself in Christ" (2 Corinthians 5:19) is too good to keep to ourselves.

KARL T. SCHMIDT

Lord Jesus, help us once again to see the outpouring of your love for us, to receive it with thanksgiving, and to share it with those who are still in darkness. Amen

Prayer concern: Christians in Ethiopia

Daily Reflections_____

_____

_____

_____

Personal encounter

As Jesus was walking beside the Sea of Galilee,
he saw two brothers, Simon called Peter and
his brother Andrew. They were casting a net into
the lake, for they were fishermen. ❖ Matthew 4:18

Evangelism is really no different now than it was when Jesus
walked the countryside and called Peter, Andrew, James,
and John. It is a personal encounter between people where
they are. Authenticity is all that is required as each believer
shares his or her faith in language and actions that are real.
Evangelism happens right where you are: at school, at home,
at the factory, in the office, in the church narthex, or at the
athletic field. It is the proclamation in word and deed that God
is good and gracious and has invaded our world.

No magic formulas, no gimmicks, and no advanced
training are required. God has placed us in settings filled with
evangelical possibility. Each of us is an evangelist by virtue of
our baptism into Christ. We have more than a model in Jesus,
who met people in the midst of everyday life and invited them
to participate in God's saving love. We have a Savior who died
on a cross to bring us that love in forgiveness of sin.

W. BRUCE WILDER

Give us fresh words to speak of your grace, O God. Amen

Prayer concern: Non-Christian friends and relatives

Daily Reflections_____

_____

_____

_____

Hard weather

> But the Lord is faithful, and he will
> strengthen and protect you from the evil
> one. ❖ 2 Thessalonians 3:3

Life itself brings "hard weather." Tragedies come without warning. Suffering comes even though nobody is at fault. Injustice abounds without anyone planning it. Death, with its muddy boots, stalks uninvited into every home. To our dismay, the lights about us seem to go out.

What can we do? We can go directly to God and rest on the clear revelation of God's word. God is faithful and will strengthen and guard us. When we are at our wits' end, God is not perplexed. We may draw on God's power in life's darkest moments and in our lowest moods if only we will trust God. Is this religious stoicism with a touch of fatalism? No, it is Christian truth, at its realistic best, ready to meet any crisis that life can bring. Peace comes to us as we put God back in the driver's seat. In his care we see all losses as temporary.

NANCY S. WILLIAMSON

O God, may we find strength this day in your everlasting arms. Amen

Prayer concern: Those in military service

Daily Reflections_____

_____

_____

_____

Silence is not golden

For Zion's sake I will not keep silent. ❖ Isaiah 62:1

When did you last keep quiet when you could have shared your faith, then realized that exact opportunity would never come again? The prophet Isaiah boldly declared, "I will *not* keep silent." Isaiah deeply felt his responsibility to the people he served. Nothing would still his message until the day of salvation dawned. Isaiah was God's spokesperson to those who lived in the darkness of exile. He kept alive the hope of release and salvation.

God still uses messengers of mercy, justice, and hope—but with an added dimension! Through Christ, God gave us the Holy Spirit, the power with which to accomplish our unique, individual task in mission. We must not be silent. Sharing can take a variety of shapes: quiet, gentle words; restraint and caution; unsophisticated simplicity; enthusiastic and joyful expression; ecstasy and excitement; perception and sensitivity; comfort and compassion.

JANET E. REINHARD

Help me to share words of grace and love every day, Lord. Amen

Prayer concern: Campus ministries

Daily Reflections_____

_____

_____

_____

Conviction

Peter and the other apostles replied: "We must obey God rather than men!" ❖ Acts 5:29

Popular culture continues to reinforce a popular song lyric from the 1970s: "It can't be wrong when it feels so right." When we follow this motto, our lives easily become like rivers without banks, spilling out in undefined directions.

While we cannot always find specific answers in the Bible, God has set down guidelines for godly living. God's word is a "lamp to my feet and a light for my path" (Psalm 119:105). Our adherence to these guidelines springs from our love of Jesus Christ. Ironically, we are not free when we choose to live independently of God, following our friends or our culture. We are free only as we hear the Holy Spirit and follow God's word.

Our first loyalty is to God, no matter what our other loyalties may demand. Peter's statement to the Sanhedrin said as much. He knew the cost. But Peter also found that God honored his courage and gave him strength to carry on.

CONRAD M. THOMPSON

Dear God, help us to love you and obey. Amen

Prayer concern: To live according to our faith

Daily Reflections_____

_____

_____

_____

Too much of a good thing

> The LORD said, "If as one people speaking the same language they have begun to do this, then nothing they plan to do will be impossible for them. ❖ Genesis 11:6

The story of the Tower of Babel foreshadows the First Commandment: You shall have no other gods. Idolatry is the fundamental sin. Idolatry is to worship the created rather than the Creator.

More damaging than the misuse of God's gifts is the subtle spoilage that occurs when we lavish too much attention on what is in itself good. That kind of idolatry is like addiction. It makes us preoccupied with one thing. It blocks out the primary interests, responsibilities, joys, and values God requires.

The family, for instance, is a wonderful gift and basic institution, but we can make our families so much the center of our concern and joy that God slips to a lesser place. In doing so, we have taken a good thing too far. We need God's grace and the Spirit's guidance lest we build our own Towers of Babel.

CARL L. JECH

Creator God, help us to worship only you. Amen

Prayer concern: Christians in the United States

Daily Reflections_____

A show of hospitality

While they ate, [Abraham] stood near them under
a tree. ❖ Genesis 18:8

It seems evident that the three men visiting Abraham represent a personal manifestation of God in visible form. When Abraham saw them coming, his response was a picture of politeness and hospitality. He ministered to them as a servant.

When Lord James Bryce (1838-1922), author of *The American Commonwealth,* came to the United States to work with Professor Jesse Macy of Grinnell College, he stayed with his collaborator for several weeks. The Macy household had no servants except for a part-time cook. However, Lord Bryce, on the basis of the experience in English country houses, assumed there would be someone to shine his shoes if he left them outside his door. Macy took the shoes and shined them himself every evening. The distinguished British statesman and scholar never knew that his host had also been his servant.

Be hospitable!

JAMES R. BJORGE

Lord, may I be gracious and generous with those who visit me. Amen

Prayer concern: Christians in Cuba

Daily Reflections_____

Ready or not

You also must be ready, because the Son of Man
will come at an hour when you do not expect him.
❖ Luke 12:40

The military is renowned for its inspections. There are inspections for cleanliness, safety, and proper procedures. Young men and women just entering the service learn quickly that everything from their personal attire and living quarters to their places of work will be regularly inspected.

When the date and time of an inspection is known in advance, it is fairly certain that everyone will be prepared. But sometimes a surprise inspection comes up. Although all military personnel are supposed to be ready at all times, there are those who are caught off guard by these surprises.

Similarly, we Christians, as members of the body of Christ, are to be ready at all times for the greatest of all "inspections," Christ's coming. Although we have been warned to expect his return, the time of this visit has not been revealed. By giving our hearts to Christ and remaining faithful, we can be ready when he comes.

BARBARA M. WILLS

Son of God, help me to prepare for your coming and to remain in readiness always. Amen

Prayer concern: Those who work in banks

Daily Reflections_____
_____
_____
_____

By example

These twelve Jesus sent out. ❖ Matthew 10:5

When a family moved into a newly built house, the two sons were 5 years old and 18 months old. One big job that had to be done was to prepare the yard for seeding. The 5-year-old helped clear away the brush and rake over the dirt. He was old enough and big enough to follow his parents' example and be a real help.

At other times, however, the parents had to tell the 5-year-old not to do certain things, because his little brother would imitate him—trying to jump from a chair to a beanbag or running down the driveway into the street. Both boys were learning by example.

Jesus had taught his disciples what to do. The day would come, however, when he would no longer be physically present. The disciples would remember Jesus' instructions, but Jesus knew they would remember more clearly if they had exercised their ministry under his eye. So he sent them out to minister, to gain firsthand experience. We have been sent as well, with the example of our Lord before us.

MARY ELLEN LARSON

Keep us in your footsteps, Lord, as we minister to others.
Amen

Prayer concern: Seminary students

Daily Reflections_____

All lives are God's

For every living soul belongs to me, the father as well
as the son—both alike belong to me. The soul who
sins is the one who will die. ❖ Ezekiel 18:4

It may seem that God's total and absolute claim upon our lives
is too much, even unfair. But "all lives are mine," God says, and
God makes no exceptions. The creator of all things, God has a
loving right to us, whether we know it or not, or like it or not.

God's claim upon us is a wonderful thing. God claims not
only the good times in our lives but also those times that are
difficult—those times of sickness, despair, loneliness, grief,
guilt, and loss of hope and purpose. All of these we can bring
to the author of life. And then we can offer our times of joy,
success, and happiness, for these also belong to God.

Surely, we can be grateful for God's claim on us, which
extends through death and beyond. That is the assurance that
God gives us in Christ's death and resurrection. Neither sin
nor death can disrupt the fact that we belong to God.

As we come to recognize that all life is God's, we no longer
will see God's claims as too much or unfair. Rather, we will give
thanks precisely because our lives are in the hands of God.

JOHN W. COFFEY

Dear God, stake your claim upon us, and never let us go.
Amen

Prayer concern: The lonely

Daily Reflections_____

Don't worry

For nothing is impossible with God. ❖ Luke 1:37

Sometimes it seems like God's promises do fail. There are times when we feel as if God does not keep promises. We might have gone out on a limb in service to God, risking ourselves and our well-being for the sake of the gospel. And then we find ourselves threatened and in danger. We feel let down by God.

When that happens, it helps to recall the word *never.* Mary had just received the startling news that she would give birth to the Son of God, the everlasting king of Israel. She questioned God's promise because the fact that she was a virgin seemed to rule out her giving birth to *any* child.

"Don't worry," God's angel said. "Look, your elderly relative, Elizabeth, is pregnant. Nothing is impossible for God. Never say, 'Never.'"

That is a good word for us too. When our lives of service are packed with risk and uncertainty, we can recall Mary's experience with God. We can hear the guarantee for us: "For nothing is impossible with God." Then we can say, "We are your servants. May it be as you have said."

DAVID FRYE

When we doubt you, God, remind us that nothing is impossible, and help us to trust you. Amen

Prayer concern: Those who have doubts

Daily Reflections_____

_____

_____

_____

Godly optimism

> Therefore, since through God's mercy we
> have this ministry, we do not lose heart.
> ❖ 2 Corinthians 4:1

We call some people "born optimists" because they always believe that things will work out. They seem to pay little attention to the facts, yet persistently hold that everything will turn out fine.

Paul's optimism was based rather on some solid facts which had been validated in his previous experience. The grace of God had been manifested in his life many times. Paul had escaped from hostile crowds, was rescued from a shipwreck, and endured numerous other hardships because of the gospel. Therefore, he could say that by God's mercy and grace he did not lose heart.

Paul could confidently say these words: "I can do everything through him who gives me strength" (Philippians 4:13); "If God is for us, who can be against us?" (Romans 8:31); "[Nothing] will be able to separate us from the love of God that is in Christ Jesus our Lord" (Romans 8:39b).

We need godly optimism, like Paul's.

ROBERT LONG

Lord, because of you, we do not lose heart. Nothing can separate us from your love. Thank you for that promise. Amen

Prayer concerns: Christians in Korea

Daily Reflections_____

_____

_____

_____

Doxology

Let the saints rejoice in this honor and sing for
joy on their beds. ❖ Psalm 149:5

A friend adopted a stray dog and gave him the unforgettable
name "Doxology." Out of gratitude, the dog followed his new
master everywhere. When my friend's brother died suddenly,
arrangements had to be made to board the dog elsewhere as
the family made hasty plans to drive across the state to attend
the funeral. On arriving at his brother's home, the grieving
widow met them at the door and asked, "Did you bring your
dog? Did you bring Doxology?"

"No," my friend replied, "I didn't think it appropriate."

"Oh, I wish you would have," responded the widow.
"Doxology always brings so much love."

My friend thought about that. *Why can't there be a doxology
even amid the sorrow and grief of death?* The doxologies of
life can be with us in whatever circumstances. Doxologies
should know no limitations. For doxologies lift us up to God.

LUTHER ABRAHAMSON

*To you, O heavenly Lord, be all praise and glory that
each day you richly fill our lives with such blessings.
Amen*

Prayer concern: Christians in Canada

Daily Reflections

Will we go?

As Jesus went on from there, he saw a man named
Matthew sitting at the tax collector's booth.
"Follow me," he told him, and Matthew got up and
followed him. ❖ Matthew 9:9

This incident is intriguing because it happens with such simplicity. Jesus and Matthew obviously have never met before,
but all Jesus says is, "Follow me." No explanation such as,
"Good day, sir. My name is Jesus, and I'm looking for twelve
men to follow me. Here's where we're going and here's what
we're going to do." No, all he says is, "Follow me." And
without any questions, Matthew rises, leaving his family, his
job, and his friends. He does not excuse himself by saying,
"But my field is taxes. I know nothing about religion." He
heard the command and he followed.

It is not very likely that you or I will ever be asked to
uproot ourselves and say goodbye to our families and jobs,
and serve instead in a capacity which requires complete self-
denial. What is much more likely to happen is that we will be
asked to serve on a committee, teach Sunday school, or fulfill
some other task requiring little if any sacrifice. What will our
answer be? Will we be too busy? Will we say that committees
aren't our line and that teaching isn't our bag?

RON MORTENSON

*Jesus, help us not to falter or question. Lead us and give
us strength to follow you. Amen*

Prayer concern: Teachers

Daily Reflections

Lifted by majesty

> I saw the LORD seated on a throne, high and
> exalted, and the train of his robe filled the temple.
> Above him were seraphs, each with six wings:
> With two wings they covered their faces, with two
> they covered their feet, and with two they were
> flying. ❖ Isaiah 6:1-2

When he beholds the glory of God, Isaiah runs out of
language. Yet he helps us to feel the grandeur of the throne
room. There stand the seraphim, unearthly creatures whose
name is from a Hebrew word that means "to burn." Beings fit
to surround the Lord are so holy that they incinerate all filth.
But even these unspeakable holy hosts must hide their faces
while hovering over the majesty of God. And as they sing to
each other, their praise is so electrifying that the foundations
of the thresholds resonate with their voices, and the house is
filled with smoke.

Can we have any idea of the grandeur of the Almighty? We
get glimpses—the tiny ears and the turned up nose of the
baby in the bassinet, or as we look back at the earth from the
television camera on the moon, or as we hear the "Hallelujah
Chorus" from Handel's *Messiah*.

ALVIN C. REUTER

*Hallelujah! For the Lord God omnipotent reigns, and
he shall reign forever and ever. King of kings and Lord
of lords. Amen*

Prayer concern: Christians in Japan

Daily Reflections_____

Not to condemn

> For God did not send his Son into the world to
> condemn the world, but to save the world through
> him. ❖ John 3:17

The "gospel in a nutshell" in verse 16 of today's Bible reading
is so precious to us that the next verse may not make the
impact on our hearts that it should.

When Jesus walked the earth, he was not like a father
saying to his son, "You're a bad boy!" Some children are so
often told they are bad it is not surprising when a relative
comes for a visit and asks, "And how are you?" that the children answer, "I'm bad," and then go about proving it. As a
matter of fact, we are all born with a sinful nature. But Jesus
did not live and die to condemn us. Rather, he lived and died
to forgive and save us.

Christians are often tempted to criticize and condemn
those who do not love Christ. Sometimes churches can be so
busy attacking social evils that they have no time left to present Christ, who came to save. But Christ died to save the
very people we are tempted to condemn. In Christ's presence
men know two things: they know they are sinners, but they
know Christ loves them. Christ came not to condemn, but to
save. Trust, and tell others.

LARRY REYELTS

*Dear Lord, help us not to condemn, but to love others as
you did. Amen*

Prayer concern: Christians in Indonesia

Daily Reflections

Only the best

> Then [Jesus] told them, "Now draw some out and
> take it to the master of the banquet." They did so.
> ❖ John 2:8

In areas where wine is made, there are places one may go to sample the many varieties offered by each vineyard. Wine connoisseurs, who are critical judges in matters of taste, can tell good wine from poor wine. The chief steward in our text was one of those who knew the difference.

Marriage festivals are always times of celebration. How embarrassing it would have been for the host to have run out of wine. Jesus, who had been one of the guests, now saved the day. The chief steward was very surprised when he tasted this batch of new wine. He knew that the poorer quality of wine usually was brought out last. By that time people's impaired taste buds and senses rarely knew the difference.

How like our Lord it is to always provide the best for his people. If we ask according to his will, he will take care of our every need. Jesus does not want to sit as a guest in our lives. He is ready to be an active participant offering us the very best. However, we, like the chief steward, usually are taken by surprise at God's wonderful generosity. Just look at the gift of life he gave us.

CYNTHIA COWEN

Dear God, thank you for giving me your best. Amen

Prayer concern: Newlyweds

Daily Reflections_____

_____

_____

_____

No enemies?

My times are in your hands; deliver me from
my enemies and from those who pursue me.
    ❖ Psalm 31:15

We hear of people who "don't have an enemy in the world."
It is good to try to live in peace with others, but imagine the
soul of such a person entering the gates of heaven. An angel
meets this individual, and says he or she is about to be
judged. "I'm not too worried," says the soul. "I didn't have an
enemy in the world." The angel asks, "Why not? You are a
Christian, aren't you?"

Jesus had enemies because of things he said and did. The
truth has a way of attracting enemies. Heaven must be full of
people who had enemies because of stands they took against
evil. If you do not have an enemy in the world, is it because
you are not as involved in resisting evil as you could be?

A prayer for deliverance from enemies is still timely and
relevant for those who resolutely face evil as servants of God.
Think about it. What would you have to do in the name of
Jesus before someone would want you to stop? Who can you
pray for who may be in real danger from enemies?

                                            FREDERICK W. BALTZ

Help us, Lord, to have the mind of Christ as we listen to
the Spirit. Amen

Prayer concern: To obey the Spirit's leading

Daily Reflections_____
_____
_____
_____

More than sparrows

> So don't be afraid; you are worth more than many
> sparrows. ❖ Matthew 10:31

Like many people, I prefer most other birds to sparrows. When sparrows come to my bird feeders, I am not nearly as pleased as when chickadees, nuthatches, and cardinals surround them. Yet sparrows, too, add cheerfulness to life by their chirping and activity.

I recall a verse I learned in childhood: "I'm only a little sparrow, a bird of low degree, but the dear Lord God who sees us all, made the sparrow and loves me."

Sometimes we feel we are sparrows among our associates. Our sense of worth and feeling that we are appreciated and loved sinks low.

"So don't be afraid," says Jesus, "you are worth more than many sparrows." Our ups and downs, even our deepest sorrows and darkest sins, do not put us beyond God's care. Jesus' death and resurrection assure us. Jesus is always present with us and will never abandon us.

OMAR STUENKEL

Dear Jesus, thank you for all you have done to give us life and joy. Amen

Prayer concern: All who mourn

Daily Reflections_____

_____

_____

_____

Finding time

> After [Jesus] had dismissed them, he went up on
> a mountainside by himself to pray. ❖ Matthew 14:23

Julie slumped down on the living room couch, bone tired. She had been gone for 14 hours, working her two part-time jobs. Her two children came racing in from the bedroom, where they were supposed to be asleep. Each had a favorite book in hand for her to read.

How do we find time for prayer? Today, many of us hardly find time for our families, let alone for prayer and meditation. Jesus too faced the problem of time. He had just fed 5,000 people, even though he was seeking refuge after learning that King Herod had killed his cousin, John the Baptist. Jesus had taken his disciples to a lonely place to have time for prayer with God, but the persistent crowds followed them. Jesus had to leave everyone and go off by himself.

Today, Jesus helps us as well to find time alone or to be alone inwardly when we are with others.

ART GRIMM

Gracious God, give us the courage and determination to find time for prayer. Amen

Prayer concern: Christians in Jordan

Daily Reflections_____

The right attitude

Serve the LORD with fear and rejoice with trembling. ❖ Psalm 2:11

Not so long, ago kids called adults "Mr. This," "Mrs. That," or at least "sir" or "ma'am." They were taught to give their chair to an adult, to let their elders precede them through doorways, and to treat others with courtesy. Much of this formality is gone today. Even teachers are called by their first names in classrooms. Perhaps greater warmth and friendliness stem from this new order, but a certain respect is missing.

I think it is this issue of respect that God doesn't want me to forget. For me, God is my Father, my friend, and my intimate prayer partner. At the same time, I need to keep in mind that God is the Creator of all that is, the Author of my salvation, the Sustainer, and the Eternal Sovereign. God's power and position demand that I not treat this lightly but rather with consciousness of God's glory and majesty.

EILEEN POLLINGER

Lord, thank you for revealing yourself, for calling me to refuge in you. But let me never forget you are the God above all else. Amen

Prayer concern: Someone who is unemployed

Daily Reflections

Jesus is Lord

But in your hearts set apart Christ as Lord.
❖ 1 Peter 3:15

One of the earliest creeds in the Christian church was the statement that "Jesus is Lord." This creed had special significance during certain periods when the Roman cult of emperor-worship was strong. In certain places, it was required of every person to go to the temple periodically and repeat the words "Caesar is Lord" in order to be certified as a loyal citizen. Some Christians paid with their lives for their refusal to say those words.

It is not that expensive for most of us to witness to Jesus now. But we do live in a world that is not always friendly to the gospel of Christ. And so we share with anyone who will listen to our sure hope of eternal life. To do that we must have the strong conviction in our hearts that Christ really is Lord.

WENDELL FRIEST

O Christ, make us believe that you are Lord, and prepare us to share the hope that is in us with anyone. Amen

Prayer concern: Church leaders

Daily Reflections_____
_____
_____
_____

God's steadfast love

I will sing of the LORD's great love forever.
❖ Psalm 89:1

The word *steadfast* could be termed quaint or archaic in today's society. Ever-changing lifestyles typify this generation. We change jobs, houses, schools, and partners. We are restless people—moving out, moving up, or moving away. Like riders on a merry-go-round, we need something immovable to which to cling as the world spins by. God is the answer.

We can grasp God's steadfast love. Daily we can observe unchanging gifts from God—the sunrise and the sunset, the surf lapping at the shore, the fragrance of a pine forest. All of these things testify to the unending love of God.

In this throw-away age, God's constant love is a real miracle. That is why we appreciate the song of the psalmist, stressing joy over God's steadfast love—love that does not change in the perfection of God's purpose or God's promises.

CAROL ANDERSEN

Lord God, bless us with your steadfast love forever. Amen

Prayer concern: Someone who is different from us

Daily Reflections

Called by our gifts

God said to [Solomon] … "I will do what you have asked. I will give you a wise and discerning heart, so that there will never have been anyone like you, nor will there ever be. ❖ 1 Kings 3:12

A confirmation teacher I know cautions his students about prayer. "Be careful what you pray for," he says, "you may get it." The teacher's warning may be understood in several ways. But his main point is that the more you are blessed, the more God requires of you.

The Lord granted Solomon's request for wisdom, but then expected the king to use his gift to honor God and rule well. Solomon was called by his gift to a life of service. Unfortunately, the continuing story of Solomon includes many times he did not use his gift well.

What about us? Our gifts call us to a life of service. Have we used God's blessings wisely?

DAVID L. MILLER

Gracious Lord, you shower our lives with many blessings. Grant us wisdom to use them according to your will. Amen

Prayer concern: Wise use of God's gifts

Daily Reflections_____

_____

_____

_____

A problem with authority

> A king who will reign wisely and do what is just
> and right in the land. ❖ Jeremiah 23:5

Many people speak of having "a problem with authority," which generally means that they have had a bad experience with a parent, a teacher, or a representative of the law, and that they are wary of being mistreated again by someone in power. Therefore, they instinctively distrust those who are in authority.

Jeremiah raises the hope that an ideal ruler would enter the scene some day. We then would enjoy a king whose reign would be marked by righteousness, wisdom, and justice. Many Christians have understood the promise of an ideal ruler as an allusion to the coming of the Messiah, a hope fulfilled in Jesus.

We are well aware that all human rulers have failings. And the Scriptures tell us that until the fulfillment of God's rule, until the Messiah comes again, all figures of authority will be imperfect. But when Christ comes again, we will behold the perfect ruler. Then we will be ruled wisely, and justice and righteousness will prevail.

GREG GABRIEL

O God, grant us compassion to accept the human limitations of those who are in authority over us. Give our rulers wisdom, and teach them to bring us justice and righteousness. Amen

Prayer concern: Those who work in our justice system

Daily Reflections

Who's a VIP?

One Sabbath, when Jesus went to eat in the house
of a prominent Pharisee, he was being carefully
watched. ❖ Luke 14:1

Have you ever imagined what it would be like if you were
famous? Have you fantasized about crowds seeking your
autograph or being asked to dinner at the White House?
Ironically, most people do not like feeling conspicuous in
public, even though we all want recognition. We all long to
hear, "You are important."

Being somewhat famous in his day, Jesus was watched by
crowds and received invitations from prominent local leaders.
But celebrity status was not important to him. The most
important invitation we can ever receive is the one that God
gives. The Lord's welcome does not depend on our social
standing or personal achievements. The Lord also invites the
poor, the sick, and the forgotten. And he invites you and me.
Imagine that! If the Savior of the whole world invites us to sit
at his banquet table, what greater recognition can we imagine
or desire?

MARY J. HENRIKSEN

*Lord, save me from too much need for personal acclaim.
Rather, direct my attention to being near you. Amen*

Prayer concern: Your governor

Daily Reflections_____

_____
_____
_____

Only doing our duty

We are unworthy servants; we have only done
our duty. ❖ Luke 17:10

"Who was your servant last year?" young Susan replied when her brother asked her to bring him a pencil. "Why should I do anything for you?"

Children are not alone in making that kind of response. By nature, we all find it difficult to put the interests of others above our own. Servanthood does not come easily.

Jesus' disciples struggled with the call to service as well. On the eve of their Lord's crucifixion and death, they argued about which of them was the greatest. And when they gathered in the upper room, none of them gave any thought to washing the feet of the others. But Jesus did: "Who, being in very nature God ... taking the very nature of a servant" (Philipians 2:6-7).

In the light of Jesus' power of example, it seems a small thing to give ourselves and our gifts in service to him and to others. Nor should we look for reward. It is a privilege, and it is our duty.

ROBERT L. ANDERSON

Lord, make us joyful servants. Amen

Prayer concern: Missionaries

Daily Reflections_____

The gift of memory

Give thanks to the LORD, call on his name.
… Remember the wonders he has done.
❖ Psalm 105:1, 5

Because of her advanced age and damage from hardening of arteries, a woman I knew had difficulty remembering recent happenings. But there was one thing she never forgot. She never forgot the wonderful way the Lord had called her to him in Baptism and confirmation. The gift of memory is one of the finest things God gives us.

Think of it! We can remember the wonderful works of God in creation. We recall the wonderful works of God in blessing the people Israel. We recollect the ways God blessed us on our way from infancy to adulthood.

When was the last time you thanked God for the gift of memory? Surely there are things that you would like to forget. All of us would. But today, let's thank God for the gift of remembering. If memory were not our gift from God, think how much poorer life would seem to be.

OLE WINTER

Dear God, thank you for the gift of memory that helps us to recall the wonderful and gracious gifts we have in Christ. Amen

Prayer concern: Those who long to remember

Daily Reflections_____

_____

_____

_____

Somewhere to run

> The men were amazed and asked, "What kind of
> man is this? Even the winds and the waves obey
> him!" ❖ Matthew 8:27

With nowhere else to run, the disciples turned to Jesus. They chided him for not caring whether they lived or died. Christ's "Peace be still!" gentled the wind and calmed the sea. Only after speaking to the wind did Jesus speak to his fear-swamped disciples. He spoke to them about their little faith. The men in the boat had fragments of faith or they would not have turned to Jesus with their problems in the first place.

What sort of man is Jesus? One who has power over the elements and the fearful hearts of people. The Word of God in the flesh changes everything. Even nature is subject to him. And he is the One who loves us enough to give himself for us. We need run no longer. We are in God's hands, storm or calm, waking or sleeping, living or dying. We need not fear loneliness, weakness, or even lack of faith. What sort of man is this? He is the Son of God, who cares about us. He is the person we can turn to.

JOHN A. SPEERSTRA

Lord Jesus, we thank you that you are all in all. Amen

Prayer concern: Those living in fear

Daily Reflections

Salt

> You are the salt of the earth. But if the slat loses its saltiness, how can it be made slaty again? It is no longer good for anything, except to be thrown out and trampled by men. ❖ Matthew 5:13

All good cooks have their share of horror stories from the days when they were first learning their craft. My sister, for example, has always enjoyed tinkering in the kitchen. When she was about 12 years old, she decided to make brownies. The recipe called for a whole can of chocolate syrup, along with other typical brownie ingredients, and 1/4 teaspoon of salt. No one knows just how it happened, but somehow 1/4 *tablespoon* of salt—three times what the recipe called for—got into the batter. There was no way to adjust the recipe. The salt had lost its original purpose, and the entire mess had to be thrown out.

People spreading the news of God's love are as important to the world as salt. It takes very little salt to improve the taste of food. Likewise, even the little things we do in our own communities with a handful of coins and a limited number of volunteers can accomplish great things in God's kingdom on earth. Even one person can make a difference.

SUE WOLF

Lord, help us to remember that even the little things we do with the little we have are blessed by you for the good of all. Amen

Prayer concern: People who are poor

Daily Reflections

Testing spirits

> This is how you can recognize the Spirit of God:
> Every spirit that acknowledges that Jesus Christ
> has come in the flesh is from God. ❖ 1 John 4:2

Our culture is filled with ideas that conflict with God's word. Yet some of these ideas may appear to follow the Spirit of God. How are we to know which ideas are good in the eyes of God? "Test them," says Scripture. "See if they confess that Jesus Christ has come in the flesh."

God does not ask us to do those things that contradict the essence of God's message of love. God's love prompted the gift of the Ten Commandments. When Jesus gave his disciples the new commandment to "love one another as I have loved you," it was an extension of that earlier covenant.

Today, God's Spirit is in the world. Other spirits exist here too. The Holy Spirit is in harmony with God and confesses that Jesus Christ has come in the flesh.

ROD C. BRODING

God, help us to discern which ideas are in line with you. Amen

Prayer concern: Those plagued by evil spirits

Daily Reflections

Light in the dark

> Your word is a lamp to my feet and a light for
> my path. ❖ Psalm 119:105

Have you ever been where it is totally dark? It doesn't happen very often for most of us. But suppose you were in a deep cave and the lights went out, or were in the woods on a cloudy night and dropped your flashlight. Then you'd know what dark is. And you'd realize the value of light.

This is the value of God's word. It is a light where we need it. The Bible says that we are in the dark because of sin—our sin and that of others. There seems to be no escape from the problems of our world. We need light to show us the way. God brings the light, and Jesus himself is the true Light. And the Bible in telling us about him brings us the light we need. It shows us a way out of the hopelessness of a world at war with itself. It lets us see the possibility of a life where evil is conquered by good. It gives us direction for our everyday living, at least enough for us to take one more step ahead.

Perhaps the verse would seem more up to date if it read, "Your word is a flashlight for my feet and a streetlight over my path." But however you put it, there's no denying that we need light. And that light comes to us from God.

ROLF E. AASENG

We thank you, God, for providing this unfailing light to guide us through life. Amen

Prayer concern: Christians in Saudi Arabia

Daily Reflections_____
_____
_____
_____

The definition of love

Love is patient, love is kind. It does not envy, it does not boast, it is not proud. ❖ 1 Corinthians 13:4

Harriet had been struggling with cancer for 13 years. As I prepared to visit her for the first time, I wondered what she would be like. She might be angry, impatient at her suffering, and justly so. She might by arrogant, thinking herself invincible after living with the disease for so long.

But Harriet was not angry, impatient, or arrogant. Rather, she was a wonderfully loving woman. She treated her daily suffering with quiet hope. She refused to concentrate on herself in conversations, but gently and gladly spoke of others. Harriet knew she was not invincible. Her ability to fight the disease made her keenly aware of God's grace.

In her approach to life, Harriet modeled Paul's definition of love. She bore witness that love is possible, in Christ, precisely where one might least expect it.

KAREN BATES

Lord Jesus, thank you for those who show us how to love as you love. Amen

Prayer concern: Hospital chaplains

Daily Reflections_____

_____

_____

_____

Lasting value

> For my flesh is real food and my blood is real
> drink. ❖ John 6:55

Because we have allergies in our family we learned to be good label readers. My children learned as preschoolers that items containing too much sugar or one of the forbidden additives would not be purchased. That was "pretend" food. "Real" food had natural vitamins and minerals.

Jesus offers real life: hope of change for destructive behavior, forgiveness for failures and broken relationships, joy in small endeavors, and a sense of purpose and continuity. We fill our lives with many pretend promises: success, accomplishment, and accumulation. These offer no real hope and only a fading sense of purpose.

Natural food may appear boring when compared with less nutritious items. and leading a life of daily, faithful commitment may seem dull when compared with the glamour and excitement offered us elsewhere. It is the long-term results that matter.

KATHY M. HAUEISEN

O Lord, we are tempted to grab the glamorous and pass up the life-giving. Create in us a hunger for your will that we may be fed by you and live. Amen

Prayer concern: Your congregation

Daily Reflections_____

_____

_____

_____

Contribution or commitment?

> For I testify that they gave as much as they
> were able, and even beyond their ability.
> ❖ 2 Corinthians 8:3

Giving to God sometimes gets lost in the materialism of our time. We may confess that all we receive our gifts from God. But when it comes to depositing that paycheck, we might think that it is our money to do with as we wish.

What a contrast this is to the example left us by the Macedonians, who gave not only "according to their means," but "beyond their means." They gave not only what they could afford, but what they couldn't afford. Such giving requires real faith that God will provide for one's needs. Continuing to give to God when one's resources dry up requires faith also.

One couple facing retirement was surprised to discover just how limited their budget would be. Yet they resolved to continue giving a portion of their income to the work of the Lord. They gave, finding security not in a bank balance but in a God who promises to supply all their needs.

MARLYS A. KORMAN

Lord, help us to keep you first in our giving, as well as in our living. Amen

Prayer concern: Faith

Daily Reflections

Bright light

> Even in the darkness light dawns for the upright,
> for the gracious and compassionate and righteous
> man. ❖ Psalm 112:4

Recall the nature of darkness. If you open a door to the outside at night, darkness doesn't come into the room. The room stays just as light as it was before, and the darkness stays outside. But if you are in a dark room and open the door to a bright outside, light pours into the room and illuminates every corner. Darkness doesn't flood into a room. Light does.

Sometimes we want to hide things from God. We feel embarrassed about something we've said. We feel ashamed of something we've done. So we hide it from others and from God in some deep, dark corners of our minds.

But God's light rises in the darkness. Even the corners that we wish to keep hidden are known to God. Is that something that should frighten us or cause us anxiety? It need not. God is gracious and merciful. And God's light in Christ brings forgiveness. Bask yourself in that forgiveness and light.

ERIC BURTNESS

Lord God, make your presence known to us. Amen

Prayer concern: Someone despondent

Daily Reflections_____

_____

_____

_____

One little ewe lamb

Then Nathan said to David, "You are the man!"
❖ 2 Samuel 12:7

This story recounts for us a confrontation between the prophet Nathan and King David, in which Nathan pointed out David's sins by telling a story. Nathan described a rich man who stole a poor man's precious ewe lamb in order to serve a fine meal to a traveler.

Nathan wanted David to recognize that he did a great wrong when he seduced the beautiful Bathsheba while her husband Uriah was at war. David then had arranged to have Uriah killed and took Bathsheba as his own wife.

The ewe lamb becomes a symbol of that which is most precious to us, that which can be lost to another person's envy, self-centeredness, or malice. All of us, like David, need to be shown our sin at times when we cannot see the implications of our own actions. The Word of God then drives us to Christ to confess our sins and receive the gift of forgiveness.

STEPHANIE FREY

Lord Jesus, keep us from coveting our neighbor's family members or possessions. Show us our sin. Give us your grace and forgiveness. Amen

Prayer concern: All who seek forgiveness

Daily Reflections_____

We, the people

> The people stood watching, and the rulers even
> sneered at him. ❖ Luke 23:35

It is always thought provoking when biblical accounts of the same incident are different. Matthew and Mark report that the people sneered at Christ. But Luke remembers them as being silent, watching, playing the part of spectators in this drama.

Luke's account creates a sense of unity of the people with Jesus. We don't know whether these people were the ones who clamored at the trial or whether they were the mournful followers. What we do know is that no matter what their thoughts or orientation, they were united for that moment, with their eyes fixed on Jesus. We are reminded that they, the people, are the ones for whom Jesus died on that cross.

And we are "the people." We can't share Christ's suffering on the cross. We can't participate in the dreadful drama. But as we hear the story, we can know that it was for us that Jesus was born, crucified, died, buried, and resurrected.

ALFREDA H. EBELING

Lord, thank you for the words of Luke and the reminder that we, too, are the people. Amen

Prayer concern: Someone in intensive care

Daily Reflections_____

_____

_____

_____

Whom do you follow?

> Andrew, Simon Peter's brother, was one of the
> two who heard what John had said and who had
> followed Jesus. ❖ John 1:40

President Calvin Coolidge once invited some friends from
Vermont to dine at the White House. Worried about their
table manners, the guests decided to do everything that their
host did. All went well until coffee was served. Coolidge
poured his into the saucer. The guests did the same. The president added sugar and cream. So did the guests. Then
Coolidge leaned over and placed his saucer on the floor for
the cat.

All of us have times when we find ourselves in some
predicament. Often the seriousness of the situation is not
revealed until it is too late. Whom do we follow in life? Possibly
the greatest danger is in having no leader but ourselves.

In today's Bible text, Andrew was concerned about whom
he followed, but when he found Jesus he shared his enthusiasm with his brother, Peter. So we are called to follow the
Son of God and to share his message with others.

ROGER A. DOMYAHN

Lord, help us always to follow you. Amen

Prayer concern: Someone who is having a difficult time
in life

Daily Reflections_____

_____

_____

_____

The gift of being heard

> [Jesus] offered up prayers and petitions with loud cries and tears to the one who could save him from death. ❖ Hebrews 5:7

When my mother was dying of leukemia, I would pray for her as I drove to work, "with loud cries and tears to the one who could save her from death." If modern medicine could not do the job, then I hoped for a miracle. Yet it was not to be.

In today's text, we see Jesus praying in distress to the only one who could save him from premature death. Jesus' prayers were not answered in the way he sought, for we know he was obedient, even unto death on the cross. Even so, we are assured that Jesus was *heard* in his prayer, because of his godly fear.

How highly we value a friend who will just listen. Although the difficulty may not be resolved, we feel restored and hopeful just by the telling of it. God in Christ is the ultimate listener. When we bring our hurts and problems to him, we can always say, no matter what the outcome, "And I was heard."

NANCY LEE SASSER

Almighty God, I praise you for hearing all my prayers and concerns. Empower me to be obedient. Amen

Prayer concern: Those who have lost a parent

Daily Reflections_____

_____

_____

_____

We have seen his star

We saw his star in the east and have come to
worship him. ❖ Matthew 2:2

The story of the magi is, in a way, our story. Their journey
must have been long and arduous, and they must have wondered what, if anything, they would find. We tend to imagine
that for them inspiration was clear and travel simple and
direct. But they may have had to work hard to maintain enthusiasm for their travels.

So it may be with us. In our journey through life we often
run into difficulties, and we worry because there are no
bright lights shining on the path ahead. We become disoriented when the path takes unexpected turns. We forget that,
with God's light, we can walk the road ahead one step at a
time, and that light will be enough. One step at a time!

The magi followed a star, and they may have had hope, but
they had received no promise. We have been given both light
and promise: As we walk onward with Jesus, the path ahead
will be radiant.

NORMA SHIRCK

*Light of the World, keep us within the safety of your light
as we journey through this life. Amen*

Prayer concern: Those away from home

Daily Reflections

A new start

> Repent, then, and turn to God, so that your sins
> may be wiped out, that times of refreshing may
> come from the Lord. ❖ Acts 3:19

When I was a child, jumping on the bed was great fun. It was also forbidden. One day the inevitable happened—the bed frame broke. For a whole week I waited, gripped by fear, until Mom found out. I said I was sorry. No doubt I was punished, but then I was forgiven. It was like being let out of jail. I was free.

Forgiveness sets us free from the past and gives us new energy to move on with our lives. When our sins are wiped out, a heavy burden is lifted: a burden of sin, a burden of guilt, fear, worthlessness, and the regrets and mistakes of yesterday. Our relationship to God is restored, as well as our relationship to others and to ourselves.

Forgiveness wipes our sins out. We are freed to start anew. Instead of dwelling on what happened in the past, our eyes are opened to the opportunities of today. How refreshing it is to get a new start. A new start is offered to us daily, as God in Christ forgives us.

LINDA HOXTELL

Lord, thank you for a chance to start over today. Amen

Prayer concern: Fathers

Daily Reflections _____

Conditioning

> Fix these words of mine in your hearts and minds;
> tie them as symbols on your hands and bind them
> on your foreheads. ❖ Deuteronomy 11:18

There are many things we do in life simply because we have been conditioned to respond in a certain way. Young children are warned against touching a hot stove or a burning match. If they do it anyway, they immediately learn that it hurts. And they become conditioned to pull back from intense heat.

Most of us were trained as children to say, "Thank you," when someone did us a favor, gave us a gift, or delivered us a compliment. Now, later in life, we say it without thinking. It is a conditioned response.

God's instructions to the Israelite people were to keep God's words in their hearts and to teach them to their children. Keeping God's word before their eyes and in their ears conditioned them to be compassionate and caring toward one another.

Jesus always was as alert to human need as is the needle of a compass to the North Pole. The fullness of God dwelt in him, conditioning with love. How about us?

JAMES R. BJORGE

Lord, may your word guide my conduct. Amen

Prayer concern: Someone looking for a job

Daily Reflections_____

Listening

They too will listen to my voice. ❖ John 10:16

Voices. Some of the most overwhelming facets of modern society are the myriad voices that seek our attention. What voices make up this babble around us? The radio broadcasts' nonstop voices: songs, commercials, political announcements, interviews, and play-by-plays of sporting events. Television offers more of the same. Telephones and fax machines also demand our attention.

In addition to mechanical voices, there are the voices of family, friends, coworkers, neighbors, and even the voices of our own conscience and sense of responsibility.

Amid the din and clamor, we read Jesus' promise, "They too will listen to my voice." What reassurance to know that nothing can still our Lord's voice! He promises that even the sheep that belong to another fold will heed his call, and all will hear the quiet, soothing words of calm and comfort he brings to our inner souls.

BETTY HEIDEMANN

Dear Jesus, keep us focused on your voice through all the noise of our world. Amen

Prayer concern: Christians in England

Daily Reflections

Christ is essential

> No branch can bear fruit by itself; it must remain
> in the vine. Neither can you bear fruit unless you
> remain in me. ❖ John 15:4

How human to nurture the notion that if we set our minds to
it, we can do anything. A young tyke with sleeves rolled up
proudly shows a bulging arm muscle to admiring parents—
and we praise the child for it. Another child proclaims, "See,
I did it all by myself," and is lauded.

Building a child's self-confidence offers long-term benefits,
for there are forces in the world that extinguish the flickering
candle of those who are timid and uncertain. Many of the
world's great leaders, such as the reformer Martin Luther,
have made a difference because they had confidence in themselves and their work. But the Christian, growing in maturity,
realizes that the *self*-confidence the world knows is replaced
gradually by a *Christ*-confidence. As the apostle Paul writes,
"I can do everything through him who gives me strength"
(Philippians 4:13).

O. Henry Hoversten

*Lord, give us the Christian maturity to rely more and
more on you and less and less on ourselves. Amen*

Prayer concern: Siblings

Daily Reflections_____

_____

_____

_____

Lord of the Sabbath

> The Sabbath was made for man, not man for the
> Sabbath. ❖ Mark 2:27

It is much easier to follow rules than to live by love. We feel much more secure inside fences. In the kingdom of God, there is a shepherd. The fences, all that we call rules, point us to the shepherd, so that we might know and follow him. The shepherd leads us, and his voice gives order to our lives.

When we grow to love the shepherd, we learn that God is for us and that the fences are gifts to us. But we find it is not enough just to do what we ought to do and stay inside the fences. We learn to follow the shepherd's greatest commandment to love. The very nature of love opens us to understand that we are given life abundantly to live it. Joy is on the menu.

Stepping outside the fences, we find a kingdom wide and wonderful before us. Leading the way is one who calls us by name and invites us to come along.

The rules have never been the point. They were given simply as guides to show us the way to know God. We are sustained by God's person, not by rules. It is the shepherd, not the fences, that shows us the kingdom.

DALE CHESLEY

Lord Jesus, help us to know you and to live the joy of your love, today. Amen

Prayer concern: Parish workers

Daily Reflections_____

_____

_____

_____

Navigators

We live by faith, not by sight. ❖ 2 Corinthians 5:7

Early navigators charted their courses by following the stars. Long ago, Phoenicians and Greeks set sail confidently into vast seas, with no landmarks except in the sky. They looked up into an explosion of stars, undimmed by pollution or the obscuring competition of manufactured lights, and knew where they were.

Even in the southern hemisphere, with no constant Polaris to guide them, Polynesians and Micronesians sailed by watching and knowing the changing constellations of the southern sky.

Now, atomic-powered submarines can sail underwater around the world, never seeing the stars to tell them where they are. Their navigators put their faith in sonar and computer-generated charts and simulations that tell them exactly where they are at all times.

Technology is miraculous. Faith is even more so. We thank God for Word and Sacrament, the means of grace that feed our faith through this life. And we thank God that someday we will see and have no need of faith.

ANONYMOUS

Lord of heaven, give us faith. Our vision is so limited. Amen

Prayer concern: Sailors

Daily Reflections

The presence of God

I did not see a temple in the city, because the
Lord God Almighty and the Lamb are its temple.
❖ Revelation 21:22

It is hard to overestimate the importance of the temple to the
faith of the Israelites. There, in that place, they experienced
the presence of God. Then came Jesus, the presence of God in
human form. Now people could know, close up, that God was
at hand. God would speak of the "temple of his body" being
raised from the dead for the life of the world.

Across the globe, God's people now gather around Word
and Sacrament. Buildings and liturgical forms vary, but Jesus,
the Lamb who was slain, has begun his reign. Jesus is present
in the proclamation of the gospel, in water and word, and in
bread and wine. We do not need to hunt for God. God is here
for us in these means of grace. We cannot overestimate the
importance of this regular nourishment for faith and life.

One day, in God's good timing, temples, sermons, and
denominations will cease. We will be brought from the east
and the west, and from the north and the south, to the eternal
presence and praise of our Lord.

BARBARA KNUTSON

In your presence, O Lord, is fullness of joy. Amen

Prayer concern: Christians in Singapore

Daily Reflections_____

_____

_____

_____

Shepherding ministry

> I will place shepherds over them who will tend
> them. ❖ Jeremiah 23:4

At services of ordination, when a person is set apart for the ministry of Word and Sacrament, these words from Jeremiah are sometimes read as the First Lesson. They are God's promise to give us faithful pastors to proclaim Christ as crucified and risen Savior. He comes through the Word, Holy Baptism, and Holy Communion to dwell in us.

Through the ministry of faithful pastors, we are reminded that in our baptism we have been crucified with Christ. We don't live for ourselves any longer. Rather, Christ lives in us. As the years pass, we experience the growth of the inner nature—Christ in us—in the very face of the outward aging of the body.

As the apostle Paul writes, "We always carry around in our body the death of Jesus, so that the life of Jesus may also be revealed in our body.... Therefore we do not lose heart. Though outwardly we are wasting away, yet inwardly we are being renewed day by day" (2 Corinthians 4:10, 16).

RICHARD J. SMITH

O Lord, fulfill your promise of faithful shepherds for your sheep. Amen

Prayer concern: Pastors

Daily Reflections_____

_____

_____

_____

The bread of life

This is the bread that came down from heaven.
Your forefathers ate manna and died, but he who
feeds on this bread will live forever. ❖ John 6:58

Children see countless ads on TV and in magazines that urge
them to eat, drink, or wear the products their "heroes" are
eating, drinking, or wearing. Many of the products advertised
are unnecessary, not beneficial, or cost too much. Among
them are some snack foods that contain "empty calories," or
no nutrition. They do not satisfy physical needs.

Do we also try to satisfy our spiritual needs with unhealthy
food? Do we fill our minds with strange ideas or philosophies,
and unchristian beliefs from the world around us? Or do we
hunger for the bread of life—for the spiritual nourishment
that Jesus can give us?

The children of Israel ate manna, food God provided them
in the wilderness. It sustained them each day in their wander-
ings, but eventually they died. In Jesus, God provides us with
a different kind of food. Jesus is the bread of life that gives us
eternal life.

ELAINE BABCOCK

Thank you, God, for Jesus, the Bread of Life. Amen

Prayer concern: Someone struggling with temptation

Daily Reflections_____
_____
_____
_____

Creation

Now the LORD God had formed out of the ground
all the beasts of the field and all the birds of the air.
❖ Genesis 2:19

All living creatures are a part of God's good creation, says
Genesis 2. It is good for us not to rush by this passage too
quickly. Rather, we need to stop and marvel at the incredible
number and diversity of wildlife created by God.

A quick reference to the encyclopedia tells us that there
are several million species of animals. The tiniest animals are
too small for the eye to see. Thousands of them could swim in
a teaspoon of water. The biggest animal, the blue whale,
weighs more than 100 tons. Not only do animals differ in size
but also in name and location. In this good creation we have
the guanaco of South America, the chamois of central Asia,
and the kudu of Africa, just to name a few.

God created and is concerned for animal life at every level
in this world. God has given it to us to name, to enjoy, and to
care for as good stewards.

JEANETTE STRANDJORD

*Thank you, God, for this good earth and for the diverse
and interesting animals you have created. Help us to
enjoy and care for them. Amen*

Prayer concern: Creation

Daily Reflections_____

_____
_____
_____

Good fruit

Produce fruit in keeping with repentance. ❖ Luke 3:8

John's declaration to the crowds who came for baptism is as valid today as it was in his time. Even though his baptism was with water only, it demanded change. John insisted that religiosity, the outward display of ritual, and pride of heritage were to be replaced with inner, spiritual renewal. Repentance and forgiveness were to be manifest by the "fruit in keeping with repentance."

John's emphasis on good fruit is reflected in Matthew 25:35-36: "For I was hungry and you gave me something to eat, I was thirsty and you gave me something to drink, I was a stranger and you invited me in, I needed clothes and you clothed me, I was sick and you looked after me, I was in prison and you came to visit me."

For us, that is the essence of personal ministry. When God claims us as children of God, we are given new hearts. We are called away from sin and to God. That turning away is called repentance. And the whole world should be able to see from our actions where our hearts lie.

JANET REINHARD

Give us hearts eager to serve you, dear God. Amen

Prayer concern: Farmers

Daily Reflections_____

_____

_____

_____

The Spirit says, "Go"

The Spirit told Philip, "Go to that chariot and
stay near it." ❖ Acts 8:29

Wouldn't be great if the Spirit always gave such clear instructions? Then we would never have to worry about making a mistake or doing something foolish. How did the Spirit speak to Philip? Through a voice? Or did the idea just pop into Philip's head? We don't know. Perhaps we too easily assume that God used miraculous means to instruct his servants in the past. They probably had just as much trouble knowing God's will as we do. But they acted in faith and God gave results.

The Spirit is still giving instructions. In general, we all know what God wants us to do: to serve the needs, physical and spiritual, of others. Maybe God will speak to you through a mysterious voice. More likely, God will do it by showing you someone in need, depending on you to find a way to meet that need. Maybe God is telling you to go to Africa; more likely God wants you to show love to someone you see every day. The Spirit is still telling God's people to go out and share their love with others.

ROLF E. AASENG

Help us, Holy Spirit, to recognize your voice. Amen

Prayer concern: Career counselors

Daily Reflections

A gentle caution

Hear, O my people, and I will warn you! ❖ Psalm 81:8

The driver's education car was normal in all respects except one: it had an additional brake pedal on the rider's side. During my first jaunt out on a country highway, I approached a 90-degree turn too fast. The instructor calmly stepped on the brake and eased us through the turn. "You took it a bit too fast," he gently warned.

I could have taken it as an insult. I didn't. Had he not interrupted my actions, I could have been hurt badly. I thanked him for his help.

Today's Scripture passage reveals that God's people will not be allowed to "bow down to an alien god." God will warn them if they do and remind them of their salvation: "I am the LORD your God, who brought you up out of the land of Egypt" (Psalm 81:10).

We may take God's warning as an insult, or we may thank God for saving us from getting hurt through our own bad judgment.

DAVID A. SORENSON

Lord, when I'm heading for a collision, use the brake on your side of my life. Amen

Prayer concern: The congregation council

Daily Reflections_____
_____
_____
_____

Pass it on

One generation will commend your works
to another; they will tell of your mighty acts.
❖ Psalm 145:4

A group of young people stand in line. The first person whispers a message to the second, then adds, "Pass it on." The second repeats the message to the third person and again says, "Pass it on." The pattern is repeated to the end of the line. Usually the message gets twisted in transmission and results in laughter.

No matter. In playing this game, these young people illustrate a simple religious truth. Our faith has come to us because others have passed the message on. It must be spoken clearly.

We didn't write the Bible. We didn't start the church. God's truth was passed on to us. The Bible provides a checkpoint so the message won't be distorted. That is why it is so important to train our children on the basis of the Bible. That is why the church maintains Sunday schools and religious education classes. For as Christians we must pass the message on to others clearly and correctly.

W. A. POOVEY

Lord, help me to guard your truth and to share it with others. Amen

Prayer concern: Sunday school teachers

Daily Reflections

Learning obedience

Although he was a son, he learned obedience
from what he suffered. ❖ Hebrews 5:8

Almost everything we do depends on our ability to learn. Without this ability, we would be unable to walk, talk, write, or do anything except involuntary actions. Consequently, through learning we become the distinct persons who we are.

The perfect obedience to God that Jesus showed on earth was also something learned. Because he was divine, as well as human, we might expect him to have been protected from pain and agony. However, the truth is that he did not escape bitter anguish. He was truly human, with a body and with feelings that, like ours, could be hurt. He was God's Son, yet he accepted the role of a servant. And as a servant, he became obedient to God's will, even when it meant his death.

Through human suffering, Jesus learned perfect obedience. Through his obedience, we learn of God's undeserved love for us.

MATTHEW DEAMES

Lord, thank you for the gift of learning. Amen

Prayer concern: A relative

Daily Reflections_____

_____
_____
_____

The great commandment

"The most important one," answered Jesus,
"is this: 'Hear, O Israel, the Lord our God,
the Lord is one.'" ❖ Mark 12:29

Getting "back to basics" seems to be the catchphrase of the day. We tell ourselves, "Simplify things. Don't muddy the waters. Keep to the point." There's something to say for making sure we're on target when setting priorities and making decisions in our life.

One of the blessings of Holy Scripture is how it can act as a guide for us. Jesus tells us that the First Commandment is to recognize that the Lord God is one. He says we are to love the Lord our God with all our heart, soul, mind, and strength (v. 30). I would call Jesus' words an instance of getting back to the basics. We have to be on target here in our faith or we'll miss the whole point of our call to live as children of God. By loving God, not just believing in God, we gain basic direction for our lives.

REBECCA M. HEBER

Dear God, let us magnify the name of the Lord! Amen

Prayer concern: Pastors

Daily Reflections_____

_____

_____

_____

The hiding place

You are my hiding place; you will protect me from
trouble and surround me with songs of deliverance.
❖ Psalm 32:7

Do you remember sitting in Sunday school as a child and
singing out the words to "Jesus Loves Me"? I remember
singing, "We are weak, but he is strong" and picturing in
my mind a larger than life Jesus who could handle any
problem I might ever have.

Somehow, between childhood and becoming an adult, that
picture faded, and more and more I wanted to count on myself
to solve my problems instead of turning them over to Jesus.
That childhood faith was replaced by a need to show everyone
how wise and strong I was on my own. Usually what I ended
up proving is how much I need to depend on Jesus.

How much easier life would be if I would learn to turn to
God first. God knows what I need and resolves every problem
in the best way for me. Just as the words of the song told me
as a child, he is a strong friend to count on.

DONNA MORGAN BERKEBILE

God, thank you for your strength. Amen

Prayer concern: Medical schools

Daily Reflections_____

_____

_____

_____

A clean slate

> Then I acknowledged my sin to you and did not cover up my iniquity. I said, "I will confess my transgressions to the LORD"—and you forgave the guilt of my sin. ❖ Psalm 32:5

I can remember sitting through my high-school math classes in terrible fear of being called to come to the blackboard to do a problem. I would always be so nervous that all knowledge left me, and my incorrect problem would be right there for everyone to see. I would stand there in agony until, at last, the teacher would let me erase my mistake and sit down.

Going to God with a confession of our sins is often a very hard thing to do. We tend to stew and worry endlessly over things we have done. We go from person to person looking for help and understanding, while all the while God waits patiently for us to bring our guilt to him. What relief we feel when we finally turn our sin over to God and in Jesus' name ask for forgiveness. And what a comfort to know that God is always there, waiting to listen and to wipe our slate clean.

DONNA MORGAN BERKEBILE

Thank you, God, for being there to erase our past mistakes and grant a new start. Amen

Prayer concern: Ministries for social justice

Daily Reflections_____

_____

_____

_____

Conscious words

> LORD, who may dwell in your sanctuary?
> Who may live on your holy hill? ❖ Psalm 15:1

A conversation with a good friend shifts to discussing a mutual friend's odd behavior of late. Or maybe a church coffee-hour conversation focuses on someone's prolonged absence from church. Gossip is insidious. For all of our good intentions about only wanting to "discuss someone's situation," it's far too easy to slip into negative comments. Why do we do this? Maybe it's a way of making the circumstances of one's own life seem better, but it's hurtful and, well, wrong.

Consider exercising. It's hard at first, but the more we do it, the stronger we become, and the easier it gets. Likewise, the more we consciously change the subject when conversations begin to slip into gossip, the easier it becomes to avoid gossip. Think of it as building our muscles of conscious concern rather than our muscles of conscious chatter.

The psalmist describes God's righteous ones as those who interact with others honestly and caringly. When we use our words for healing rather than hurting, we claim the psalmist's promise of a place next to God from where we "can never be moved." It's a promise worth claiming!

DENICE STRADLING

God, help my words to reflect your love. Amen

Prayer concern: Those who have been hurt by the words of others

Daily Reflections_____

_____
_____
_____

Goodness and love

> My cup overflows. Surely goodness and love will
> follow me all the days of my life. ❖ Psalm 23:5-6

One of the special blessings that accompanies teaching elementary Sunday school is having to think in simpler terms. As adults, we think on higher planes, so simpler terms can be refreshing and enlightening.

In the process of teaching a class, my students and I established the following definitions:

❖ *God's goodness* (or grace) is getting something good that you don't deserve.

❖ *God's mercy* is *not* getting something bad that you do deserve.

As children of God, we have the privilege of being sheep of the Good Shepherd. We know there are times when we wander from the path he's chosen. At those times we have the privilege of asking for forgiveness. What an outpouring of love and peace comes with knowing we are forgiven children of God! As we heed the call of the Good Shepherd, we experience holy grace and mercy in boundless measure. In this way and many others our cups overflow.

GRACE E. HAMMOND

Lord, thank you for your love. Amen

Prayer concern: Confirmands

Daily Reflections_____

_____

_____

_____

Who can fathom?

> This is what God the LORD says—he who created the
> heavens and stretched them out, who spread out the
> earth and all that comes out of it. ❖ Isaiah 42:5

At creation, the Lord "stretched" out the heavens. That's a
mild way of putting it. God created a gargantuan universe!
The star Alpha Centauri, the one nearest to our sun, is more
than 24 trillion miles away. Some astronomers theorize that
the outer edges of the universe (with a probable radius of
13,000 million light years!) could be expanding at the rate of
nine-tenths of the speed of light, or 5.5 trillion miles per year.

The psalmist was right in asking the Lord, "What is man
that you are mindful of him?" (Psalm 8:4). Who can fathom
God's creation?

Our overwhelming universe causes some to see humanity
as puny specks. But for Christians, humanity has been loved
into significance. Planet Earth was chosen as home for the
covenant-bringer, the light-maker, the blind-healer, and the
prison-opener—our Lord Jesus Christ.

WILLIAM A. DECKER

*O Lord, what can we do but bow before such a great God
as you? In Jesus' name. Amen*

Prayer concern: Astronomers

Daily Reflections_____
_____
_____
_____

God goes with us

Comfort, comfort my people, says your God.
❖ Isaiah 40:1

The word *comfort* means "strengthened by being with." The Bible frequently reminds us of our great God who will not forsake us or fail us. God will be there with loving arms to uphold and sustain us. That is our comfort.

In our human relationships too often the reverse happens. "For better, for worse, for richer, for poorer, in sickness and in health, to love and to cherish." Those definitions of commitment are frequently defaulted. We turn our backs on each other. The comfort of someone standing by you ceases.

I heard about a salesperson who had been working the New England area and was being transferred to California. The move had been the major topic of conversation around the house. The night before the big move, when the man's five-year-old daughter was saying her prayers, she said, "And now, God, I'll have to say good-bye forever because tomorrow we move to California." She will discover, though, that God is alive and well in California just as in New England.

JAMES R. BJORGE

Lord, thanks for sticking with us always. Amen

Prayer concern: Christians in Canada

Daily Reflections_____

_____

_____

_____

It's water we need

Whatever he does prospers. ❖ Psalm 1:3

Just before his death, Joshua challenged the Israelites: *Choose this day whom you will serve—the gods your fathers served, or the Lord, whom I and my house will serve.* This psalm offers the same choice: to take the way of doom and destruction or the road of life and blessedness.

The way to doom starts with little decisions—to take the advice of the wicked on how to get along; then to seek friendships among them; and finally to become one with their actions.

The way to life starts similarly, with decisions of the mind—this time to seek the advice of the law of the Lord and to meditate on its words. The result? Like a tree nourished unceasingly from underground streams, the Christian life yields fruit and foliage ever green. It prospers.

ANONYMOUS

Dear God, I want to choose life. So remind me where the water of life is found. Then I shall be nourished in prosperity from your day-and-night Word. Amen

Prayer concern: Clean water

Daily Reflections

Part of life

> Give everyone what you owe him: If you owe
> taxes, pay taxes; if revenue, then revenue;
> if respect, then respect; if honor, then honor.
> ❖ Romans 13:7

No one likes to pay taxes. It sometimes seems like money
thrown into a bottomless pit. But governments need money to
build roads, maintain order, and provide for people in need.
To think that someone else is better able to pay the cost is
tempting, but Christians are reminded by Paul that citizens
should pay taxes willingly—and he was writing in a day of
persecution.

Paul challenges Christians to be exemplary also in other
relationships that make up ordinary life. Pay your bills;
acknowledge your status and age; show courtesy to those
who have special dignity for whatever reason—these are
some attitudes Christians are to accept and practice. This all
stems, of course, from God, who brought order out of chaos
at creation. By following Christ, we can be positive examples
for others.

ANONYMOUS

*Almighty God, prepare us to be good citizens always.
Amen*

Prayer concern: Congressional representatives

Daily Reflections_____

_____

_____

_____

Separation will come

As the weeds are pulled up and burned in the fire,
so it will be at the end of the age. ❖ Matthew 13:40

Several years ago we left for a two-week vacation. I had arranged for people to check our house and our mail; but I forgot to ask someone to tend our garden. By the time we returned, the weeds had taken over. My bold attempt to separate the weeds from the plants failed miserably. Separation had to wait until fall.

The parable of the weeds among the wheat is a graphic description of human life. God and the devil are busy sowing their seed. Both kinds of seed sprout and grow together, sharing the same soil. But the day of separation will come. There will be surprises on that day. Some that we think are weeds will enter the kingdom. The opposite will also be true. We need to consider our words and actions. Are we stumbling blocks to others? Do we sow seeds of doubt?

DAVID L. MILLER

Lord, move us to proper repentance. Amen

Prayer concern: Someone you have injured

Daily Reflections_____
_____
_____
_____

Jams and jellies

Then the land will yield its harvest, and God,
our God, will bless us. ❖ Psalm 67:6

At harvest time there is a glorious color everywhere. Apples,
colored lemon-yellow a month ago, now are 24-karat gold.
Ones that were faintly pink now are richly red. I pick one—
still warm from the sun—and polish it on my sleeve until it
blushes, showing faint freckles beneath its skin. I carry boxes
of them to a cool basement corner and place them alongside a
pile of pie pumpkins—like fluorescent-orange beach balls—
brightening a spot downstairs.

I pause to look over the storeroom shelves at jellies, fruits,
and vegetables I've put up in recent weeks. Tomatoes,
peaches, pears, corn, blackberry, and apricot jams. The colorful contents of the jars seem like little faces pressing against
their glass prison walls, peering back at me.

God blesses us when a great variety of food is available
every harvest season!

ISABEL CHAMP WOLSELEY

*Dear Lord, "thank you" seems pathetically inadequate to
express our gratitude to you at harvest time. Amen*

Prayer concern: A school-age child

Daily Reflections

Free the captives

I will free your prisoners from the waterless pit.
❖ Zechariah 9:11

When asked to contrast people in the United States to people in China, a student in Hong Kong wrote of Americans: "Their minds are full of freedom."

The minds of God's people, too, were full of freedom as they suffered in exile. Unable to farm, trade, travel, or worship as they had done at home in Judah, the people of God felt as if they were at the bottom of a waterless pit. But God promised to free the people of Judah, just as their ancestor named Judah had freed his brother from another waterless pit long ago (Genesis 37:24-27). God often works through people like Judah to set people free, even today.

We all have the responsibility to work for the freedom of those who are in modern-day "waterless pits" of torture, discrimination, political imprisonment, and denial of basic human rights. As Abraham Lincoln said, it is a tremendous thing to be an instrument of the liberation of the human race.

ANONYMOUS

Show us the waterless pits today, Lord, and the ways to free their captives. Amen

Prayer concern: Peacemakers

Daily Reflections_____

Twice mine

Into your hands I commit my spirit; redeem me,
O LORD, the God of truth. ❖ Psalm 31:5

One day a young boy ran to the river to launch the sailboat he had made. As he skipped along the river bank, holding the tow string, he watched with delight as his boat floated smoothly downstream. But as he rounded a bend he lost his grip on the string. He watched in tears as his treasured creation sailed out of sight.

Weeks later, so the story goes, he spied his precious boat in a pawnshop window. Delighted, he ran inside to claim it. But the pawnbroker said, "You must pay my price."

"The boat is *mine!*" the boy protested.

But the shopkeeper was firm. "Pay the price."

The boy saved his nickels and dimes until he had enough money to claim his boat. Cradling it in his arms, he spoke gently to it. "Now you're *really* mine. First I made you, now I bought you. You're *twice* mine!"

Just like the sailboat, we are redeemed. We are twice God's—first created, then bought back.

INEZ C. SCHNEIDER

Thank you, Lord, for redeeming us. Amen

Prayer concern: Kindergartners

Daily Reflections_____

The Lord is our healer

If this man were not from God, he could do nothing. ❖ John 9:33

These words of the "man born blind" witness to Jesus' person and power. They are a response to the Pharisees' judgment of Jesus because of the healing he performed on the Sabbath. Some intellectuals and philosophers today imitate the Pharisees' attempt to prove that Jesus was not the Son of God. Today people may substitute scientific data for the Pharisees' religious standards to challenge Jesus. Skeptics may scoff at miracles and say that supernatural power does not exist. The event from John 9:1-41 is a fairy tale to them. These unbelieving persons reject biblical evidence.

Uptight Pharisees asked the man who was healed to repeat his account of what happened, hoping to trip him up. Modern skeptics, too, try to show that some biblical accounts were false. The healed man affirmed his simple, unanswerable defense that an imposter could never do what Jesus had done. The miracle of Jesus testifies to his person and to do his power: He is the Son of God.

M. EUGENE FOEHRINGER

God, thank you for your Word, which confirms your person and power. Amen

Prayer concern: An unbelieving acquaintance

Daily Reflections_____

_____

_____

_____

Promises, promises

I will make you into a great nation and I will bless
you; I will make your name great, and you will be
a blessing. ❖ Genesis 12:2

❖ "I *promise* I won't have another dish of ice cream."

❖ "I *promise* I'll call you promptly at 7:30."

❖ "I *promise* not to forget your birthday again!"

For most of us such pledges, usually broken, only serve to
demonstrate our human frailty. A synonym for *promise* is
covenant. In today's passage, the Lord promised Abraham
that his seed would be a blessing to many nations—through
the saving act of the Messiah. Jesus made a covenant with the
disciples (John 14). He promised them the energizing power
of the Comforter. Through the Sacrament of Baptism, we
accept our Lord's promises to us.

With a human being, a promise is imperfectly kept, at best;
with God a covenant is eternal. Through Christ, we too can
receive salvation and spiritual power, the blessed promises of
our Lord.

NANCY NAU-OLSON

*Gracious Lord, I thank you for your promises, which
abide forever. Amen*

Prayer concern: Homemakers

Daily Reflections_____

_____

_____

_____

Like chaff

Not so the wicked! They are like chaff that the
wind blows away. ❖ Psalm 1:4

Each autumn I remove seeds from marigolds blooming in our
yard. In the spring these seeds produce new flowers. One particular year my efforts at this task were in vain. As I held the
many newly extracted seeds in the palm of my hand, a sudden
gust of wind swept them away. All plans for new flowers suddenly became dependent on store-bought seeds or florist-
grown shoots. In a fleeting second, assured planting had
been eliminated. If only I had been more caring!

God gives us countless opportunities to do God's will.
Again and again, God forgives our careless ingratitude for the
many blessings we receive daily. We need to remember the
reality of the coming final judgment. Only reliance on God's
mercy in Christ can save us. For at that time God will decide
the fate of all people. Those who have been like worthless
chaff will be doomed by their own fault.

JEAN R. SWEIGERT

*Dear God, let us never forget your blessings or our respon-
sibility. Help us to trust Jesus and instill in us the will to
follow you always. Amen*

Prayer concern: Greek Christians

Daily Reflections

Prayer for the present

Restore us again, O God our Savior, and put away
your displeasure toward us. ❖ Psalm 85:4

The so-called "good old days" may not have been as good as
we sometimes think they were. But even if they were, there is
no turning back the clock. Still, it is a good idea in facing the
present to recall the past.

When we consider the past, the goodness of God is evident. In the past there is also likely to be some guilt—guilt
that can blind us to God's goodness. This goodness never
fails; it can be found in the present as well as in the past.

The cynic might say that prayer is just talking to oneself.
The cynic is partly right. When we put our feelings into
words, what we hear ourselves say can be quite revealing. But
prayer is more than that. It opens the way to God and invites
a response from God. "Let me hear what God the Lord will
speak." God always has a word of peace for the present.

ANONYMOUS

*Show us your steadfast love, O Lord, and grant us your
salvation. Amen*

Prayer concern: Christians in Taiwan

Daily Reflections_____

_____

_____

_____

A glorious church

Strength and glory are in his sanctuary.
❖ Psalm 96:6b

I remember feeling faint when I entered St. Peter's church in Vatican City. Its beauty is overwhelming, and its vastness stuns the imagination. The interior of this building, the largest Christian church in the world, is lavishly decorated with marble, gilding, and mosaics. But it is the 400-foot-tall dome that stirs the heart.

Ten architects with vivid imaginations planned this magnificent structure to express the power and majesty of the Almighty God. People can view such sermons in stone and marble, like the majesties of mountains, deserts, and oceans, to stimulate at least a beginning concept of our Creator.

Yet the really glorious church is the one that humbles itself in true worship of God because of Jesus, our Savior, and declares "his glory among the nations."

HILDEGARDE KAMPFE

Dear God, we want to be your church on earth so that we may sing your praises in heaven. Amen

Prayer concern: Congregational leaders

Daily Reflections_____

_____

_____

_____

It's not fair!

> Don't I have the right to do what I want with my own money? Or are you envious because I am generous? ❖ Matthew 20:15

How can it be fair for someone to start work at 6 A.M., and for another to begin at 5 P.M., and for them to receive the same amount of pay? This parable offends our expectations of being paid fairly for work done.

However, the house-holder wasn't operating according to expectations. A denarius was a good wage for a day's work, so, far from being stingy with those who had worked all day, he was being generous with those who hadn't. He had much to give and he chose to give freely.

We are told this generosity is like God's action in the kingdom of heaven. We don't work a lot and get "a lot" of God's care, or work less and get "less heaven." God's grace is distributed with great generosity to us all, not because we have earned it, but because God chooses to give freely. We can rejoice for all who enter the kingdom of heaven and be thankful for God's generous gift of salvation.

ANN KLEMAN

God, thank you for this parable to remind us of your generosity to us all. Amen

Prayer concern: Entertainers

Daily Reflections_____

_____

_____

_____

Follow the leader

> As Jesus went on from there, he saw a man named Matthew sitting at the tax collector's booth. "Follow me," he told him, and Matthew got up and followed him. ❖ Matthew 9:9

A high-school senior applied for admission to a small college. Among the application forms was a questionnaire to be filled out by his father. The father was asked, "Do you consider your son to be a leader or a follower?" The father, an honest man, replied that he thought his son was a follower.

Later, the son was notified of his acceptance. With the letter was a note from the school's president to the father. He wrote, "We're glad your son is enrolled. Furthermore, out of 227 students, it is good to know we have at least one 'follower' in the incoming class!"

Although it doesn't sound very glamorous, being a follower can be important. To some extent, everyone has to be a follower. Much depends, however, on what kind of parents, teachers, heroes, or leaders we follow. Following a leader can be a stimulating force in our life, depending on whom we follow. Jesus invited Matthew to follow him. It was one of the most significant decisions in his life.

WILLIAM LUOMA

Lord, teach us how to follow you. Amen

Prayer concern: Followers

Daily Reflections_____
_____
_____
_____

Intercessory prayer

> The Spirit intercedes for the saints in accordance
> with God's will. ❖ Romans 8:27b

There are many ways to pray. We can tell God what we need. This is called a *petition*. We can *thank* God for our blessings. We can *praise* and celebrate God's goodness. We can pray for others. Such prayers are called *intercession*.

One meaningful service in the life of the church today is a service of intercession. In this service, people can go forward to the altar and share burdens with a pastor. This is followed by a time of prayer for those in need.

It is a privilege and a blessing to pray for one another. Paul, for example, in his epistles often tells others of his prayers for them. In his biblical writing, James also encourages praying for others.

We frequently have such heavy burdens for others that we hardly know how to pray. At those times, the Spirit intercedes for us according to the will of God.

ALICE HEIL

Thank you, God, for hearing and answering our prayers for others. Amen

Prayer concern: Someone who is lonely

Daily Reflections_____

_____

_____

_____

Growing up

Brothers, stop thinking like children. In
regard to evil be infants, but in your thinking
be adults. ❖ 1 Corinthians 14:20

Carol, a college student reminiscing about her childhood, now
chuckles in recalling an absurd threat from her older sister:
"If you don't let me color in your coloring book, I won't be
your sister anymore!"

Another student, Anne, remembers her sister saying, "If
you don't let me play with your doll, I'll never, ever speak to
you again!" Both young women can now laugh at words that
sounded so ominous then.

As children, there are occasions when we accept what
someone else says, because we are unable to think for ourselves. We may be afraid to stand up to others because of who
they are. That's one good thing about growing up. It helps us
to realize that we can think for ourselves and make our own
decisions without being intimidated.

The apostle Paul encourages us not to be swayed in our
thinking by fear or by what seems impressive or spectacular,
but to use the intelligence and wisdom God has given us.

WILLIAM H. LUOMA

God, give us perspective in our lives. Amen

Prayer concern: Teenagers

Daily Reflections_____
_____
_____
_____

Second sight

> Then Jesus told him, "Because you have seen me,
> you have believed; blessed are those who have
> not seen and yet have believed." ❖ John 20:29

A friend told me about an elderly woman who had worn glasses for 70 years. When she went to have her eyes tested the doctor said, "You don't need glasses anymore. You are one of those rare people who receive *second sight*."

When Thomas placed his hand in Jesus' wounded side and palm, he said, "My Lord and my God!" He had received second sight.

Thomas had to see and touch in order to believe. But Jesus said to Thomas, "Blessed are those who have not seen and yet have believed."

It is comparatively easy for us to believe in Christ when God gives us good health, plenty to eat, and a happy home life. But do we still believe in Christ when our marriage is in trouble or when we have lost our job?

Believing, having spiritual second sight, requires faith in the Word of God. It means trusting the Lord's presence with us when it is not apparent. Faith is second sight.

CONRAD M. THOMPSON

Holy Spirit, help me to believe without seeing. Amen

Prayer concern: A faith that will not shrink

Daily Reflections

A matter of priority

[Martha] came to him and asked, "Lord, don't you care that my sister has left me to do the work by myself? Tell her to help me!" ❖ Luke 10:40

When Jesus was visiting Mary and Martha, Mary sat at his feet, listening to his words. Meanwhile, Martha was busy with the pots and pans, cooking up a storm. Martha was a good host, but she was preparing a banquet when only a picnic was needed. In the midst of her frenzied activity, she got upset that Mary was just sitting in the other room. Exasperated, she confronted Christ with a request to get Mary into the kitchen.

Well, Jesus did not condemn Martha for being a good cook, but neither did he send Mary into the kitchen. Instead, Jesus replied that Mary had chosen the basic need of the moment and that her decision was appropriate.

It has been said that in every situation the most basic question is not "What must one do?" but rather "What must one do first?" It is a selection of priorities. In today's text, conversation with Jesus ranked above cooking.

JAMES R. BJORGE

Lord, may we take time to talk to you. Amen

Prayer concern: Sisters and brothers

Daily Reflections_____

_____

_____

_____

God's new way

See, I am doing a new thing! Now it springs up;
do you not perceive it? I am making a way
in the desert and streams in the wasteland.
❖ Isaiah 43:19

The first time I drove over the Allegheny Mountains from Ohio to the east coast, the road was narrow, winding, and very steep at places. Today the road has been straightened and leveled by tunnels through the mountains, filling in of valleys. It is faster, easier to travel, and more direct. Only a visionary could have imagined that the old road could ever have become what the new one is today.

Isaiah reminded the captives in Babylon that the same God who opened up the Red Sea for their forebears in the exodus from Egypt would open up a new road for them for their return to their beloved Jerusalem. To believe such a thing would require faith and vision on their part.

So it is that, when the road before us seems to be blocked and treacherous, the Lord beckons us to look ahead. God's promise still stands, "See, I am doing a new thing!"

ROBERT LONG

When our horizons are limited to only that which we can see, help us to trust you, O Lord, for you are able to do new things. Amen

Prayer concern: Christians in Nepal

Daily Reflections_____

_____
_____
_____

Love and Balaam's jackass

> If I have the gift of prophecy and can fathom all
> mysteries and all knowledge, and if I have a faith
> that can move mountains, but have not love, I am
> nothing. ❖ 1 Corinthians 13:2

The truth surely is important, for we know of a Savior who
was the truth and who died for the truth, but he *did not* say,
"By this shall all men know that you are my disciples, that you
have the right doctrine." Rather, he *did* said, "By this all men
will know that you are my disciples, if you love one another"
(John 13:35).

There's an odd story in the Old Testament of how God
once spoke the truth through the mouth of Balaam's jackass.
I've often wondered what this incident means. Perhaps that if
all we needed do was to clobber people with the right doctrine
and call them names to get them to subscribe to your beliefs,
then God could just as well speak that truth through a jackass.
As Paul said, "If I have the gift of prophecy and can fathom
all mysteries and all knowledge ... but have not love, I am
nothing."

ALVIN C. REUTER

*Christ, our way, truth, and life, we thank you for bringing
us your firsthand report of God. Abide in us, that we may
be liberated from arrogance. Amen*

Prayer concern: Christians in China

Daily Reflections_____

_____
_____
_____

Causes of blindness

[Jesus'] disciples asked him, "Rabbi, who sinned,
this man or his parents, that he was born blind?"
❖ John 9:2

When the disciples asked this question, they echoed a
common view at the time—that misfortune resulted from sin,
that bad things happened to bad people, and that good things
happened to good people. In many ways, little has changed
over the years. We still tend to blame victims of misfortune:
"If she had stayed home, she wouldn't be sick now." Or, "If he
had been paying attention while driving, he could have
dodged that deer."

At the root of such statements is fear. When something
bad happens, we want the situation to be someone's fault;
otherwise, we have to face the fact that some problems are
random and can befall anyone, even our loved ones or ourselves. These kinds of judgmental statements also betray the
fact that in our own sinful blindness we believe that we earn
any good fortune we receive—that we do not need God,
except to reward us for our good behavior. Just as Jesus cured
the man of his physical blindness, Jesus also sought to heal
the disciples of their spiritual blindness. Jesus seeks to help
us as well, challenging us to place our faith in God.

MARK A. HINTON

Lord, help us to see those who need our help. Amen

Prayer concern: The strength to show mercy toward
others

Daily Reflections_____

_____

_____

_____

It's a mystery to me

> I became a servant of this gospel by the gift of
> God's grace given me through the working of his
> power. ❖ Ephesians 3:7

Chosen last for softball—again. Assigned to the cleanup crew
for the big party. Given just a small part in the play. Not even
called for an interview for the job you wanted so much.
Excluded, ignored, cast out—so many of the world's people
treated as outsiders. Who's in and who's out? And why is it
that only some people seem to get to make up the rules?

It's a challenge to understand how a tattered assembly of
outsiders who didn't "know the rules" could become the body
of Christ. Who understands the mysteries behind this odd
mix of Gentiles of God's plan for all creation, so that even
"rulers and authorities in the heavenly realms" (v. 10)
acknowledge God's wisdom? Who could guess that the
apostle Paul, once a prosecuting attorney for the authorities,
would lead this motley crew as its prisoner and servant?

The world is turned upside down. Insiders and outsiders
no longer exist—only those who belong to Christ. Who could
guess that God kept you in secret, waiting until now to show
the boundless grace in Christ Jesus? It's a mystery. Claim it
in confidence today.

THOMAS S. HANSON

Gracious God, make me neither insider nor outsider.
Make me yours alone. Amen

Prayer concern: Those who feel overlooked

Daily Reflections _____

_____

_____

_____

Walking with God

Enoch walked with God; then he was no more,
because God took him away. ❖ Genesis 5:24

What an epitaph! Enoch walked with God—to have this honestly said of one is to receive the supreme tribute. Walking with God may not be easy; it isn't always quite as cozy as the familiar song, "In the Garden," may lead one to believe. God is more than a friendly companion along the way. And while God's eyes and ears are open to our needs and prayers, God's will is still our command. God is God.

God loves us and expects us to "act justly and to love mercy and to walk humbly" with God (Micah 6:8). Jesus summed it up this way, "Love the Lord your God with all your heart and with all your soul and with all your mind and with all your strength…. Love your neighbor as yourself" (Mark 12:30-31).

There are no loopholes in this command. This is a call to total commitment. This is walking with God. In this fellowship, we enjoy the peace of God's pardon, the power of God's presence, and the pledge of God's promises—truly a partnership that must result in joyous witness and service.

HERBERT NOTTBOHM

Lord, let me live and labor in faith and hope and love at your side till journey's end. Amen

Prayer concern: Christians in Africa

Daily Reflections_____

_____

_____

_____

Christ is risen

He is not here; he has risen, just as he said. Come
and see the place where he lay. ❖ Matthew 28:6

During a recent heart attack, it was my experience to face
death. As I recall that day I see it as a great blessing. It
became very clear at the time that the material was of no
value. The faith to know that Christ is risen was all that really
mattered. In Christ the sting of death had been removed.

The Lord has restored me to health. I now find an ever
greater desire to live for him with all that I have. I know that
to die to self and live for Christ while still in this present life,
is the only kind of life that counts. Paul said it is then that
Christ can live in us because we too have died and therefore
have risen with him. Life becomes an exciting adventure.
We have been set free to serve just as we are.

In this urgent, mixed-up age, Christ gives a peace that
passes all understanding. Easter was then, now, and forever.
It is to be meditated upon every day, but vacation time gives
us an especially profitable time for considering that Christ did
not remain where his body was placed. He is risen.

Alleluia! Jesus lives! Won the battle glorious!

AL E. DOERRING

Thank you, Lord, for being alive and living in us.
Empower us to be busy declaring the message that you
want us all to quit living for ourselves and to live for you
who died and is risen. Amen

Prayer concern: Christians in Iraq

Daily Reflections_____

_____
_____
_____

Life is a choice

> For whoever wants to save his life will lose it, but whoever loses his life for me and for the gospel will save it. ❖ Mark 8:35

This paradox was written to a church facing persecution. But these words have a universal meaning that challenges an era that flaunts, "You have to look after yourself." Much is invested in the preservation of looks, health, money, and position. The preservation of life, however, attracts much less attention.

The real heroes of the human family are those who forgot themselves in the service of others. Have you not found your greatest happiness when you forgot yourself in assisting and caring for another? Many people whose lives were burdened with boredom or grief, with emptiness or pain, have been born again in the giving of love to others. The greatest demonstration of life-giving love is Jesus.

LUTHER ABRAHAMSON

In faith and love, O God, help us deposit today something on which interest can be drawn tomorrow. Amen

Prayer concern: Women in your congregation

Daily Reflections_____

_____

_____

_____

That all may know

> God blessed them and said, "Be fruitful and
> increase in number and fill the water in the
> seas, and let the birds increase on the earth."
> ❖ Genesis 1:22

The people of Cameroon hold feasts to honor a marriage, mourn at a funeral, or celebrate the harvest. Luxuries such as meat are usually eaten only at these times. In our country, we also have great feasts, such as Thanksgiving dinner. At these times, people pause to give thanks for their many blessings. Unlike the people of Cameroon, however, we often continue our "feasts" with year-round self-indulgence. Affluence may distort our concept of blessing. While some of God's children are "filled with good things," others starve.

There's a story of a poor woman taunted by an unbelieving neighbor, who asked, "If your God is so generous, why are you so poor?"

In response, the poor woman said, "God is generous enough; it's just that some whom he blessed too much forgot how to share."

Old Testament scholar Walter Breuggeman says God wants honest friends who will come into God's presence and groan to God along with the poor and oppressed. Only then can we give praise and thanks for God's blessings.

JULIE DENNISON

God, help us let others know about your blessings. Amen

Prayer concern: People who help others

Daily Reflections_____

Why the thirst?

> My soul thirsts for God, for the living God. When
> can I go and meet with God? ❖ Psalm 42:2

What is it that creates within us the longing to know God?
Who or what restlessly calls us to prayer? What do we seek in
those moments set aside for the quiet contemplation of our
faith? The thirst for God, persistently spanning the genera-
tions, must certainly be God's way of calling us into a closer
relationship.

"Knock and the door will be opened" is the promise for all
who long for God. Those who seek God will find God. But we
do not need to find God in the burning bush, the parting seas,
or the splashy miraculous. Few of us can point to these. For
most of us, it is in the still small voice, the unexplained peace,
the unexpected insight of joy, or the undeniable flooding of
love into an otherwise isolated experience that leads our souls
to meet God. And it is God who creates the thirst that nothing
else will satisfy.

CAROLYN MOWCHAN

*Dear Lord, give us eyes to see and ears to hear, that we
may better comprehend your presence. Amen*

Prayer concern: Keeping promises

Daily Reflections_____

_____
_____
_____

He came for life

The thief comes only to steal and kill and destroy;
I have come that they may have life, and have it to
the full. ❖ John 10:10

After a child dies in a tragic accident, some people try to comfort one another by saying, "It was the will of God" or "His time was up." An earthquake or a tornado destroys the homes—and maybe the lives—of our loved ones and we may shake a fist at God and demand, "Why did you do this?"

The problem of evil in the world is a terrible one with which to struggle. We believe in a faithful God. It seems more difficult to believe in such faithfulness when horrible things happen day after day.

It's difficult unless we face the reality that God does not force his will on everyone and everything. We need not blame God for everything that happens—even though God may permit things to happen that are against God's will. This helps us make more sense out of why Jesus came into the world in the first place. He came to help us say no to evil, to endure it, to survive it, and to overcome it.

DAWN M. PROUX

Lord, lead us to abundant life. Amen

Prayer concern: Those who face death

Daily Reflections_____

Seen and unseen

Blessed are those who have not seen and yet have
believed. ❖ John 20:29b

I inherited from my father the hobby of doing magic tricks.
One of a magician's favorite ways of getting a reaction from
the audience is to say something like this: "The ball has now
moved magically from this closed box to this closed box. But
the *difficult thing* is to return it to the original box!" The ball
is then shown to be right back where it started.

The audience hasn't seen a thing, and usually some of
them will yell, "You didn't show it in the other box!" It's fun,
then, to do the trick over and show them what really
happened, but actually the whole routine would not be half
as effective without the little tug of war over seeing and
believing!

While a magician's magic depends on deception (and is
therefore the opposite of faith in a faithful God), magic
reminds us of this truth: belief does not demand seeing
evidence. Christian faith does have to do with "all that is, seen
and unseen" (revised Nicene Creed). But the deeper meaning
of the resurrection is something that cannot be seen.

CARL L. JECH

*Thanks, Lord, for blessing us with a grasp of the unseen
meaning of your resurrection. Amen*

Prayer concern: Struggling congregations

Daily Reflections_____

_____

_____

_____

Real servanthood

Instead, whoever wants to become great among
you must be your servant. ❖ Matthew 20:26b

Watch a group of children on the playground or in a lineup in
a large auditorium. The pushing and shoving tell us what their
normal desires are. They all want to be first.

Imagine a world where all people thought of elders before
themselves—or more specifically, a community of believers
operating on that principle. Gone would be the little power
struggles, the petty jealousies, and the feeling of having been
slighted when honors were due. Sounds like heaven, doesn't it?

The disciples were rightfully indignant with the sons of
Zebedee for cozying up to Jesus. Yet Jesus wasn't really surprised. They were in line with the system of the world around
them. How can we behave differently? There is only one way.
Christ must live in us. Only the power of the Holy Spirit can
accomplish this.

ARLET VOLLERS

*Jesus, we realize more and more how helpless we are in
our own strength. We need you before we can know real
servanthood. Amen*

Prayer concern: Construction workers

Daily Reflections_____

_____

_____

_____

Beyond all bounds

> And if someone wants to sue you and take
> your tunic, let him have your cloak as well.
> ❖ Matthew 5:40

An Old Testament law said you could sue a person for his shirt but not for his coat. The coat was like a blanket worn over the shirt. It was used by the poor as a cover at night.

In effect, Jesus is saying that we are not to let the law determine the extent of our love. Unlike the world's definition of love, with its qualifications and limitations, the life of love to which Jesus calls us goes beyond all bounds. It may even mean exposing ourselves to some danger.

Doing more than is expected, giving more than is customary—that's the kind of love that makes people stop and take notice. It opens the door for witness to the love of Christ who went beyond all bounds to give of himself totally for our salvation.

CHARLES KNORR

Jesus, fill me with the love which goes beyond all bounds. Amen

Prayer concern: People who are unemployed

Daily Reflections

Fill it up

Jesus said to the servants, "Fill the jars with water";
so they filled them to the brim. ❖ John 2:7

When Jesus gave the command, the servants followed it exactly. They didn't hesitate to fill the jars to the brim! There was no chance for additives or spiking with old wine. Their obedience resulted in an abundance of wine. Yet it was not their obedience but the power of God that worked the miracle.

In our obedience to the words of Jesus, are we too cautious? He says: "Come to me"; "Take up your cross and follow me"; "Forgive, and you will be forgiven"; "Take my yoke upon you, and learn from me"; "Ask and it will be given to you." Have we done these things?

God delights in those who trust God to fill their lives with an abundant supply of grace. "From the fullness of his grace we have all received one blessing after another" (John 1:16).

BORGHILD GISSELQUIST

Fill us with your abundance, Lord. Make us instruments of your peace. Amen

Prayer concern: Agnostics

Daily Reflections_____

_____

_____

_____

Top priority

[Jesus] sets aside the first to establish the second.
❖ Hebrews 10:9

The statement that Christ "sets aside the first to establish the second" sounds as though either Christ or the writer to the Hebrews had the priorities confused. What the writer refers to as the "first" is the sacrificial system and its priestly orders. In reality, the rituals of the tabernacle and the temple worship were to signal God's grace in providing salvation. Both priests and people in this time commonly thought of the sacrifices as their means of courting God's favor.

Either way, Christ as high priest comes to abolish the system. He is the sign of God's grace for us. He is the best sign. But we are not to think of his sacrifice only as an example for our obedience. His perfect sacrifice of obedience is also an offering for us. We remember how this Coming One gave top priority to his sacrifice that we might be "made holy through the sacrifice of the body of Jesus Christ once for all" (v. 10).

HARRY N. HUXHOLD

Christ, help us keep our priorities in order. Amen

Prayer concern: Engaged persons

Daily Reflections_____

_____

_____

_____

Knowing God

> Hear, O Israel: The LORD our God, the LORD
> is one. ❖ Deuteronomy 6:4

The Israelites were an unusual people. Unlike other cultures of the day, they worshiped not a host of gods and images but only one unseen God. Their conquering neighbors viewed them as foolish and scoffed at their God. But many times the God of Israel revealed himself in power to these skeptics. Sometimes they even believed.

The prophets of Baal were silenced when God sent fire from heaven to kindle Elijah's water-soaked wood to flames. Nebuchadnezzar decreed that none could speak against the God of Israel after he saw that same God save three young men from the furnace. King Darius's order was that all should tremble and fear before the God who spared Daniel from the lion's jaws.

How those men must have rejoiced when God became known to them. We, likewise, rejoice that the one, true God has been revealed to us in Jesus Christ.

NANCY LEE SASSER

Lord, we pray that all might see and believe. Amen

Prayer concern: Your pastor

Daily Reflections

One plus one equals one

> For this reason a man will leave his father and mother and be united to his wife, and they will become one flesh. ❖ Genesis 2:24

For centuries, these words of Scripture have been read in cathedrals, churches, and chapels as an integral part of wedding ceremonies. The mathematics has never changed: One plus one equals one.

A husband and a wife each have a separate and distinct identity. Each has a personality shaped by experience and education. Each has a unique catalog of feelings, fears, hopes, and ideals. The differences are not destroyed by marriage. Instead, a new bonding takes place. Two separate individuals become one. The love each has for their parents and for themselves reaches a new dimension as each cleaves to and enfolds the other.

God's design for oneness in marriage is not an outmoded idea. It has stood the test of time and brought blessings to countless homes. It will continue to do so.

MILAN C. INGMAN

Dear Lord, may your abiding love reach into every heart and every home. Amen

Prayer concern: A widow or widower

Daily Reflections_____

_____

_____

_____

Praise to the Creator

> Sing to the LORD a new song, his praise in the
> assembly of the saints. ❖ Psalm 149:1

Our daughter learned to sing on the prairies of North Dakota. The 45-mile drive between the two rural churches we served was often a time of joyful singing. Until then we did not realize what an advantage it was that our car had no radio!

Often the songs we sang together were new and made-up. Sometimes there were songs about family and friends. Sometimes a song became a prayer for a parish member recently hospitalized or for a family who had suffered the loss of a loved one.

On one memorable day, we saw a wondrous rainbow, whose beautiful color bands crossed the vast North Dakota sky in a full arch. This rainbow became an occasion to "sing to the LORD a new song" in praise for created beauty. The drive and our song ended too quickly. How we wished we could stay and admire God's handiwork and sing forever.

CHERYL MATTHEWS

God, our creator, open our eyes to the beauty of your handiwork, and open our mouths to sing your praise. Amen

Prayer concern: Rural communities

Daily Reflections_____

Enslavement

What cause fights and quarrels among you?
❖ James 4:1

Wars and battles, conflicts and quarrels, feuds and fighting occur everywhere on our planet between nations, within communities, among the members of Christian congregations, and, unfortunately, in families. The cause is the same the world over—the desire for power and prestige, for possessions and money, for domination and authority over the life of another person or group of people. It comes from something inside of us that wants something we do not have. It is enslavement to pride, to a heart that has scant moral or ethical sensibilities, which loves self too much and has slight need of God. It sees little to be gained in serving God and humankind.

But such disharmony need not be. For we are loved by a God of grace, who calls us despite our unworthiness, who stoops down to us to initiate our redemption, and who willingly reconciles us time and time again. God never gives up, and God loves beyond human comprehension.

JANET REINHARD

Call us, forgive us, and renew us, O Lord. Amen

Prayer concern: Those enslaved by drugs

Daily Reflections_____
_____
_____
_____

When the gift obscures the giver

Jesus answered, "I tell you the truth, you are looking for me, not because you saw miraculous signs but because you ate the loaves and had your fill."
❖ John 6:26

This story of Jesus and the Capernaum crowd gives a classic example of ingratitude. On the previous day, Jesus had performed the miracle of expanding the bread and fish into a great banquet. Nowhere is there any evidence of gratitude. The people sought only a repeat of his miracle.

Perhaps the crowd ought not to be faulted. They did not forget or reject Jesus. They wanted him to be king. They crossed the lake to find him. But somehow the crowd has lost sight of Jesus in their excitement. They allowed the gift of bread to obscure its giver. The fringe benefits had become more important than the giver of life.

The gift without the giver is bare. Jesus is not feeling sorry for himself when the people clamor around him. Rather, he is sorry for the crowd because all they received was a meal. They did not receive the giver. Jesus' best gift to us is himself. As we worship today, we too can receive that gift.

LUTHER ABRAHAMSON

God, give us the wisdom to trace our blessings to their source that we may love you more and more. Amen

Prayer concern: Your family

Daily Reflections_____

_____
_____
_____

Two by two

Calling the Twelve to him, he sent them out two
by two and gave them authority over evil spirits.
❖ Mark 6:7

At its beginning, Christianity didn't have large edifices. Small
"house churches" (Romans 16:5), with gatherings of small
groups, was all it could boast. Throughout the ages, renewal
in the church regularly arose from such small groups that
were fueled by their convictions. In our generation, Christians
in China survived the most deadly persecutions, destruction
of their buildings, and banishment of their pastors by holding
unobtrusive and often secret meetings in their tiny house
assemblies.

Jesus sent out his disciples in groups of two so they could
encourage and support each other. He made a promise about
that kind of partnership: "Again, I tell you that if two of you
on earth agree about anything you ask for, it will be done for
you by my Father in heaven" (Matthew 18:19).

Why not seek a prayer partner, a witness partner, a small
group where spiritual power flows?

GEORGE H. MUEDEKING

*Help me to find and strengthen another. And always,
may I be your partner, Jesus? Amen*

Prayer concern: Leaders of the congregation

Daily Reflections

Sabbath spirit

*The Pharisees said to him, "Look, why are they doing
what is unlawful on the Sabbath?"* ❖ Mark 2:24

A highly respected school principal told me he believed in
establishing few rules and keeping those general. He said that
rules that are specific can be twisted. They can compel
choosing between the letter and the spirit of the law.

The Pharisees in Jesus' day loved the letter of the law. In
their view, Christ was a rule-breaker, and they made the most
of it. They even construed rubbing out a few handfuls of grain
to be unlawful harvesting.

In response, Jesus pointed out to them their own inconsis-
tencies. He reminded them of why they were given the
Sabbath. It was a day for renewal, not a day for rigid rule-
observance.

We set our Sunday aside for the same purpose. It is a day
for our mental, physical, and spiritual renewal. We choose our
use of the day in response to God and according to our need.
What matters is the spirit in which we use it.

EINARD WAISANEN

*The Sabbath is your day, Lord. Let me find new strength
of body, mind, and spirit. Amen*

Prayer concern: Principals

Daily Reflections_____

_____

_____

_____

An abiding place

> If you obey my commands, you will remain in my
> love, just as I have obeyed my Father's commands
> and remain in his love. ❖ John 15:10

When we inquire about someone's state of mind or health, and that person flatly replies, "Oh, I'm living," we don't get a message of enthusiasm. Even "Now I'm really living!" sounds as though the person is experiencing only temporary thrills.

But to have an abiding place says, "Here is life with a new quality to it. Here life will not wear down, wear off, or even wear out." When Jesus says, "Obey my commands," he calls us to a place that feels like home.

We sing, "Abide with us, our Savior, O Light of endless light, Bestow on us your blessings, And save us by your might" ("Abide with Us, Our Savior," *Lutheran Book of Worship* #263). But as we sing those words we sometimes lean back in our padded pews and think that the rest of the world can take care of itself. It is then that we remind ourselves abiding in his love involves loving others also.

JOHN A. SPEERSTRA

Abide with us and in us, our Savior. Amen

Prayer concern: All elected officials

Daily Reflections_____
_____
_____
_____

I believe

So Moses made a bronze snake and put it
up on a pole. Then when anyone was bitten
by a snake and looked at the bronze snake,
he lived. ❖ Numbers 21:9

Faith is, in a way, unexplainable. It is a gift of God. Therefore,
thank God if you find yourself believing in Jesus. Yet we have
responsibility too.

When Israelite rebellion against God and Moses resulted
in an infestation of poisonous snakes, people cried for help.
At the Lord's direction Moses raised a bronze snake on a pole,
so that whoever, when bitten, would look at this bronze
serpent and live. Some people believed, and some did not.

From this incident, Paul draws the following exhortation in
1 Corinthians 10:9: "We should not test the Lord, as some of
them did—and were killed by snakes." In John 3:14-15, our
Lord draws an even more significant lesson when he says:
"Just as Moses lifted up the snake in the desert, so the Son
of Man must be lifted up, that everyone who believes in him
may have eternal life."

ANONYMOUS

Lord, I do believe. Help me overcome unbelief. Amen

Prayer concern: Christian day schools

Daily Reflections_____

A room of my heart

> Very early in the morning, while it was still dark,
> Jesus got up, left the house and went off to a solitary place, where he prayed. ❖ Mark 1:35

In my house, I have the luxury of a room that is totally mine. I keep all my books and files there, so it is a good place to work. At times it is also a good place to retreat when I want to be alone, because I know no one will disturb me there.

Jesus rarely had the luxury of being by himself, and he never had a place that he could call his own. He was always on call, ready to respond to the needs of those around him. Yet he seemed to know he needed time to be alone, to renew his relationship with God.

In today's busy world, it often is hard for us to find time to be alone. Many people never learn to appreciate the joys of time alone to think and renew themselves for the day's tasks. Will you accomplish more today because you took a few minutes to be alone in order to renew yourself and your relationship with God?

DONNA MORGAN BERKEBILE

God, thank you for times of silence. Amen

Prayer concern: Those in need of the good news

Daily Reflections_____
_____
_____
_____

Exodus and Easter

Remember the wonders he has done. ❖ Psalm 105:5

The wonderful work remembered in this Bible verse was God's exodus of Israel from slavery in Egypt (Psalm 105). God gave the gift of freedom and a new lease on life.

The wonderful work remembered by the people of the *new* Israel (the Christian church) is the resurrection of Jesus. This is Easter! God expands the meaning of both freedom and life!

Must we place this world in competition against the world to come? God wants us to sing, celebrate, and remember *all* of God's wonderful works—creation *and* redemption, the heavens *and* the earth, life now *and* the life to come!

Sometimes we hear something so regularly that we don't really listen to it anymore. We say or hear, "God loves you," "God be with you," or "God bless you," so often that the words can become hollow. Ancient miracles are complete *for us* when long ago events come alive *today* with fresh meaning.

CARL L. JECH

Thank you for true freedom and real life, God of Exodus and Easter. Amen

Prayer concern: Refugees

Daily Reflections_____

_____
_____
_____

Unlimited love

[God] set them in place for ever and ever; he gave
a decree that will never pass away. ❖ Psalm 148:6

All of creation has boundaries and limits. Day follows night.
Rivers run downhill. Trees lose their leaves in autumn,
and crocuses bloom on the same hillside each spring.

We also are creatures with limited time, energy, and
resources. Often we try to overcome these limits. We strive
for personal perfection, drive ourselves to seek success, or
neglect our physical or spiritual selves, only to find that our
goals seem to elude us. We become restless within our
boundaries and long for freedom.

Only God's love knows no bounds. There is no limit to
God's love. God loves and accepts each of us. God even sent
Jesus to die for us, so we could know how great and unlimited
the love is. It is in that love that we can experience freedom—
freedom from yesterday's guilt and regrets, freedom to love,
freedom to trust ourselves and others, and freedom to fulfill
God's intentions for us.

LINDA HOXTELL

*God of love, thank you for your limitless love. Help us in
turn to love one another. Amen*

Prayer concern: Mothers

Daily Reflections

Heart condition

Therefore God, your God, has set you above your
companions by anointing you with the oil of joy.
❖ Psalm 45:7b

"I believe that the heart of the nation is strong, but it has
become encased in fat," Kaj Munk, a Danish pastor, said that
in a sermon after the occupation of Denmark by Hitler's
troops. In the 1930s, Munk had admired Hitler, but when
his homeland was invaded Munk saw how he had become
insulated from the truth. His sermons and writings sparked
the resistance and eventually resulted in his death at the
hands of the Gestapo.

Just as a weight problem develops gradually while we are
distracted by other concerns, we also can lose touch with the
new life God has given to us. God has given us hearts of faith,
strong with the spirit of truth and great in its capacity for love.
That heart needs to be nourished and exercised.

We all can afford to lose some *emotional* weight, especially
if what we are carrying has already been carried to the cross
of Christ.

DEBRA R. GRANT

*Lord, help us to hear the certain sound of our own strong
hearts of faith. Amen*

Prayer concern: Terrorists

Daily Reflections_____
_____
_____
_____

Sudden crisis

> The Ninevites believed God. They declared a fast,
> and all of them, from the greatest to the least, put
> on sackcloth. ❖ Jonah 3:5

The people of Nineveh were stunned by the announcement of their coming destruction. The prophet Jonah helped them see the hand of God in this turn of events. It was the hand of judgment upon them. They were not innocent victims in this crisis—they were its cause.

The people accepted Jonah's word. They fell on their faces before God in repentance. They did not know what would happen, but they threw themselves on God's mercy and waited.

Not all of our crises are announcements of judgment from God. But crises jolt us into realizing our frailty, vulnerability, and our persistent sinfulness. We may not understand our crises and may not know the likely outcomes, but through repentance in prayer, we can ask God to forgive, illuminate, guide, and care for us.

KURT T. MEYERS

Dear Lord, in time of crisis, draw me closer to you and your Son, Jesus. Amen

Prayer concern: Churches in crisis

Daily Reflections_____

_____

_____

_____

Good conduct

> Since everything will be destroyed in this way,
> what kind of people ought you to be? You ought
> to live holy and godly lives. ❖ 2 Peter 3:11

Peer pressure often paralyzes the truth within us. We become controlled by the crowd and are squeezed into the mold of the majority. Thus we lose the calling of the "light set on a hill," which Jesus challenges us to be. The standards of holiness and godliness are dimmed.

Christians are not to change colors in order to fit into the background of the world. Too often we act like breakfast cereal that is supposed to "snap, crackle, pop" but instead just lies at the bottom of the bowl.

Paraphrasing Caesar, a church committee member once confessed, "I came, I saw, I *concurred*." Agreeableness is not a good trait when it tampers with truth and justice. Nearly every great historic change has been based on nonconformity. The church has been great and pulsating with life when it has flown high the flags of godliness and holiness and has not gotten comfortable and cozy with the world around it.

JAMES R. BJORGE

Lord, help me to live a Christlike life. Amen

Prayer concern: The president

Daily Reflections

With a song in our hearts

Sing to the LORD with thanksgiving; make music
to our God on the harp. ❖ Psalm 147:7

Take a minute to sit back and look out your window. Reflect
on all that you can see that was created and continues to be
cared for by God. An amazing array of things can be seen in
even a short time of reflection, each one planned to perfection
by our Creator.

Can we ever cease to wonder at the beauty of our world, at
the changing of seasons, and at the variety of creatures that
fill our world? The psalmist tells us to "sing to the LORD with
thanksgiving" for all that God has done. That song needs to be
constantly on our lips, not necessarily in the form of a musical
melody, but in the rhythm of our daily lives. Every act and
every thought should be an act of praise given in response to
all that God has done for us. Our lives should become a living
prayer of praise for God's sustaining love and care.

DONNA MORGAN BERKEBILE

*Creator of all things, we offer you our praise and thanks-
giving for the miracle of creation. Amen*

Prayer concern: Those who suffer

Daily Reflections

Ten ways to say love

I am the LORD your God who brought you out of
Egypt, out of the land of slavery. ❖ Exodus 20:2

God knows how tough it is for parents to help children grow
into free, happy, healthy adults. It takes lots of patience and
forgiveness, lots of direction and guidance. Parents lovingly
teach children rules so that children may have safe, fulfilling
lives as they grow, knowing what is wise and good.

God knows how difficult it is because the children of Israel
required much patience, forgiveness, direction, and guidance.
Because God loved the Israelites so much and rescued them
from captivity in Egypt. Yet after leaving Egypt, the Israelites
acted like children in many ways. They didn't really know how
to live as free people. Because God loves them so much and
gave them the Ten Commandments to help them in their
journey through life.

God loves us just as much. We are children of God. So God
also gives us the Ten Commandments out of love. God wants
us to know what is right or wrong.

THOMAS REHL

Thank you, Lord, for the gift of your law. Amen

Prayer concern: Missionaries you know

Daily Reflections_____

_____

_____

_____

Called a new name

The disciples were called Christians first at
Antioch. ❖ Acts 11:26b

Antioch was known as the "Oriental Rome" because it was a
cosmopolitan city, a colorful ethnic center, and a gateway to
Asia. When the bad times came following Stephen's death,
Christian believers were scattered from Jerusalem to many
parts of the civilized world. The scattered ones met at the
synagogues to share the good news of Jesus. But this name
was meant for all—Jews and Greeks alike.

The Greeks first heard the name Jesus and what that name
meant for them from some Cypriots and Cyrenians. Soon
Barnabas was sent for. He in turn brought Paul to help him.
For a whole year they worked together. Great numbers
believed this new teaching and became followers of Jesus.

It wasn't long before the church could no longer be mis-
taken for just another sect in Judaism. They had a name. For
the first time they were called "Christians." It happened in
Antioch.

JOHN A. SPEERSTRA

*Lord Jesus, we rejoice that we too are called by your holy
name. Amen*

Prayer concern: New Christians

Daily Reflections_____
_____
_____
_____

Peter

> And I tell you that you are Peter, and on this rock
> I will build my church, and the gates of Hades will
> not overcome it. ❖ Matthew 16:18

Controversies arise over this text. Does it mean that Peter is the foundational leader of the church and that all bishops are his successors? Does it mean that Jesus will build his church on the confession of Peter? Whatever institutional meaning the text has, the personal application is important for each of us.

First, Peter is a model of faith. He believes that Jesus is the Son of the living God. Second, Peter is a model of confession. He speaks out to say he trusts in Jesus. True, Peter later denied his Lord. He was human and moved by fear. But Peter later confessed his denial and received forgiveness from the risen Christ. This text shows that faith life is about forgiveness—releasing repentant sinners from the sins that weigh them down.

ROLAND SEBOLDT

Lord, give us the faith of Peter to confess our sins and our faith sincerely and boldly. Amen

Prayer concern: The church

Daily Reflections_____

_____

_____

_____

Remembering

> Remember that you were slaves in Egypt and that the LORD your God brought you out of there with a mighty hand and an outstretched arm. Therefore the LORD your God has commanded you to observe the Sabbath day. ❖ Deuteronomy 5:15

It is so easy to get caught up in the law concerning the Sabbath that we forget the grace. The Sabbath day is one of God's richest gifts. God provides a time for us to be reminded of the continual love and care we have been given. The Sabbath is time God gives us to worship.

We violate the Sabbath not when we do a certain work, but when we forget to worship, when we get so involved with life that we act like it all depends on us. If we do not worship, we forget that we belong to God.

People who forget they belong to God live for themselves. This kind of living not only creates a distance between us and God, it is the very thing that is tearing the world apart.

God provided the gift of the Sabbath that we should have time for worship. It is in worship that we remind ourselves and others that we are God's. We remember that we are God's through the grace we received in Holy Baptism, which tells us we are children dependent on God's hand.

DALE CHESLEY

Sabbath Giver, may we never forget that we are yours and you are ours. Amen

Prayer concern: Persecuted Christians

Daily Reflections

So now . . .

And now I bring the firstfruits of the soil that you,
O LORD, have given me. ❖ Deuteronomy 26:10

Action and *Response.* The history of God's relationship with us follows this sequence. God acts, then we respond. The people of Israel also recounted this history, basically saying, "The Lord brought us out of Egypt, so now ..." Deliverance and gratitude. God's generosity and human gratitude. This is a pattern we can trace throughout the Bible.

Where do you experience God's action in your own life? Unless we prayerfully can recount our own faith history of deliverance, blessing, comfort, and hope, our gratitude is likely to be perfunctory. Have you felt the hand of God leading you from death-like life to the fullness of joy? Whether leading through our own droughts, or subtly prodding us toward maturing wisdom and faith, God's Spirit continues to work for blessing in our lives. So after the harvest God has helped to bring about, what is our response?

CAROLYN MOWCHAN

Dear Lord, we ask for the eyes of faith to trace and trust your presence in our lives. Help us to respond as faith stewards. Amen

Prayer concern: Those who are new to Christianity.

Daily Reflections_____

_____

_____

_____

Among enemies of Christ

But he who stands firm to the end will be saved.
❖ Matthew 24:13

Most of us are among the world's fortunate. We gather for our congregational worship and work without hindrance. We join in Christian mission in a society that is overwhelmingly tolerant, even encouraging, of our efforts. When the hurts and tragedies of life assail us, we openly seek each other's comfort and strength. When we are upset with our shortcomings as a church, we are free to exhort each other and to take action toward effective change.

Yet as we read the Scriptures, we keep encountering those strange passages that talk about tribulation and persecution. They remind us that many people have a different lot. They tell us that we have no guarantee that these signs of the time will not catch up with us. We cannot take for granted the privilege of living among other Christians. There may be much falling away. You may belong to a family in which you alone count yourself one of Christ's. Others have known what it means to stand in the midst of unconcern and even enmity. Certainly our Lord did! So, as far as you are able, be ready, knowing that "he who stands firm to the end will be saved." We will love both friend and foe in all our strife.

DAVID W. PREUS

Give us such faith as will enable us to stand, O Lord, whatever shafts Satan unleashes at us. Amen

Prayer concern: Christians in India

Daily Reflections_____

_____

_____

_____

Filled to the brim

All of them were filled with the Holy Spirit and
began to speak in other tongues as the Spirit
enabled them. ❖ Acts 2:4

We often ask that our coffee cup be only partially filled. We do
not desire it filled to the brim. And in life's opportunities, we
are often hesitant about giving ourselves to something in a
wholehearted manner. Doing so, we are afraid, would smack
a bit of fanaticism or overzealousness. Therefore, we frequently commit ourselves with some reservations.

But Christianity requires not just a part or even most of
our hearts. God wants us to occupy the whole house. God
wants to fill our hearts to the brim with his love and power.

There's a story about a man who boasted that he was
God's gift to women. But his friend disagreed, saying, "The
Lord would never be that chintzy."

The Lord is an extravagant giver who wants to fill you with
the presence of God. Great things happen when people are
willing to be "filled with the Holy Spirit."

JAMES R. BJORGE

Fill my cup, Lord. I lift it up, Lord. Amen

Prayer concern: Executives

Daily Reflections

Praying helps

> For my house will be called a house of prayer for
> all nations. ❖ Isaiah 56:7

It would be an interesting experiment to stop 100 people at random to ask them one question: "What is your principal occupation when you attend the church of your choice?" No doubt, some of them would answer, "Listening to the sermon," "Teaching a class," "Singing in the choir," or "Fellowship with others." Certainly these answers are admirable. Yet none of the above is the one God prefers to hear.

God put it plainly: "For my house will be called a house of prayer." Prayer should be our primary occupation while we are at church. And with good reason! Elsewhere in the Scriptures, our prayers are likened to sweet aromas rising toward God, who is pleased with prayers. We should be pleased as well. Praying helps us ward off temptations and prepare for daily duties. And most of all, praying develops our acquaintance with our heavenly Creator.

ISABEL CHAMP WOLSELEY

*Lord, show me how to make prayer a vital part of my life.
Amen*

Prayer concern: Church leaders

Daily Reflections

Knowing God

No one knows the Son except the Father, and no one
knows the Father except the Son and those to whom
the Son chooses to reveal him. ❖ Matthew 11:27

This passage might bother a serious student. It is discouraging to be told that study and learning will not necessarily result in a deeper knowledge of God. Independent study, degree programs, academic excellence—none of these will necessarily reveal God to us. This does not mean that formal education is useless, only that it is limited.

How then do we discover God? God becomes known to us in Christ. This knowledge is not a secret, but it is a mystery. It cannot be understood by our own efforts, no matter how studious. Instead, it is the Holy Spirit who calls us.

The Spirit often works through an older sister or brother in the faith, one who becomes the spiritual teacher of Christ's younger disciples.

ANONYMOUS

*Reveal yourself to us, Lord, as you once revealed yourself
to your first disciples. Amen*

Prayer concern: High-school students

Daily Reflections_____

_____

_____

_____

Repent

In the past God overlooked such ignorance,
but now he commands all people everywhere
to repent. ❖ Acts 17:30

The apostle Paul knew that the people of Athens were quite religious. He had traveled through the city and seen for himself the various shrines and altars built for the Roman gods. Yet he knew that people could be extremely religious and still remain in spiritual ignorance. Paul brought to the Athenians the truth for which they hungered, as evidenced by their many religious idols. He brought to them the truth of the gospel.

People in every land and every generation hunger for meaning and truth. In an attempt to create spiritual life and peace, human beings will construct gods of their own imagination. Paul recognizes this as deep and profound yearning for the one, true God whom we know through Christ. Like the ancient Athenians, we are taught to repent from our trust in these false gods and turn to the living God, whose Word is truth. God mercifully has overlooked this human ignorance but now calls all people to hear the good news of a Savior and trust in Jesus Christ alone.

BRUCE WILDER

Almighty God, forgive us for our trust in any power other than you. Turn us from all false hopes and direct us to your saving gospel. In Jesus' name. Amen

Prayer concern: Those who do not know Christ

Daily Reflections

Come as you are

For the foolishness of God is wiser than man's
wisdom. ❖ 1 Corinthians 1:25

The Corinthians were impressed by worldly notions of power
and wisdom. Paul wanted them to understand that God's
saving work in the cross turns upside down such notions:
"For the foolishness of God is wiser than man's wisdom, and
the weakness of God is stronger than man's strength." Paul
knew that one doesn't need worldly knowledge and power to
believe in God and proclaim the gift of salvation we receive
through the cross of Christ. To the world, God's way through
this cross does not make sense. Yet with infinite wisdom, God
beckons us to come exactly as we are and sends the Holy
Spirit to strengthen our faith.

Have friends or family members ever told you about their
concerns of the struggles in their lives? Have you struggled to
find the words to tell them about the reality of God's presence
and love? Have you ever been amazed, then, when just the
right words came into your mouth? If so, you know the joy
of how God's power is able to work through our apparent
weaknesses. God is able to work through us as we believe and
share who we are as God's children. There is no greater
wisdom.

DENISE STRADLING

*Wise God, help me to use all that I am to tell others of
your saving love. Amen*

Prayer concern: Those anguished by doubt

Daily Reflections_____

Calling all believers!

> Brothers, think of what you were when you were called. Not many of you were wise by human standards; not many were influential; not many were of noble birth. ❖ 1 Corinthians 1:26

"How can I lead the Bible study at the women's shelter this month?" Mary lamented. "I don't have the Bible background necessary to explain the lesson. The women might reject God's message just because of me!"

The believers in Corinth may have struggled with similar concerns. They wanted non-believers to see them as new creations in Christ. They wanted to share the good news of Jesus. But would people in such a corrupt society reject them and their message? Paul reminded these believers to remember their own call in Christ. God had not chosen them because of who they were—gifted teachers or speakers. God had chosen them because of who God is.

When you question your own abilities, remember that God has called you and provided you with the gifts you need to share. God only asks you to be available when called.

JUDY HEREEN

Thank you, God, for calling us to serve you. May we be willing to answer your call. Amen

Prayer concern: Persons with feelings of inferiority

Daily Reflections

A new beginning

> The people walking in darkness have seen a great
> light; on those living in the land of the shadow of
> death a light has dawned. ❖ Isaiah 9:2

When Ben's wife died, he felt his world had come to an end.
When Sue lost her job, she became very depressed. When the
church council voted against Pastor Arnie, he was devastated.

Each of us has experienced the darkness. There are those
times when we have cried out, "God, have you forgotten me?
Why, God?" During dark and lonely nights we have wondered,
"Does anyone care?"

But again and again, the pain has healed and there comes
the light of a new day, a new beginning. It is God who gives of
a new day, a new beginning. How fitting it is that the words of
this ancient promise from Isaiah reach into our lives today
reminding us that we who walked in darkness have seen a
great light. It is the light of Jesus Christ.

Wherever we are this day on the spectrum that goes from
darkness to light, let us remember that God's light has overcome all the darkness of this world.

TED VINGER

*Thank you, dear God, for new beginnings in Jesus Christ
who heals the past and gives us hope for today and
tomorrow. Help us to walk in the light. Amen*

Prayer concern: Those struggling to begin again

Daily Reflections_____
_____
_____
_____

Peter's denial

Then Peter remembered the word Jesus had
spoken to him: "Before the rooster crows twice
you will disown me three times." ❖ Mark 14:72b

It's easy for us to judge and condemn Peter. He had fair
warning. When Jesus had said, "You will all fall away," Peter
seemed so sure of himself, announcing "Even if all fall away,
I will not" (Mark 14:29).

What can we say as this story unfolds? We know how often
we have had to swallow our brave words, to drop our rash
promises. Even our intentions fail us.

What is amazing about this whole incident is the love Jesus
shows to Peter. Even when the denial happened, Jesus did not
say, "I told you so." He simply looked at this miserable man
who was strong—and weak, brave—and cowardly.

When Jesus had risen from the dead, he met Peter again.
Three times Jesus asked gently, "Do you love me?" Three
times Peter replied, and Jesus restored him to the company of
his witness. We remember—and pray for strength.

CHESTER M. PATTEN

*Lord Jesus, in whatever ways we offend or disappoint
you, stand by us and lead us again to your presence, your
peace, and your glory. Amen*

Prayer concern: Those suffering from feelings of guilt

Daily Reflections_____
_____
_____
_____

New purpose

Elijah replied, "I am the only one left, and now they are trying to kill me too." ❖ 1 Kings 19:14

Despair is a complex emotion. Usually it is based on a very real problem. The loss of a loved one, the betrayal of a friend, and the guilt of old sins are all actual sources of desperate concern. After wrestling with the problem logically and directly without avail, people may begin to approach it more emotionally. They find no easy solution. Their mental and emotional resources fail and despair seeps in. Disillusionment joins despair and they feel abandoned, as Elijah did. Terror and depression begin to fester and grow.

Elijah shows us, however, that we need not yield to despair. He moved, physically and emotionally, from the point of despair. He sought out a friend, Elisha, and regained his perspective on life. God led him to new purpose and direction. Despair lost its grip to trust in God and new purpose in life. God's loving guidance lifted him, as it can help us all.

JUDY CHRISTIAN

Help us, O God, to get up and move when we find ourselves in a dark corner. Send us to the friendship of other believers. Amen

Prayer concern: Those in need of hope

Daily Reflections_____

_____

_____

_____

Peace of heart and mind

I will lie down and sleep in peace, for you alone,
O LORD, make me dwell in safety. ❖ Psalm 4:8

If I had a dollar for every hour of the day when I have been at
odds with myself or those around me, and one for every hour
of the night when I was unable to sleep because of worry,
or anger, or exasperation—if I had a dollar for each of these,
I would be a wealthy person. I would be wealthy or, as the
psalmist puts it, "my grain and my wine would abound." But
I would be in distress, for we are made to live in fellowship
with each other and with God. Wealthy as I might be, I would
not have fellowship even with myself.

The psalmist tells us a great truth: that we are made for
peace, for wholeness, for fellowship, and that this comes from
God. Whether in good times or bad, in good days or bad, all
peace comes from God.

CHARLES ANDERSON

*In peace, I will walk and work, lie down and sleep for you
alone, O Lord. Make me dwell in safety. Amen*

Prayer concern: Nations that are at war

Daily Reflections_____

The narrow door

Make every effort to enter through the narrow
door. ❖ Luke 13:24

What is the narrow door? People interpret it in various ways:
a particular brand of Christianity, a set of rules for eating or
abstaining, an enlightening experience, a standard of poverty,
a particular interpretation of the Scriptures, or a turning away
from those with whom they do not agree.

The main problem with most attempts to identify the
narrow door is that we too often end up with narrow vision
and a narrow God. It becomes our symbol for salvation, and
we pursue it relentlessly. Yet when we seek salvation as an
end in itself, our vision clouds, and we stand in danger of
missing it altogether.

It is only when we serve our Lord because we *love* him,
in response to his sacrificial love for us, that we finally come
near the narrow door. It is when we quit keeping score to
balance bad deeds with good deeds that we are free to do
God's will out of adoration. The Lord forgives us and admits
us into his loving presence only by grace through faith.

BARBARA M. WILLS

Lord, thank you for grace. Amen

Prayer concern: Christians in Russia

Daily Reflections_____

Children and the kingdom

> Jesus said, "Let the little children come to me, and do not hinder them, for the kingdom of heaven belongs to such as these." ❖ Matthew 19:14

Jesus put a special value on children. His words set down the disciples who were saying something like, "Don't bother Jesus with your children." But what Jesus said was plain. Children were important in the kingdom of God.

Remember that these words were spoken in a time when Roman society allowed people to destroy unwanted infants. But in every land where these words of Jesus have been heard, there has been some form of protection and care for children. Children's homes, child-care in temporary and adoptive homes, and other ways of aiding children come from earliest Christian times.

And children have something to teach us. They provide models for adults at times: models of love, and trust, and faith, and hope. It's a pity that the openness and honesty of children is soon eroded—and that sometimes mistrust, doubt, and fear grow in children as they grow older. What kind of example do we offer to children?

JULIE ELIOT

Help us to trust and love you, good Lord, even as you loved children and they loved you. Amen

Prayer concern: Christians in Europe

Daily Reflections_____

_____

_____

_____

How long?

But I pray to you, O Lord, in the time of your favor; in your great love, O God, answer me with your sure salvation. ❖ Psalm 69:13

"Are we there yet?" How familiar we all are with the impatient excitement of children on a trip! To young minds, even a short trip seems to last forever. Every moment is filled with the anticipation of joyful surprises waiting to be discovered around the next corner.

"How long can this go on?" We utter these words with far less excitement. Watching a dear one suffer a terminal illness, hearing of the endless injustices of this world, waiting for deliverance from a painful crisis, our endurance is tested. Time seems to drag endlessly onward. There seems to be no relief from the decay we sense all around.

As people of faith, we, like the psalmist, can trust in God's action in God's own time. We can dare to wait with hope, even in the bleakest situation, knowing that all our minutes, hours, and days are indeed in God's hands.

Donna Hacker Smith

Lord of our lives, help us to trust that you act at the time that is best. Grant us patience. Amen

Prayer concern: Those awaiting death

Daily Reflections_____

Assurance

> Thomas said to him, "Lord, we don't know
> where you are going, so how can we know the
> way?" ❖ John 14:5

Very often families in mourning ask me to read today's Scripture text at the burial of a loved one. Jesus' encounter with Thomas seems to be helpful in two ways for those of us who face the reality of death.

First, we are comforted by knowing God provides a place for each one of us who die in the Lord. But second, Thomas's thoroughly human question puts into words our own speechless wrestling. When we try to come to terms with the fact that we will die and find ourselves wondering whether God's love can overcome death, Thomas's words become our own.

Because everyone we know eventually dies, we are forced to struggle with the mystery of life: Is this all there is, or does God have more in store for us? Like Thomas, we look to Jesus to lead us through the valley of death's shadow.

Jesus answers Thomas and us with his assurance that he is our way, our truth, and our life. That is enough to help us face the questions of death and life.

DAVID FRYE

God, when we seek to face our doubts, help us to trust that Jesus is the way, truth, and life for us. Amen

Prayer concern: People who ask challenging questions

Daily Reflections_____

_____

_____

_____

Embodied praise

And Mary said: "My soul glorifies the Lord and
my spirit rejoices in God my Savior." ❖ Luke 1:46

Take a deep breath and let it out slowly. Feel your lungs
expand and the air move back through your nostrils. Now
think about how that simple breath of air is your breath of life.
Even if breathing is a struggle, it is still a gift and, in a very
real sense, a victory over death.

Mary's words liken breathing to praising God, the creator
of life. We tend not to envision Mary, as she speaks, stroking a
swollen stomach and feeling the changes in her body as a
fetus grows within. We tend to put *soul* or *spirit* on a different
plane from the *body* and its *senses*. But in the Jewish tradition,
body and *spirit* are not thought of separately. The unity of the
two is clear when Mary speaks of her spirit. She means her
breath—ordinary, bodily breath. From the depths of herself,
she says, "My spirit—my very breath and the whole of my
being—rejoices in God!" (v. 47).

Praising God with our *spirit* is an appropriate gift of
thanks. We simply return to God the breath of life that God
first gave to us.

LYN GESCH

With soul and body we praise you, God. Amen

Prayer concern: Christians in Mozambique

Daily Reflections _____

Beyond tradition

And [Joseph] went and lived in a town called
Nazareth. So was fulfilled what was said through
the prophets: "He will be called a Nazarene."
❖ Matthew 2:23

In the stage play *Fiddler on the Roof*, the song "Tradition" has
an important place. Tradition is given credit for binding the
community together. But there is more than just tradition in
life. Jesus frequently said, "But I say unto you ..." With these
words, Jesus brought a new era of thinking about faith. Luke
4:16-19 illustrates how he gave new meaning to ancient
prophecies. But not everyone was happy about this.

In life, we also face change. If we lived only on tradition,
there would be no modern medicine, modernized transporta-
tion, or new forms of worship. We need to reach out for a new
day, welcome a new age, and appreciate a new generation.

The manger of Bethlehem became a new "hinge of history."
Nations and peoples entered into a new era. Jesus said,
"Today this scripture is fulfilled in your hearing." Advent is
not the beginning of the end but the end of the beginning.

NORMAN G. ANDERSON

*Help us, O Lord, during this Advent to fling wide the
portals of our hearts. Amen*

Prayer concern: History teachers

Daily Reflections_____

_____

_____

_____

The dwelling

Surely goodness and love will follow me all the days of my life, and I will dwell in the house of the LORD forever. ❖ Psalm 23:6

One time when we were on vacation, our hotel room was broken into and some camera equipment worth about $700 was stolen. We were bothered by the loss of things, even though the equipment was insured. But more important, we were upset and felt insecure that someone had come into our room uninvited. Dwellings should be places of security, love, and safety.

Our homes are important to us. We remember our home even when we are far away. It reminds us of the love and caring that is there for us.

In the same way, we sense the protection and power that the house of the Lord, the temple, gave to David. We too can live in the presence of God, in daily communion with the Lord on high. How glorious to dwell in the house of the Lord, in his protection and care!

MARCUS G. ENGLEHADT

Lord God, keep us in your house, your home, so that as the world around us gets more chaotic we will always be secure. Amen

Prayer concern: An adopted or foster child

Daily Reflections_____

_____

_____

_____

Mine and thine

All I have is yours, and all you have is mine. And glory has come to me through them. ❖ John 17:10

The name of Jesus appears more often in the Gospel of John than in any of the other Gospels. Of the 879 verses in John, nearly half identify Jesus by name. In other words, this is a book largely composed of the words of Jesus. Think of how many people have read these words and begun the trip to eternal joy. Haven't you ever wished you'd been the one to write such a volume telling about Jesus and containing his words? Or wouldn't it have been a rich experience at least to have been the scribe who copied the words? Don't you wish you had been that close to Jesus and his words?

The truth, of course, is that we *are* close to our Savior. We have never heard him speak in a face-to-face encounter. Yet he speaks to us daily in words like the ones we have read. We may never have written a book about him, but our daily lives speak volumes about our lives with him. We haven't felt the warmth of his nail-scarred hands on our shoulder, yet he is over us, beside us, under us, behind us—and in us.

We belong to Christ, and Christ's prayer was a strong one: "I am not praying for the world but for those you have given me, for they are yours." This prayer for the apostles? Yes, but for you and me too.

OMAR BONDERUD

Lord Jesus, we thank you for making us yours. Amen

Prayer concern: Christians in Russia

Daily Reflections

Body building

Because there is one loaf, we, who are many,
are one body, for we all partake of the one loaf.
❖ 1 Corinthians 10:17

Even though our preference is for harmony, church members
do have disagreements. Every congregation includes
members with differing opinions on any number of subjects—
some important, some not. A disagreement over a decorating
question is less important than a conflict about changing the
baptismal practices. Some quarrels can help build community
when members work together respectfully and create a reso-
lution to the issue. Other conflicts create gaping wounds in
the body of Christ, tearing the church apart.

Disagreement in the church dates back to the earliest
Christians. The apostle Paul often addressed issues that created rifts in the fledgling church. In today's passage, Paul
describes the corporate dimension of repentance, when all
members act to build unity in the body of Christ. Paul advised
the Corinthians not to place their own opinions above the
need for accord, even if they were in the right. Unity in the
church does not develop without the Holy Spirit's guidance.
In Holy Communion, the unity of the church is reinforced.
Through loving actions we help make unity a reality.

DONNA HACKER SMITH

*Lord, may my words and actions help build your church.
Amen*

Prayer concerns: Congregations in the call process

Daily Reflections_____

_____

_____

_____

Proper work for Christians

> Jesus went throughout Galilee, teaching in their
> synagogues, preaching the good news of the
> kingdom, and healing every disease and sickness
> among the people. ❖ Matthew 4:23

When Jesus went to Galilee, he lived under the reign of the
Roman emperor Tiberius, who used coins to publicize himself. We could take one of those coins to see what Tiberius
looked like. Yet we have no likeness of Jesus anywhere.
Matthew and the other writers did not describe him with so
much as a sentence. When they spread the word of Jesus,
they told what he said and did—not how he looked.

Matthew makes it very plain to us that Jesus engaged in
teaching and preaching, and helping and healing. When Jesus
taught, people heard how they should to live and what they
should do. When he preached, they learned of the wonderful
goodness and mercy of God. As helper and healer, Jesus
restored bodies to health, protected boatsmen in a storm, and
fed the hungry. He showed what happens when God moves
among people with wisdom, power, and rule. Matthew wrote
these words to help us believe in Jesus, to teach and preach,
and to help and heal. That is how salvation comes to us.

ARTHUR J. SEEGERS

O God, you came to people in Galilee when Jesus walked
among them. Come to us here. Help us to believe and do
the truth that Jesus is for us. Amen

Prayer concern: Christians in Iran

Daily Reflections_____

_____

_____

_____

The baptism of our Lord

And the Holy Spirit descended on him in bodily form like a dove. And a voice came from heaven: "You are my Son, whom I love; with you I am well pleased." ❖ Luke 3:22

Today we remember Jesus' baptism. Luke paints a graphic picture of the event. We see that Jesus was not baptized privately, but along with many others. We see that Jesus used his baptism as an occasion for prayer. We see that a dove—the Holy Spirit—descended upon him, and hear that a voice from heaven proclaimed him as God's beloved Son.

All of these images help us understand Jesus' baptism, and our own. In both, the washing conveys an identity. But there is a distinction. In his baptism, Jesus is identified as the beloved Son; the one through whom all others receive salvation. Baptism names us as those who have been promised the life and forgiveness won by the Son.

Jesus' baptism also reminds us that the life of the baptized is public, not private. And it reminds us that the life of the baptized is a life of prayer.

KAREN BATES

Lord, let us live our baptism. Amen

Prayer concern: Faithfulness in prayer

Daily Reflections_____

Amazing grace

> The life appeared; we have seen it and testify
> to it, and we proclaim to you the eternal life,
> which was with the Father and has appeared
> to us. ❖ 1 John 1:2

The writer of 1 John sounds astounded. He seems to be saying, "I can hardly believe it!" Yet he did believe it, amazing though it was. To think that the inexpressible was expressed—the Word became flesh! To reflect that the eternal became time-bound, "that which was from the beginning" was doomed to die! To remember that he and the other apostles had actually seen, heard, and touched the incarnate God. All of this was thoroughly overwhelming.

But John is eager to share his experience with others. It was no dream or vision, but amazing reality, he says. He repeats the phrase "seen and heard" three times. If we believe this to be true, we have fellowship with the apostles, and their fellowship is "with the Father and with his Son, Jesus Christ," to "make our joy complete."

HERBERT F. LINDEMAN

God, we thank you for sharing your life with us in Jesus Christ. Amen

Prayer concern: World peace

Daily Reflections_____

Rejoice!

Then you will look and be radiant, your heart will throb and swell with joy. ❖ Isaiah 60:5

Perhaps nothing is more dramatic or moving than a beautiful sunrise. Whether we are alone on a mountain or out on the plains, watching from a bedroom window or driving along the highway, it is exciting to watch the veil of darkness begin to fade as the morning sun slowly rises and then bursts into crimson light. As the world is bathed in new beauty, we find ourselves ready to rise, shine, praise, and sing.

The truth of Isaiah's prophecy runs throughout the Bible. All nations will be drawn to God's light. Though darkness has covered them, the dawn breaks. We who hear Isaiah are challenged to witness to the Light that has come so that under God's guidance all nations may come together to see and to be radiant, to thrill and rejoice.

NORMA SCHIRCK

Radiant God, may we share with others the light that has come to us. Amen

Prayer concern: Artists

Daily Reflections_____
_____
_____
_____

Teach us your paths

> Show me your ways, O LORD, teach me your
> paths. ❖ Psalm 25:4

When we come to God through faith in Jesus Christ, we are not a finished work. Our faith still needs a lot of guiding and molding. And the way life works, it seems that our faith goes three steps forward and then two steps—maybe even four steps—back. That is why we pray that God would continually teach us to follow the right path.

I suspect it was that way for Francis of Assisi. Until the age of 20, Francis assisted his father in business. But after much inner struggle, Francis decided to devote his life to prayer and service of the poor. This was the path that God opened to Francis. His generosity, devotion to God and humanity, love of nature, and deep humility made him one of the most cherished saints in the history of the church. Francis learned well what God had to teach.

We never arrive at Christian perfection. Rather, in lives of devotion, worship, and prayer, we learn the truths and the paths that God teaches us. And then, like Francis, we have the foundations for serving both the economically poor and the spiritually poor.

JOHN. W. COFFEY

Make us to know your ways, O Lord, and teach us your paths. Amen

Prayer concern: All who serve the poor

Daily Reflections_____

_____

_____

_____

Following Christ

If anyone does not remain in me, he is like
a branch that is thrown away and withers.
❖ John 15:6

What a contrast between a branch just removed from a tree,
and that same branch several hours later. While the wood
looks the same, it is the leaves that tell the story. In both
instances, having lost their life support, the leaves are dead,
although they appear to be alive when the branch is freshly
severed.

Jesus uses the image of a branch cut off from the tree to
illustrate the consequences of trying to survive without an
abiding faith in him.

When a person first detaches from the source of life, it may
seem that things are no different from before. But in a short
time, with the nourishment of faith cut off, we are hopelessly
adrift. Our life support is gone.

Consider the prodigal son, who thought he was free when
he cut himself off from his father's household. He soon found
himself an outcast, fit to live only with the swine. Thank God,
who knows our weaknesses and stands ready to reclaim us.

O. HENRY HOVERSTEN

*Lord God, help us to spurn the temptations that cut us
off from you. Amen*

Prayer concern: Runaways

Daily Reflections_____

_____
_____
_____

Complain, complain, complain

Who is this that darkens my counsel with words
without knowledge? ❖ Job 38:2

Job was angry. Tragedy had befallen him. He has lost his
family, possessions, and land. *God was responsible for the evil
that he had experienced*, Job complained. *God was not treating
him fairly!* Job considered himself to be devout in his religion
and one of the most righteous of men. He thought he
deserved better.

We are very similar to Job. We complain, and God often
takes the brunt of our anger. We may think, "If only God
would answer our prayers. If only God would bless us as
much as God does others. If only God would be fair."

God spoke to Job and reminded him that God is the
Almighty. God's will is beyond comprehension. Rather than
complain, we can rest in God's power and be secure in God's
love. Though tragedies befall us, God will not forsake us.

ANONYMOUS

*Lord, forgive our complaining. Move in our lives and
deepen our faith. Amen*

Prayer concern: Those struggling in their faith

Daily Reflections

Called to hope

I pray also that the eyes of your heart may be enlightened in order that you may know the hope to which he has called you, the riches of his glorious inheritance in the saints. ❖ Ephesians 1:18

Renewed hope often accompanies the arrival of spring. There is a newness and a freshness about everything. The fish are spawning, the flowers are blooming, and the golf course is open. But the hope in our lives cannot be a seasonal thing, rooted in the cycles of nature. Springtime might refresh us, but it cannot sustain us. We need far more than fishing, gardening, and playing golf to enlighten the eyes of the heart.

To know the hope that Paul had in mind for the Ephesians, to know the hope that endures through all seasons, seems to be a matter of having the eyes of the heart enlightened. Our son-in-law is an ophthalmologist, an eye doctor, and he can do marvelous things to enlighten the eyes, but only God can enlighten the eyes of the heart.

The great light from God that opens our eyes to the glorious inheritance that awaits us has been beamed to us in Jesus Christ. He is the light of the world, and he calls us to a firm and steady hope. Spring may capture us with a flicker of hope, but Christ captures us with eternal hope.

ANONYMOUS

God of light, enlighten the eyes of our hearts so that we may see the great hope to which we are called. Amen

Prayer concern: Those who serve in the military

Daily Reflections

Winning ways

You shall see greater things than that. ❖ John 1:50b

Society revolves around a system of rewards and punishments. Throughout life, we are subjected to judgments that result in either acceptance or rejection of our actions. As we mature we become increasingly adept at how to weigh the scales of judgment that register disapproval or approval of our conduct. Call it manipulation if you will, it can become a way of inducing positive response to our behavior or performance.

Too often we also attempt to use this deceptive method to win God's favor. But we cannot fool God with exaggerations of what we have done or fabrications of what we will do for him in the future. God does not look at outward appearance but at the inward spirit.

Before God, we do well to confess our weakness, seek mercy, and trust in grace. If we believe, we shall see great things and our hearts will change toward honesty.

JEAN R. SWEIGERT

Dear Lord, be with us to guide us in the path of truth. Help us to overcome our doubts and to believe, so we may see great things. Amen

Prayer concern: People who don't judge others by their appearance.

Daily Reflections

Do I belong here?

*The man who enters by the gate is the shepherd
of his sheep.* ❖ John 10:2

When I was young, I used to go to the movies every Saturday.
Sometimes between features, kids would leave by the big
EXIT door down in front by the screen. Often they'd leave the
door open—sometimes on purpose, sometimes by mistake.
Sometimes they would hold it so their friends could sneak in
for a free show.

Naturally, I wondered what it would be like to sneak in
through the EXIT door. One thing I noticed about those who
did sneak in was that they always ran and hid. Sometimes the
usher would come and ask to see their tickets—and make
them leave because they didn't belong there.

There's no doubt about it—going in by the proper door is
costly. But it's a price worth paying. If we try the shortcuts,
other people tempt us with, we'll always hear the nagging
question: *Do I belong here?*

Jesus tells us that he is the proper door; it is through him
that we are welcomed into new life. Instead of looking for
other doorways, let's come into life by the sure one.

DAWN M. PROUX

Jesus, help us know where we belong. Amen

Prayer concern: People who are alienated

Daily Reflections_____

_____

_____

_____

Shalom and shalah

> Again Jesus said, "Peace be with you! As the father
> has sent me, I am sending you." ❖ John 20:21

Jesus says *shalom* (which means "peace") and *shalah* (which means "Go," or "I send you"). His full greeting is "Peace! Go!" We are used to thinking of peace as rest, quiet, or inaction. But the Hebrew word *shalom* has a much fuller meaning. That is why this same word is used in several ways—to say "hello," "good-bye," "best wishes," or "God bless you." Yet *shalom* really means, "May you have wholeness, health, a well-balanced life." Rest and quietness are only one part of that balance.

To quote a religious folk song, "The peace of God, it is no peace." Jesus says, "I give you peace; now get a move on!" Jesus gives us the kind of peace that is most real to us when we are in the thick of things.

I know two theologians, one who carries on an incredible schedule of writing, lecturing, and teaching, and another who does difficult counseling in a medical center. Both are famous for their ability to take a catnap in the midst of a hectic schedule. They understand the connection between *shalom* and *shalah*.

CARL L. JECH

Thanks, God, for the peace to go. Amen

Prayer concern: Theologians

Daily Reflections

Fasting that helps

Is not this the kind of fasting I have chosen?
❖ Isaiah 58:6

We usually think of fasting as abstaining from food and drink. About the only time we do it in our society is when we want to lose weight. We seldom fast as a religious discipline. Maybe that's a good thing. Isaiah deplored the kind of fasting that led people to be proud of their humility. The trouble was that their fasting was too inner-directed.

Look at the text and note the kind of fasting God desires. It is a fast that sets captives free, that clothes people, and that won't tolerate starvation in famine-torn nations. It is not a fast that is inner-directed, but one that is *other*-directed. It is the kind of fasting born of an eagerness to give up selfishness and greed for the sake of the poor and oppressed of the world. From this perspective, our whole lives can be thought of as a kind of fast—a fast that is acceptable to the Lord.

CHARLES KNORR

Lord, teach us to fast in a way that will help others and not only ourselves. Amen

Prayer concern: People who are fasting

Daily Reflections

According to script

Then I said, "Here I am—it is written about me in
the scroll—I have come to do your will, O God."
❖ Hebrews 10:7

The writer to the Hebrews gives us a well-composed essay on
the role of Christ. A theologian rich in Hebrew tradition, the
writer takes great pains to demonstrate the superiority of the
Christ over angels, patriarchs, and the best in the history of
God's people. The writer also elaborates on the role of the
Christ as our high priest. As high priest, Christ comes to
make a sacrifice for us.

Using a quote from Psalm 40, the writer indicates that
Jesus served as high priest according to script. He did not
come to make ritualistic sacrifices but to offer himself in obedience to God. Obedience brought him to the cross. However,
his obedience was vindicated. God raised his Son from the
dead. This is proof positive that the fellowship and unity of
the Father and the Son remained unbroken. Through Christ,
we too have fellowship with God. We can yield trust and
obedience to God—no matter how imperfect it may be.

HARRY N. HUXHOLD

Christ, our King, help us do your Father's will. Amen

Prayer concern: Bible translators

Daily Reflections_____

_____

_____

_____

The life that is the light

On no day will its gates ever be shut, for there will
be no night there. ❖ Revelation 21:25

Today's passage paints a mind-picture of God's holy city.
But to visualize the brightness therein defies the imagination.
No sun, no moon, yet light of lights. How awesome!

It is hard to comprehend, yet it was in this same setting,
in the glorious presence of God almighty, that Satan deceived
perhaps one-third of the angels. They were persuaded to
follow the Prince of Darkness and as a result were cast out of
this bright and holy place.

Is it any wonder that we, too, are deceived by this
imposter, living as we do in a world that often seems to be
filled with all the elements of darkness? The darkness we
point to is human inhumanity to people, but the trail of dark
guilt leads back to our own hearts also. Greed, pollution, war,
jealousy, crime, apathy to human need—these and many
other tragedies are evidence that darkness springs from the
human heart.

NANCY LEE SASSER

*Lord God, how glorious it will be to come victorious in
Christ, through the ever-open gates, into your holy city.
Amen*

Prayer concern: Someone being tempted

Daily Reflections_____
_____
_____
_____

Pass the salt

Have salt in yourselves, and be at peace with each other. ❖ Mark 9:50b

Technicians use tons of salt on the sound stage of a major movie studio to create the illusion of a frigid arctic landscape. Real snow could not match salt for authentic looking texture and brilliance.

In ancient times, salt was considered one of the purest elements in the world because the light of the sun and the water of the sea combine to make those glistening white deposits. Salt was a symbol for purity.

The words of Jesus in today's text are a lasting reminder to his followers about purity and peace. When selfishness, greed, bigotry, jealousy, hatred, and suspicion contaminate the heart, there can be no peace between people. Only the Spirit of Christ can rid us of these impurities and inspire in us the selfless love and trust upon which harmony depends.

MILAN C. INGMAN

Lord, purify our hearts and minds so that peace may abound. Amen

Prayer concern: Church unity

Daily Reflections

Partiality

> For whoever keeps the whole law and yet stumbles at just one point is guilty of breaking all of it.
> ❖ James 2:10

Church members become guilty of sin if they fail to make the stranger welcome at worship. They fail to keep the command to love your neighbor as yourself. James warns us not to cater only to those who conform to our image of what a worshiper should be. When those who are different are rejected, James calls it the sin of partiality.

Partiality denies the dignity of someone who is excluded—that individual's worth in the eyes of our God, who created each one in God's image. It also degrades the one who does the excluding.

Jesus never allowed power, position, social standing, wealth—or the lack of it—to shut out any of God's people whom he came to save: "For God did not send his Son into the world to condemn the world, but to save the world through him" (John 3:17). He is aware of our inability to love as he did. He is always ready to forgive when we come to him in repentance and faith. He truly loves!

JANET REINHARD

Dear Savior, help us to fight the sin of partiality. Amen

Prayer concern: A pastor

Daily Reflections_____

_____

_____

_____

The shortcuts

> You were taught, with regard to your former way of
> life, to put off your old self, which is being corrupted
> by its deceitful desires. ❖ Ephesians 4:22

Sin has been described as a shortcut. Cheating is a shortcut
for studying. Stealing is a shortcut for work. Lying is a
shortcut for trust. Hardly a day goes by when a person is not
tempted to take shortcuts. Our first instinct is to believe that
the shortcut might work. The old nature looks for instant
gratification: "I want what I want *now*!"

Following the short-term payoff come the consequences.
The Christian has discovered that what may be apparent on
the surface is not really so. The shortcuts have a kickback.
Because such shortcuts leave God out of consideration, they
inevitably result in regrets. God's way is the way of truth and
honesty. God guarantees deep-seated satisfaction immediately
and a wholesome outcome ultimately. No person can fail when
on God's side. Throughout life, a person who avoids moral
shortcuts can live with himself or herself because God's
peace rules within.

LUTHER ABRAHAMSON

*We have found out, O God, that we cannot do wrong and
feel right. Help us to do right. Amen*

Prayer concern: Journalists

Daily Reflections_____

_____

_____

_____

Why me, Lord?

> He predestined us to be adopted as his sons
> through Jesus Christ, in accordance with his plea-
> sure and will. ❖ Ephesians 1:5

In adversity we are quick to ask, "Why me?" Less frequently we ask that question when a great happiness is ours. Even less often do we ask when we become aware that, out of the billions of earth's peoples, our hearts have been among the few to whom the good news of eternal life through Christ's death and resurrection has been told.

The apostle tells us why. Our destiny as God's daughters and sons in Christ was not an accident or luck. God was moved by love: "God so loved the world …"

Moreover, God had a profound purpose in mind when freely bestowing glorious grace on us in Christ. So that we might praise that grace, he gave us redemption through his blood, the forgiveness of our sins. That is why I—and that is why you—were chosen and destined as God's children.

GEORGE H. MUEDEKING

*O Christ, may I treasure my destiny to be united with you
in the eternity you have gone to prepare for me. Amen*

Prayer concern: Young couples

Daily Reflections_____

Worthy homes

> If the home is deserving, let your peace rest
> on it; if it is not, let your peace return to you.
> ❖ Matthew 10:13

Suppose Jesus' disciples came to your home and asked for lodging, or made inquiries about a suitable place to stay. Would your home be worthy? What sort of home would they be seeking? I don't know the answer, but I do know a lot of homes I would recommend. I have been a guest numerous times, and what I have experienced in worthy homes is remembered with fondness.

In every case, my hosts put me completely at ease. They made no demands on me and gave me to understand that their home was at my disposal. I was invited to join them at social events and at church, but the choice was mine. When I left, it was always with the understanding that I would be welcome anytime.

These gracious people differed in ethnic backgrounds, religions, occupations, and financial status, but they had one thing in common. That one common ingredient was open-hearted caring.

EINARD WAISANEN

Lord, make mine a worthy home. Amen

Prayer concern: Young adults

Daily Reflections

According to ability

> The disciples, each according to his ability,
> decided to provide help for the brothers living
> in Judea. ❖ Acts 11:29

When any part of the body of Christ is in need, the other parts respond out of love. It was true of the new congregation in Antioch, and it is still true.

The disciples sent relief. Did they collect used soap from motels? Money? Gifts? Quilts? Whatever they sent, surely it did not differ significantly from what we send today when people are hurting, hungry, cold.

Not all of us can sew quilts or children's clothing. Not all of us can haul and load clothing into boxcars bound for a place we may never go. But in whatever small way we can help, a part of us is also shipped to our brethren in need. A part of me is sent in the dollar, in the grain, in the warm coat. Because I too am a disciple I decide, according to my own abilities, how much to give. One of the hallmarks of the church is to help those in need.

JOHN A. SPEERSTRA

Lord, put my abilities to work for you today. Amen

Prayer concern: Church colleges

Daily Reflections_____

_____

_____

_____

In God we trust

The LORD is the stronghold of my life—of whom shall I be afraid? ❖ Psalm 27:1b

My high-school coach always reminded us that"the best offense is a good defense." The fewer points you give up, the better chance you have of winning. Now it seems rather simple!

A good defense *is* important for nations, for individuals, and for teams. Defense was so important to the Chinese that in the second century they built the Great Wall of China. At 1,400 miles long, the wall proved ineffective because the guards could be bribed.

The psalmist knew that life can be tough. Psalm 27 is about "enemies and foes" out there—an "army" of them! But he also wrote that he was not afraid because of his defense: he trusted in the God of all creation.

We often trust our own abilities and financial security to see us through tough times. Such things *may* help, but they cannot give us the victory. In God we trust!

THOMAS REHL

Walk with me this day, my Lord. Amen

Prayer concern: More understanding between different ethnic groups and cultures

Daily Reflections_____

_____

_____

_____

Walk in the light

But if we walk in the light, as he is in the light,
we have fellowship with one another, and the blood
of Jesus, his Son, purifies us from all sin. ❖ 1 John 1:7

We pulled into the campground about midnight and promptly
got settled and went to sleep. Only in the morning's light did
we become aware of the beautiful scenery and of the
sparkling river that flowed beside us.

In the light, we see things differently. Walking in the light
does not mean that we are sinless. Rather, it is seeing ourselves as God sees us. Walking in the light means being
honest about ourselves. It is admitting our sins, acknowledging our need of God, and following God. We often prefer
the darkness because it hides from us the things we do not
want to see. But in the darkness, life becomes a constant
cover-up and rarely makes us happy.

God, who knows us, calls us out of darkness to walk in the
light of God's love. We need not fear what we might see in
ourselves, for God loves us unconditionally. In God's light,
we find forgiveness through Jesus Christ.

LINDA HOXTELL

Gracious God, help to walk in the light of your love. Amen

Prayer concern: Emergency responders

Daily Reflections

To boast

> Not only is this so, but we also rejoice in God through our Lord Jesus Christ, through whom we have now received reconciliation. ❖ Romans 5:11

Christians can be boastful. Ours is not the "anything you can do I can do better" kind of boasting. And it's not the "my dad can beat up your dad" kind of boasting. And it surely is not the "we have the only true and right understanding of theology" kind of boasting. Christians can boast only *after* we say, "While we were still weak, Christ died." Christians can boast only *after* we assert, "While we were still sinners, Christ died." Christians can boast only *after* we understand that "while we were God's *enemies*, we were reconciled to God."

In the face of God's act of reconciliation through the death of Jesus, it requires amazing pride for us to be boastful over the rightness of our own human thoughts and actions. But I boast, and you boast, and God still continues to reconcile us to God and to one another. This truly is worth boasting about! Even as we boast, though, we remember that we have nothing to do with our being reconciled. God, through our Lord Jesus Christ, is the one who has reconciled us.

MARY ELLEN LARSON

O God, keep us ever mindful of your grace at work for our salvation. Amen

Prayer concern: World hunger

Daily Reflections_____
_____
_____
_____

Musings at the family plot

Amen. Come, Lord Jesus. ❖ Revelation 22:20

I recently visited for the first time the graveyard where my paternal ancestors are buried, and I saw my family name on two tombstones. One of my reactions was to ponder the fact that, at age 40, I have outlived both my father (who died at 39) and my grandfather (who died when he was only 30).

"The LORD gave, and the LORD has taken away; may the name of the LORD be praised" (Job 1:21). Have these words bothered you when used in relation to the untimely death of a young person? They bother me if taken as an *explanation* of tragedy. But if they are understood not as an explanation but as an expression of *confidence*, then I find the words comforting. In spite of what has happened, we say, we can trust God to bring good out of an apparent evil.

I do not take this final prayer in the New Testament as meaning that I should be in any hurry to die. I take it as a simple statement of confidence that death is not a static end but rather a waiting for the dynamic coming of the Lord.

CARL L. JECH

Come quickly, Lord Jesus. Amen

Prayer concern: Those who grieve

Daily Reflections_____

_____

_____

_____

God's promise

All who ... hold fast to my covenant—these I will
bring to my holy mountain and give them joy in
my house of prayer. ❖ Isaiah 56:6-7

Some things go together as though they were made for each
other; a walk and a beautiful day; a friend and a great time;
obedience to God and a joyful heart. As today's verse says,
those who hold fast to God's covenant will receive joy.

The people of Israel had endured conquest by the
Babylonians, exile in a distant land, and the despair of finding
their temple and city in ruins when they returned to
Jerusalem. Yet one thing remained to give them identity. One
thing remained to give them new courage in the face of great
disappointment: the covenant of God, given to Abraham and
Sarah centuries before. God promised, "I will bless you ... and
you will be a blessing" (Genesis 12:2).

Today entire countries face starvation. Our planet is criti-
cally ill from pollution and toxic waste. And in our own lives we
face disease, despair, or deep grief. Yet one thing remains at all
times: the ancient promise of God, which took flesh in Jesus.
We are blessed with the presence of Christ, so that we may
bless others in his name. And in obedience to this promise,
there is joy.

DARLENE BOWDEN MUSCHETT

*O God, enable us to know the joy of following Jesus,
regardless of the circumstances. Amen*

Prayer concern: People in difficult situations

Daily Reflections_____

_____

_____

_____

The stain

Create in me a pure heart, O God, and renew a
steadfast spirit within me. ❖ Psalm 51:10

Jeff came home from school with a large blue spot on his
pants. "My pen broke and leaked," he explained when confronted by his mother. "When I saw it, I couldn't do anything
about it."

His mother understood but was still faced with the task of
getting the stain out. "I'm not sure I'll be able to get it all out,"
she said. "These pants may always be stained."

As we go through life, we pick up stains. They are called
"sins" in the church. We try various ways to wash them out.
We try to wash them out by doing good things, by increasing
our attendance at church, or by dropping a few dollars more
in the collection plate. But nothing takes away the stains.

Nothing, that is, except Jesus Christ. When we trust his
grace, we are washed clean by his death and resurrection and
stand shining bright before God in Christ's righteousness.

KEVIN E. RUFFCORN

Lord, I have sinned. Forgive me. Amen

Prayer concern: Civic leaders

Daily Reflections_____

Good shepherd

> When Jesus landed and saw a large crowd, he had
> compassion on them, because they were like
> sheep without a shepherd. So he began teaching
> them many things. ❖ Mark 6:34

As adolescents, what our peer group thought, said, and did
was important for us. We often took our guidance from them.
But eventually we learned that it is not uncommon to receive
unreliable cues from our peer group. Where do we turn, then,
for guidance? To another group? To an individual? To the
state? The psalmist says we are not even to put our trust in
princes (Psalm 118:9).

In such a situation, we could feel like members of the great
crowd in Jesus' day who were like sheep without a shepherd.
Jesus had compassion on them. He has compassion on us.
Through his Word, audibly proclaimed in preaching and
physically shared through the Sacraments of Baptism and
Communion, we hear the message that Christ is our good
shepherd. We were crucified with him, and now he lives in us.
Guidance comes from Christ, who has bonded himself with
us and dwells within us.

ELAINE BABCOCK

*Lord Jesus, you are our shepherd. In our inner persons,
teach us many things. Amen*

Prayer concern: A friend in need

Daily Reflections

_____

_____

_____

Love acts

Dear children, let us not love with words or tongue
but with actions and in truth. ❖ 1 John 3:18

Love consists of more than words. Truth, to be established,
requires more than speeches. To show love and to confirm
the truth of our words we must act. The world knows this.
"Put up or shut up," it says as it points to the gap between
what Christians say and what they do.

We pray for the poor but do little to eliminate poverty. We
pass resolutions against discrimination but avoid those who
are different. We tell the church not to invest in companies
that cooperate with apartheid, but we continue to buy their
products.

Those people who are most particular about how to word
Christian truth are often the most negligent in acting it out.
Jesus commended the church at Ephesus for its pure doctrine
but said they had abandoned love (Revelation 2:2-4). If we did
more we wouldn't need to say so much. When you befriend
people who are different, you don't need to say, "Some of my
best friends are...."

Jesus proved his love and the truth of his words by giving
his life for us. He can help us to follow his example.

ROLF E. AASENG

Lord, help us to love by acting. Amen

Prayer concern: A church custodian

Daily Reflections

What Joseph didn't do

*But Joseph said to them "Don't be afraid. Am I in
the place of God? ❖ Genesis 50:19*

Joseph's brothers didn't know what to expect. Their father,
Jacob, was dead. Would Joseph now want to strike back at
them for selling him so many years before? Fearing the worst,
they begged forgiveness. To their amazement, Joseph
responded with kindness. He accepted his brothers and
assured them they would be cared for. What he didn't do was
to take on the role of God and judge them.

Perhaps Joseph thought about punishing his brothers.
(He must have been sorely tempted at least to give them a
lecture.) But he didn't chastise them. Joseph recognized God
as the rightful judge and left matters in his hands.

We shouldn't be quick to judge either. It's not always easy
to refrain from judging others, and it's certainly not easy to do
as gracefully as Joseph did. But we can let God be the final
judge. And like Joseph, we can respond to others not in
unmerciful judgment, but in gracious kindness.

ANN KLEMAN

*God, when we're tempted to judge others unmercifully,
help us remember Joseph, who reacted with kindness.
Amen*

Prayer concern: Family members who don't get along

Daily Reflections_____
_____
_____
_____

Reach out

> If your brother sins against you, go and show
> him his fault, just between the two of you. If he
> listens to you, you have won your brother over.
> ❖ Matthew 18:15

A Roman Catholic nun spoke at a community ecumenical service held at a Methodist church. She mentioned some of the things that have separated Christians for all these years and offered her opinion about what keeps them from getting together. The nun said that three of the most difficult things for someone to say to another are "I was wrong," "I'm sorry," and "I love you."

She pointed out that each of these three statements touches a sensitive nerve, not only in the personal circle of family and friends but in ecumenical relations as well. Christians of all kinds have problems saying these things to one another. But when such admissions and feelings are expressed they have power to bring healing to broken relationships. Jesus' words chart a course to reconciliation: Try to gain your brother.

WILLIAM H. LUOMA

Lord, when there is a problem between me and others, help me say the right things and with the right intentions. Amen

Prayer concern: Renewers of the church

Daily Reflections_____

Treasure that surprises

> The kingdom of heaven is like treasure hidden in
> a field. ❖ Matthew 13:44

It's exciting to think of finding hidden treasure. When our son
was younger, he and his dad used a metal detector to look for
"buried treasure." Sometimes they found nothing more than
old bolts or worthless metal scraps. Once in a while, however,
a coin or piece of jewelry turned up. What excitement there
was then imagining how valuable the discovery might be!

Jesus says that our relationship to God is like a valuable
treasure, which we should seek and desire. Unlike people
with metal detectors, the person in Jesus' parable discovered
the treasure quite by accident. It surprised him! Often that's
the way God's kingdom comes to us.

The crucial question we must answer is, what shall we do
when the awareness of God's action of love in Christ breaks
upon us and surprises us? We have found a treasure!

ALICE HEIL

*God, it's wonderful to live in your kingdom here. Keep
us faithful. Amen*

Prayer concern: Church choirs

Daily Reflections

Our hope

In that day the Root of Jesse will stand as a banner
for the peoples; the nations will rally to him, and
his place of rest will be glorious. ❖ Isaiah 11:10

The more attention we pay to the news, the more depressed
we tend to feel. We ask ourselves, "Will we ever get a break
from all this trouble? Will it ever be the way we imagine the
'good old days' were—peaceful, trusting, and secure?" People
in every age have asked the same questions. Because sin and
death still have power in the world, love and peace have never
been the norm.

Yet the Christian lives by trust, hope, and faith. We trust
God's promises to nurture and sustain us are true. Our hope
comes through the Holy Spirit, who will never leave us com-
fortless. We have faith in our Lord Jesus Christ, by whose
grace we have been saved.

In due time, God will give us peace. We will enjoy peace
in its entirety: human and beast will dwell together, the beast
so very tame. All people will know the love of Christ. The
world cannot endure without the Lord. The Root of Jesse
reminds us that the day of God's glory will come.

OFELIA CAVAZOS-MADDEN

*Lord God, we pray that we will not despair but hold on
to your promise, through Jesus Christ. Amen*

Prayer concern: People who were recently baptized

Daily Reflections

Blood is good

As for you, because of the blood of my covenant with you, I will free your prisoners from the waterless pit. ❖ Zechariah 9:11

As if he is seeing far into the future to a cross on Calvary, Zechariah gives the promise of salvation through the blood of a dying Savior.

We sometimes become squeamish about the language of blood. Blood means violence—and even death. But blood means life. Blood carries food to the cells of our bodies. Blood gives us oxygen and carries away poisonous carbon dioxide. It is the river of life coursing through our veins and arteries. To say that the Lord shed his blood for the sins of the world is to say he gave his life. And that is the most glorious language in the Christian's vocabulary.

Jesus said that no greater love exists than someone who lays down his life for a friend. Then Jesus did the extraordinary: he made us all his friends. Jesus died for us all. Through his death we are free from the pit of sin and death, and free to live with him forevermore.

ALVIN N. ROGNESS

Thank you, Lord, for shedding your blood for our salvation. Amen

Prayer concern: Victims of domestic violence

Daily Reflections_____

_____

_____

_____

Now I know

> Then the woman said to Elijah, "Now I know that
> you are a man of God and that the word of the Lord
> from your mouth is the truth." ❖ 1 Kings 17:24

Like Thomas and like Elijah's hostess, I would like proof.
My years in the engineering disciplines prompted me to seek
a rational basis for everything. Including God.

But that approach won't do it. God is not out to *prove*
anything to us. Even the cross of Christ *proves* nothing. Does
the father of a household *prove* to his children that he is their
father? No, he simply loves them, cares for them, encourages
them, and disciplines them. For the children, that is enough;
they trust him.

Our response of trust is to a heavenly Creator who loves,
cares, encourages, and disciplines us. Through Christ, we can
see deep into the heart of God—a God of incredible love and
forgiveness. We see all of this by faith; by faith we understand;
by faith we know. The unveiling of God in Jesus Christ is
enough. We need no proof, for now we can know. Christ is
sufficient.

JOHN W. COFFEY

*Dear God, I keep thinking I need some proof about you.
Remind me again that Jesus Christ is what I need. Amen*

Prayer concern: Those having trouble with trust

Daily Reflections_____

_____

_____

_____

A new day

For I will forgive their wickedness and will
remember their sins no more. ❖ Jeremiah 31:34

Margaret entered the shop where she worked. Her heart
pounded as she closed the door behind her and walked to the
back room to hang up her coat. She felt miserable. She had
been under a lot of stress the past few months and was
becoming depressed. Yesterday she had said some nasty
things to one of her coworkers. Carlos had not said or done
anything wrong. It's just that everyone and everything
annoyed her lately.

Carlos came into the room, whistling and sporting his
usual smile. Carlos's love for people and life was evident in
his words and actions. "Good morning, Margaret!" Carlos
exclaimed. "I hope you're feeling better today. We need you!"

Margaret was surprised. She had expected to be shunned,
but Carlos had acted as if nothing had happened. Margaret
felt as if a great weight had been lifted from her shoulders.
The slate had been wiped clean. What joy!

SUE SPRANG

*God of Glory, thank you for giving me a fresh start each
day. Amen*

Prayer concern: Those who cannot let go of their sins

Daily Reflections_____

_____

_____

_____

Honesty brings healing

> Then I acknowledged my sin to you and did not
> cover up my iniquity. ❖ Psalm 32:5

Carrying the burden of wrongdoing and sin can create havoc
in our bodies. Sometimes we actually feel the heaviness of the
burden in our heart. Other times we lose much-needed sleep,
tossing and turning through the night due to the "dis-ease"
that unresolved guilt has created in us.

In a marvelously simple way, the psalmist reminds us that
when we bring our confession to the Lord and speak honestly
to God, we receive the kind of healing that comes with the
freeing word of forgiveness. Hearing the promise of forgiveness can in turn bring healing of the body and restful sleep.
Confession and forgiveness restores us; it restores not only
our relationship to God but our physical well-being too. Such
healing is truly our salvation.

STEPHANIE FREY

*Gracious God, help us to understand that when we keep
silent about our guilt, our bodies waste away—but when
we speak our confession to you, you offer the healing
balm of forgiveness. We thank you for that gift. Amen*

Prayer concern: Courage to confess

Daily Reflections_____

_____

_____

_____

Obedience

Peter and the other apostles replied: "We must
obey God rather than men!" ❖ Acts 5:29

While I was pondering these words, the thought that came
was, "That's easy for you to say, Peter, the day after an angel
released you from prison." A bittersweet reaction, to say the
least. In thinking through my response, I found that my reaction arose from my fear of being caught in a position like
Peter's. Just how far would I go to obey God rather than
people? All the way, like Peter? I really don't know.

What I must remember is that I am not Peter. But like
Peter, I do know that Christ endured much for me, that he
died and rose from the dead for me. He gives me the Holy
Spirit to sustain me through my struggles to obey him. And,
if I fall, he's ready to forgive and help me learn from past mistakes. Because of this, most of the time I can face each new
day knowing God is with me. God will help me to accomplish
the purpose set out for me. I want to obey God, not people.

MARLYS A. KORMAN

*Thank you, Jesus, for what you have done. Help me to do
what you want me to do. Amen*

Prayer concern: A chronically ill person

Daily Reflections_____

The great light

> The people walking in darkness have seen a
> great light. ❖ Isaiah 9:2

The sun rose and set. There were dawns and sunsets. Winter
and summer followed in order. Yet a curtain of darkness lay
over the land and the people, the prophet says. There was an
evil gloom of division and strife, of the threat of destruction and
desolation. Oppression and almost constant war was the rule.

Even today, this kind of darkness takes away hope in parts
of the world. Isaiah brought new hope. He pointed to a time
to come when the saving grace of the Messiah would shed
a glorious light among God's chosen people.

We know Isaiah's words of hope: "For to us a child is born,
to us a son is given.... And he will be called Wonderful
Counselor, Mighty God, Everlasting Father, Prince of Peace"
(Isaiah 9:6). We also know that this prophecy was fulfilled.
There are still people who walk in darkness. Our great Light
is Jesus, the Savior. We can reflect the Light that has given us
hope into the darkness around us.

MILDRED BRENDEN

Lead us, O God, in the light of your truth for Jesus' sake.
Amen

Prayer concern: Christians in Sudan

Daily Reflections_____

_____

_____

_____

Jesus' invitation

Jesus came and stood among them and said,
"Peace be with you!" ❖ John 20:19b

In the nation of Cameroon, huts have no doors. To announce their visits the Fulani people clap their hands and call out, "Salaama alekum" (meaning, "Peace to your house").

"Shalom alekum" was Jesus' first greeting to his disciples after the resurrection. In this everyday greeting, Jesus wished them the wholeness of mind, body, and spirit expressed in the Hebrew word *shalom* (which means "peace").

Yet Jesus' peace was unique, and only his peace could still their fears. "Peace I leave with you, my peace I give to you. I do not give to you as the world gives" (John 14:27). By his life, death, and resurrection, Jesus' peace restored a covenant relationship with God.

Today, Jesus still calls out, "Shalom alekum." He invites each of us to daily reconciliation with God and promises us the wholeness of his peace.

JULIE DENNISON

Jesus, thank you for your invitation. May we respond like the Fulanis: Amina—yea, yea it shall be so. Amen

Prayer concern: Peacemakers

Daily Reflections_____

Overflowing love

> For God so loved the world that he gave his one
> and only Son, that whoever believes in him shall
> not perish but have eternal life. ❖ John 3:16

What more can be said? This verse is the gospel in a nutshell. It is God's nature to pour out love upon us. "From the fullness of his grace we have all received one blessing after another" (John 1:16). In love, God created us. In love, God provides for us. And in love, God grants us eternal life. Grace upon grace! Overflowing love!

God even judges us in love. Thank God that our final judge will not be our neighbor, our boss, our spouse, or even our own conscience. Our final judge will be the Savior of the world, the wounded and crucified One, the risen and victorious One! Trace this promise upon your memory every day. Digest it as food for your soul. God loves us with everlasting love! We can depend on it.

LYLE RICH

Lord God, we praise you for your saving love in Christ. Our hearts overflow with thanks. Amen

Prayer concern: Someone in the news

Daily Reflections_____

_____

_____

_____

Promised return

At that time they will see the Son of Man coming
in a cloud with power and great glory. ❖ Luke 21:27

General Douglas MacArthur was the commander of the Allied
forces in the Pacific during World War II. At the close of the
war, in August, 1945, MacArthur was named supreme commander. He received the surrender of Japan aboard the
battleship *Missouri*. This famous general had a long and distinguished military career. He was wounded three times,
decorated 13 times, and cited for bravery in action seven
times.

At one point, MacArthur was ordered from the Philippines
to Australia. He was reluctant to leave his troops in the
Philippines, and in a departing speech, he made what was to
become a famous promise: "I shall return." That promise
meant a great deal to the troops. It gave them hope and confidence for an ultimate victory. MacArthur did return in
triumph.

Our Lord has promised to return. We remember that
promise every time we express our faith: "He will come again
to judge the living and the dead." Christians, too, look for
Christ's return as a sign of ultimate victory.

WILLIAM H. LUOMA

We look for your coming with confidence and faith,
O Lord. Amen

Prayer concern: POWs

Daily Reflections_____

_____

_____

_____

Coming into the house

I will dwell in the house of the LORD forever.
❖ Psalm 23:6b

Herding sheep in David's day was a rough job. The shepherd's psalm reflects this outdoor life. It pictures outdoor scenes of pastures, waters, and valleys. The shepherd, like his sheep, spent a lifetime in the wilds.

The scene changes only in the last verse. There the psalmist looks forward to spending eternity in the house of the Lord. What a powerful image that is. Imagine what it must have meant to a shepherd to look forward to a heaven where he will be forever warm, dry, and safe. That promise must have helped him through many a long cold night.

We too have the promise of heaven to help us through this life. Whatever our own image of heaven is, it's a pleasure to think of it—not as a means of avoiding the problems of earth, but as simple reassurance that we will be in God's care forever.

INEZ M. SCHWARZKOPF

Shepherd of our souls, thank you for your promise to keep us with you forever. Amen

Prayer concern: Elected officials

Daily Reflections_____
_____
_____
_____

More than adrenaline

Strengthen the feeble hands, steady the knees
that five way; say to those with fearful hearts,
"Be strong, do not fear." ❖ Isaiah 35:3-4

When the parking brake failed, the family car came to a rest
with one wheel on Tony's thighs. Although she weighed only
115 pounds, Tony's mother pushed the 3,000-pound car back
up the drive and freed her son. Miraculously, Tony suffered
no broken bones. His mother had a slightly strained back.

After examining mother and son, the family doctor shook
his head in wonder and said, "I guess the increased flow of
adrenaline in a moment of great stress …," but Pastor Jensen,
knowing the mother's great faith in God and her love for
Tony, interrupted, saying, "Doctor, it wasn't all adrenaline."

Certainly, there is a limit beyond which flesh and blood
cannot go. But when it comes to conquering fear or anxiety,
lifting burdens of sin, saving one's life for eternity, it isn't
adrenaline at all. There are no limits to God's strength, love,
and desire to save.

HAROLD W. PENNINGTON

*Omnipotent Lord, make me strong and unafraid. In your
love, save me. Amen*

Prayer concern: Parish workers

Daily Reflections_____
_____
_____
_____

What it takes

Since you are eager to have spiritual gifts,
try to excel in gifts that build up the church.
❖ 1 Corinthians 14:12

Have you ever wondered why it seems to take more energy to clean a house than it does to get it messy? It has to do with the Second Law of Thermodynamics: It takes more effort to restore order than it takes for things to fall into disorder.

This is an interesting concept to apply to the church. If no one cared, the church might soon tend to fall into disorder. This refers, of course, to much more than the building. It has to do with the people and the programs and the church's work and witness.

Unless the church is built up continuously, it will lose its effectiveness. God's Spirit moves people of every generation to keep the church strong. The Spirit can use us to keep the church from becoming weak.

Today's Scripture verse offers powerful encouragement to all people who are concerned about the future of the church. Strive to excel in building up the church.

WILLIAM H. LUOMA

Dear Lord, give us the grace to be church-builders. Amen

Prayer concern: Christians in Cameroon

Daily Reflections_____

_____

_____

_____

Wish I may, wish I might

> Set your minds on things above, not on earthly
> things. ❖ Colossians 3:2

If you had a magic genie that could grant one wish, what
would you request? The foolish rich man in one of Christ's
parables sought to build barns for his excess grain so he
would never have to work again. The prodigal son asked for
an early inheritance. In both cases, the granted wish failed to
satisfy: the rich man died before he could enjoy his leisure,
and the prodigal wasted his inheritance.

The unavoidable fact is that nothing in this earthly life is
permanent. People die, objects are destroyed, and satisfied
desires invite dissatisfaction and a desire for more. God alone
endures. Further, there is no genie.

Jesus told us to lay up for ourselves "treasures in heaven"
(Matthew 6:20). Paul reinforces this thought in today's verse.
Better than any earthly wish is a prayer for eternal values, for
peace with God.

BARBARA M. WILLS

*Eternal God, thank you that no genie is required for
the most important wish of all—that I may live in your
eternal love. Amen*

Prayer concern: Those who are suffering from chemical
dependency

Daily Reflections_____
_____
_____
_____

Humility

This is the one I esteem: he who is humble and con-
trite in spirit, and trembles at my word. ❖ Isaiah 66:2

Every Sunday after worship, she walks one mile—rain or
shine—to the house of her dear friend. Her friend is older
than her own 70 years and unable to go to church anymore.
She always brings some kind of baked treat for her friend, and
something for her friend's cat. Her friend is blind, so she
reads the Sunday newspaper to her. Sometimes they talk
about the sermon and worship. On Mondays, she volunteers
at a retirement center, playing the piano and leading sing-a-
longs. She often spends Wednesdays at the church, cleaning
and caring for the flower gardens. If you compliment her on
all she does, she gets embarrassed. She says she's not a
leader or a role model. She does what she does and wants no
fuss about it. She honors God's word with her life.

Isaiah prophesies that God will seek those people who live
with true humility and in obedience to God's word. Who are
these humble ones in your midst? What have you learned
from their example? When younger people look at your life,
what do they learn about humility and service?

MARK A. HINTON

*Mighty God, make me a humble and obedient servant
formed by your Word. Amen*

Prayer concern: Those who serve behind the scenes

Daily Reflections

A bruised reed

> A bruised reed he will not break, and a smoldering
> wick he will not snuff out. ❖ Isaiah 42:3

I have felt like a bruised reed. I have felt, at times, like a dimly burning wick. And I have seen loved ones feel the same. To feel oneself as a bruised reed is to feel weak, pained, and torn. To feel oneself as a dimly burning wick is to feel energy-spent and hopeless.

But the world is not often gentle with the bruised, or tolerant of those whose light is dim. We are expected to handle rejection by denying its hurt. It is assumed we will find hope by single-handedly pulling ourselves out of despair. We are told that weakness must be made into strength; spiritlessness forced into joy.

By its demands, the world can leave us feeling more bruised, yet more dimly lit. But God is not like the world. God will not demand strength when we are weak, or hope when we are hopeless. God's way is to heal the bruised by becoming their strength, and lighten the dim by becoming their hope, in Jesus, of whom Isaiah sings.

KAREN BATES

Lord, thank you for your great love. Amen

Prayer concern: Those who have hurt us

Daily Reflections

Step by step

Leave your simple ways and you will live; walk in
the way of understanding. ❖ Proverbs 9:6

The longest journey begins with a single step. The greatest
change of behavior begins with deciding to try something
new. One day at a time is the only way to introduce change.
The way soon becomes a comfortable and familiar routine.
Then not doing the new behavior feels awkward and foreign.

There is so much I would like to do, to change, and to
accomplish in my life that I begin to feel overwhelmed, frozen
in a state of inertia. My goals seem unobtainable. But if
I consider what I might do with this next hour, I have hope
and new inspiration. Then I can move forward in faith, one
step at a time.

When I focus on all I want to learn and do, my ignorance
seems to drown me. But when I focus on what I have already
learned or done, the unknown seems more manageable. I can
keep learning and doing, step by step.

KATHY M. HAUEISEN

*Dear Lord, grant us faith to trust you for our inspiration.
Amen*

Prayer concern: People with physical disabilities

Daily Reflections_____

_____

_____

_____

Guard the truth

> Guard the good deposit that was entrusted to
> you—guard it with the help of the Holy Spirit who
> lives in us. ❖ 2 Timothy 1:14

The Great Wall of China was constructed to keep out the barbaric hordes to the north, but it failed to provide the security the Chinese sought. When their enemies came to invade the country, the Chinese people did not break down the wall nor did they climb over it. They simply bribed a gatekeeper and walked through the gate.

We have been called to stand guard over something more critical than a nation's border. Like Timothy, we have been entrusted with the truth that is Jesus Christ. He is the way to God and to life.

Anything so precious as the truth is subject to being stolen away. We could be easily deceived or led astray. How can we guard against such loss? "The Holy Spirit who lives in us," also helps us. Relying on God's presence and power, we can stand firm in the truth.

ROBERT L. ANDERSON

Holy Spirit, power divine, fortify this will of mine. Amen

Prayer concern: Christians in China

Daily Reflections

What's the message?

For even when we were with you, we gave you
this rule: "If a man will not work, he shall not eat."
❖ 2 Thessalonians 3:10

There was once a self-made man who was extremely critical
of those who used food stamps. It didn't matter to him what
their situation was because he had already decided their
plight was their own fault—no matter what reason they might
give. If that self-made man had a favorite Bible verse, this was
probably it.

At first glance, Paul's statement to the Thessalonians does
seem to justify the man's attitude. Should we take Paul's
words literally? Is it God's will that we treat others this way?
If so, what do we do with Matthew 7:1? ("Do not judge, or you
too will be judged.") Or with Matthew 25:35? ("I was hungry
and you gave me something to eat.") If these verses have
merit, then what do we make of the verse in Thessalonians?

The letter was written to specific individuals who were
foolishly idle. Paul wanted them to contribute, to set a good
example as others were doing. He wanted them also to be
worthy of imitation (v. 13) and encouraged them to do well.

ALFREDA H. EBELING

Lord, stop us from using the Bible for self-justification.
Amen

Prayer concern: Someone experiencing grief

Daily Reflections_____

_____

_____

_____

The centenarian

> This is the message we have heard from him and declare to you: God is light; in him there is no darkness at all. ❖ 1 John 1:5

According to Christian tradition the apostle John lived to be almost 100 years old. And it appears that the older he became, the simpler the gospel seemed to him. At the end of his life, the story goes, he kept repeating, "Little children, love one another." This admonition is contained in Paul's first epistle. In the text quoted above, he again reduces a complicated situation to its essential components: the evangelical message, he says, is that God is light.

The application of this message to Christian living is that ideally the children of light have nothing to hide. They have been brought into a loving relationship with God and with the members of God's family, and they prayerfully try to do nothing that would disturb that relationship. It's too precious a thing to lose. What's more, the joy of it may be increased by deliberately fostering the ties that bind.

HERBERT F. LINDEMAN

Help us, O Lord, to obey your new commandment: to love one another as you have loved us. Amen

Prayer concern: Someone with cancer

Daily Reflections

Glory land

The LORD will indeed give what is good. ❖ Psalm 85:12

This psalm remembers the past favor of the Lord upon the Israelite nation. It affirms that the land will again be a glory land if the people's iniquities can be forgiven and their sins pardoned.

Can our nation expect comparable consideration? Certainly God is willing. We read: "Surely his salvation is near those who fear him" (v. 9). Then "righteousness and peace will kiss each other." The nation must answer with faithfulness, however, as the plants of springtime burst forth in response to the sun's warming rays.

Dietrich Bonhoeffer said that God's appointed task for human government is to make a safe and untroubled opportunity for the church to tell the good news about Jesus Christ. If we turn to God in our hearts, as the psalmist says, the Lord will give what is good. God's righteousness will make traceable footsteps in our national culture and life.

GEORGE H. MUEDEKING

Beyond all else, Lord of all nations, bless us with the unhindered proclamation Jesus. Amen

Prayer concern: The United Nations

Daily Reflections_____

_____
_____
_____

A universal realization

No longer will a man teach his neighbor, or a man his brother, saying, "Know the LORD," because they will all know me, from the least of them to the greatest. ❖ Jeremiah 31:34

A teenager invited her friend to a Communion service. "What's Communion?" the friend asked.

What is more sobering? The realization that there are millions of people who have never heard of Jesus? Spending time with family, friends, or colleagues who have no interest in our faith—who may even mock or scorn it? Knowing Christians who are complacent about growing in the Lord?

Today's reading assures us such will not always be the case. Whether lowly or important, wise or foolish, rich or poor, all will know who Christ is, and all will know the promise, "I will remember their sins no more."

The apostle Paul adds to that good news: "Therefore God exalted him to the highest place and gave him the name that is above every name, that at the name of Jesus every knee should bow ... and every tongue confess that Jesus Christ is Lord, to the glory of God the Father" (Philippians 2:9-11). What a joyous day it will be when everyone knows that Jesus is Lord!

NANCY LEE SASSER

Almighty God, I praise you for forgiving me. Empower me to believe. Amen

Prayer concern: Teenagers

Daily Reflections

Quiet restoration

[God] leads me beside quiet waters, he restores
my soul. ❖ Psalm 23:2-3

For so many people, life today has become a hectic rush to
keep schedules, meet deadlines, and fulfill all the obligations
placed on us, whether by choice, by chance, or by necessity.
How treasured are those moments when we can sit down,
relax, take a deep breath, and spend some time thinking. Are
these moments few and far between? Are more needed?

Jesus is our shepherd. While he lived on earth, "he went
up on a mountainside by himself to pray" (Matthew 14:23).
Jesus invited the disciples, "Come with me by yourselves to a
quiet place and get some rest" (Mark 6:31). Our shepherd
knows we need quiet times beside still waters, lonely places
where we can meet with him as he restores our souls.

If we resolve to set apart time for God, are we not adding
one more demand to our already too busy life? Rather, let's
ask Jesus to lead us himself to a quiet place where he will
work renewal and peace within us.

BETTY HEIDEMANN

*Lord, thank you for the quiet moments of restoration you
plan for us. Amen*

Prayer concern: Doctors

Daily Reflections_____

The visitation

> Blessed is she who has believed that what the
> Lord has said to her will be accomplished!
> ❖ Luke 1:45

Mary believed the word that she heard from the Lord, and she received in her body, that which God had promised. There was nothing she could do to make it happen, and yet by faith, she experienced what God was doing.

We can do nothing to make God part of the fabric of our lives. But like Mary, we do participate in the drama. We receive a rich word of all that God has done for us. Then comes the invitation to join in. Covenants and promises are made. Sacraments are given, and we live as children in the kingdom.

We can count on God to do what has been promised. We are free to respond with confidence and receive by faith all the gifts God gives. We then have all we need to live in grace. Even though Mary could do nothing to conceive Jesus, without faith, she would not have been the mother of our Lord. We can do nothing to bring to life our own salvation, but because of the gift of faith, Jesus is made known to us and in us. We, too, can be bearers of Jesus.

DALE CHESLEY

Be alive in us today, Jesus, that we might believe and be saved. Amen

Prayer concern: Expectant mothers

Daily Reflections

Healing

[God] forgives all your sins and heals all your
diseases. ❖ Psalm 103:3

Forgiveness and healing are placed alongside one another in
David's song of thanksgiving. Long before modern medicine
recognized the interaction between mind and body, the
psalmist sensed its reality. A mind that is at leisure from itself,
resting in God's peace, disposes the body to live in health.

This is not to say that the peace of God automatically con-
fers bodily wholeness. One cannot ignore that some people
are born healthy and physically strong while others may have
less of physical endurance and may be more susceptible to
disease. And even the most faithful people can become seriously ill. No matter what our physical condition, though, all
healing ultimately comes from God.

This is a work that is constantly going on in every person.
God has endowed the human body with marvelous powers
of recovery. These powers may be inhibited and blocked by
fretfulness, worry, hatred, and resentments. And they may be
released for the healing God has intended when peace and
love live in the heart. The apostle Paul wrote to the Colossian
Christians, "Let the peace of Christ rule in your hearts"
(Colossians 3:15).

FRANK A. SCHIOTZ

*O Lord, fill our hearts with trust in you, that your healing
work may not be hindered. Amen*

Prayer concern: Christians in Algeria

Daily Reflections_____

_____

_____

_____

Have you seen it?

And they were calling to one another: "Holy, holy, holy is the LORD Almighty; the whole earth is full of his glory." ❖ Isaiah 6:3

It's in the whisper of a snowflake, the trill of a wren, the opening of a rosebud, "the whole earth is full of his glory." It's in the chatter of children, the warmth of friends, the embrace of those who grieve, "the whole earth is full of his glory." It's in the tenderness of a nurse's aide, the dedication of a teacher, "the whole earth is full of his glory."

Although Moses saw it at the burning bush, and the favored three disciples saw it on the Mount of Transfiguration, and the intimate friend of Jesus saw it on the Isle of Patmos in the Revelation, the vision of the Lord's majesty is not withheld from any worshiper. As this verse reminds us, "the whole earth is full of his glory."

Moments of ecstasy—but to what purpose? The same earth that nourishes a rose also drinks in the blood of war. The same air that carries the melody of a meadowlark also transmits the moans of mourners. Is the glory of God of any value over against the plight of the human race? Isaiah's vision says yes.

ALVIN C. REUTER

Lord, keep our eyes open to your glory. Amen

Prayer concern: Christians in Egypt

Daily Reflections_____

_____

_____

_____

Hope—Next Right

You have made known to me the path of life.
❖ Psalm 16:11

As one drives south of Minneapolis on Interstate 35, there is a most interesting road sign. It simply reads, "Hope—Next Right." Now, obviously there must be a small community named Hope near the interstate. Someday I am going to take that turnoff to see what kind of place Hope really is. I wonder how it got the name. That makes me wonder what *hope* is really like—for you and for me.

When I read this passage from Psalm 16, with the words "You have made known to me the path of life," I thought of that sign. God is constantly putting before us signs that say something like, "Hope—Next Right."

When we bring a child to the baptismal font, we are witnessing to the hope that God has reserved for us. As the youth of a congregation gather at the altar for the rite of confirmation they are taking a turnoff from the "interstate" of everyday life. They are saying that there really is hope. When we walk away from a casket at a grave site, it is as if we follow a sign that says, "Hope—Next Right." A cross marks the spot where we turn off and Christ shows us the path of life.

OLE WINTER

Thank you, Lord, for the hope you provide. Amen

Prayer concern: Those in need of hope

Daily Reflections_____

_____

_____

_____

A heart to listen

John replied in the words of Isaiah the prophet, "I am the voice of one calling in the desert." ❖ John 1:23

We usually think literally about John in the wilderness, living in the desert on a diet of locusts and honey. But think for a minute of a desert's relation to green, fertile land. A desert is on the margins, while the center of social and economic life is found where there is water and arable land.

John spoke from the geographic margins of the world, but also from the margins of religious life in his day. He lacked the official credentials for a religious leader, and the established religious leadership viewed John's message as a threat.

A "voice calling" from the margins of social and religious life; a voice calling the church to redirect itself toward a living God. Are there voices like that today? What message shakes us from our comfortable faith? There are voices today that call us to care for abused children, people who are homeless, or those suffering from AIDS—to touch with God's love those on the margins of social life. While we may find it hard to listen, the gospel calls us to care for everyone. We respond by redirecting our lives and faith toward Christ.

LYN GESCH

Lord, teach us to listen, to pray, to care. Amen

Prayer concern: People who have AIDS

Daily Reflections_____

Not I, but Christ

> I want to know Christ ... sharing in his suffer-
> ings, becoming like him in his death, and so,
> somehow, to attain to the resurrection from the
> dead. ❖ Philippians 3:10-11

Besides physical dying, there is another death. It is to die to
self and to live for Christ. To die to our self-righteousness, to
give up the pride of self is so difficult that "apart from me
[Jesus] you can do nothing" (John 15:5).

Luther used the phrase "curved in upon oneself." You have
seen a cat chasing its tail. It gets nowhere. So it is also when
we try to pull ourselves up by our spiritual "bootstraps" to
save ourselves. The reverse is required. Paul cries, "What a
wretched man I am! Who will rescue me from this body of
death?" (Romans 7:24). To recognize this need is to die to self.
To take the leap of faith into Christ is to live the resurrection
now and eternally.

KARL T. SCHMIDT

O to be saved from myself, dear Lord, O to be lost in thee.
O that it might be no more I, but Christ, that lives in me.
Amen

Prayer concern: Christians in Madagascar

Daily Reflections _____
_____
_____
_____

The mountain spring

Love and faithfulness meet together....
Faithfulness springs forth from the earth.
❖ Psalm 85:10-11

A family looked at possible mountain sites for their log cabin
home. It was late winter and many streams and springs were
flowing freely. The water supply seemed to be no problem. By
late August, however, everything had dried up.

The family told a neighbor farmer of their problem. He
smiled and said, "T'ain't no problem. There's a good spring
not far above where yer thinkin' of puttin' yer house. It's
probably buried with leaves and stuff but it's bin a good spring
for as long as I've hunted ginseng in these woods. I call it
'steadfast love.' It's jist always there."

Amid all the changes of life, we can count on God's steadfast love and faithfulness. Our health fails, friends desert us,
love goes sour; but like a spring of pure water, God's faithfulness springs eternally fresh.

JOHN AND MARY SCHRAMM

Thank you, God, for steadfast love. Amen

Prayer concern: Children

Daily Reflections

Silencing the critic

> For it is God's will that by doing good you
> should silence the ignorant talk of foolish men.
> ❖ 1 Peter 2:15

The easiest thing to find is a critic. No matter what you do, someone might criticize you. Nineteenth-century evangelist Dwight Moody once said the best things he ever did were the things men criticized him for most bitterly.

The critics of this world, however, have their heyday when a Christian does something wrong. People are quick to point fingers of scorn at a believer who falls into sin. Let a church member get caught in wrongdoing and newspapers are sure to mention that fact. Thus, great harm is done by weak actions on the part of believers.

Of course no one in this life is perfect, and Christians don't always delight in the law of the Lord. If we do something wrong, we have a Savior who forgives. Nevertheless, Christians must remember what sinful actions on their part can lead to. Sin always hurts others, and when a believer commits a major sin, the whole church suffers. This is one of the reasons why God encourages us to walk in a holy way.

W. A. POOVEY

Lord, help me to talk carefully so that no one will stumble in faith because of me. Guide me in your way, and when I fall short, forgive. Amen

Prayer concern: Our critics

Daily Reflections

How then can we live?

Our offenses and sins weigh us down, and we are
wasting away because of them. How then can we live?
❖ Ezekiel 33:10b

For all our clever rationalizing, we often do not escape awareness of our sin. Sometimes we are unable to keep track of how
sin takes concrete form, but we can't avoid it. How then can
we live?

We begin by being honest with ourselves. We are imperfect. But if we are honest, we can identify sin as a part of who
we are. Once it is identified, we can ask for forgiveness and
begin again. Forgiveness is dependent on a relationship.
Being rescued from our sinful selves comes from our relationship with God. We ask because we have been promised that
God is forgiving. We receive because God loves us. God has
not given up on us.

How then shall we live? With freedom and the confidence
that God won't abandon us, even in our lowest times. God has
no pleasure in our death but waits with patience and devotion
for us to ask for help and forgiveness. When we face our self-
disappointment, guilt, and shame, we discover how good it is
to live.

JUDITH MATTISON

*Gracious God, we are flawed and we carry heavy burdens
of sin. Forgive us, as you have promised, and help us to
turn back to your loving ways. Amen*

Prayer concern: Those who cannot let go of their guilt

Daily Reflections_____

The greatest sacrifice

While they were stoning him, Stephen prayed,
"Lord Jesus, receive my spirit." ❖ Acts 7:59

Many believers gave up their lives to pass the Christian faith down through the centuries. The account of Stephen's martyrdom reminds us that in many times and places, it has been life-threatening to be a Christian.

In most parts of the world today, it is quite safe to practice Christianity. What is it like for those who risk freedom and life itself to proclaim Jesus? For those of us living in free societies, it is difficult to comprehend.

While we are just as valued by God as martyrs who have gone before us, their supreme sacrifice reminds us of the radical nature of the gospel. Their example encourages us to devote ourselves to Christ above all other people or things.

MARY BRAUCH

God, help me grow in faith to understand the unshakable devotion of all martyrs who have died for their beliefs. Amen

Prayer concern: Those who suffer for their faith

Daily Reflections_____
_____
_____
_____

Nobody and somebody

And whoever wants to be first must be slave of all.
❖ Mark 10:44

Wanting to be somebody is a very human desire. The disciples shared it. They also shared the common idea that success is measured by wealth, position, and honor. Such success they expected to have after Jesus, in some miraculous way, shoved the Romans out of Jerusalem and became a king there. So Jesus discussed with them what greatness really is.

In God's kingdom, the real *somebodies* are often those whom people outside call *nobodies*. Jesus himself is the perfect example of this. He came to the world as a servant, obedient to God's will. Jesus' one wish was to help all human beings. Being great was not about getting dressed up, strutting around, and yelling orders. Being great meant being humble, unselfish, compassionate, and forgiving—all the things our sinful nature doesn't want to be.

Yet Jesus promises a reward for those who give their trust and service to him. He died for our sins. So Jesus can hold out to us a crown of life in his kingdom, where everybody is a special and beloved somebody.

LOUISE LINCOLN

Savior, may we serve you here in love and be with you in glory forever. Amen

Prayer concern: The humble

Daily Reflections_____

_____

_____

_____

Something for nothing

> The Spirit and the bride say, "Come!" And let him who hears say, "Come!" Whoever is thirsty, let him come; and whoever wishes, let him take the free gift of the water or life. ❖ Revelation 22:17

God's grace is a free gift to all people. We cannot buy, sell, trade, earn, bargain for, or borrow God's love and grace. All people are invited to share in this gift of love. All people are invited to receive the promises of God of life and salvation. All people are equal in the eyes of God and receive the same promise.

God's free gifts of forgiveness, love, and grace, come to us through the suffering and death of our Lord, Jesus Christ. God really gives us something for nothing. The gifts of life and salvation are free to those who accept Jesus as Lord and Savior.

We are God's messengers to invite others to share in these gifts. We cannot earn God's love and grace. But we can share the good news of God's grace with others.

JAMES E. LESCHENSKY

O Lord, you have given us the greatest gifts that could ever be given. Bless our efforts to share these great gifts from you. Amen

Prayer concern: People who spread God's message

Daily Reflections_____

_____

_____

_____

The appeal of love

> And while they were eating, [Jesus] said, "I tell
> you the truth, one of you will betray me." ... Then
> Judas, the one who would betray him, said,
> "Surely not I, Rabbi?" ❖ Matthew 26:21, 25

In the closing events of the Gospel story, Jesus and Judas
seem to be together in a world alone. Judas must have gone
about the business of betrayal in secret. Otherwise the other
disciples certainly would have interfered. Judas may have
kept his plans hidden from them, but not from his master.

It is always that way. We may hide our sins from others,
but we never hide them from the eyes of our Lord. He sees
into the depths of our lives. Jesus knew what Judas was doing.

Here we see Jesus' reaching out in love to a sinner. He
chose not to resort to exposure, or ridicule, or finger-pointing.
Rather, Jesus appealed with love to a man caught in the web
of his own ambition.

When Jesus reaches to us in love, he does two things.
First, he confronts us with our sin—he makes us take a hard
look at the harsh realities. Second, he invites us to look at
him—can we sin against him who gives us such love?

LUTHER ABRAHAMSON

*Lord Jesus, you have invited us to follow you. Keep us
from such temptation that would cause us to turn back
and deny you in our hour of trial. Amen*

Prayer concern: Christians in Uganda

Daily Reflections_____

_____

_____

_____

Come and see

You shall see greater things than that. ❖ John 1:50

When Nathanael responds skeptically to Philip's excitement about having found the Messiah, Philip can only answer, "Come and see." Sometimes when it seems impossible to explain or describe a person or situation well enough, it is simplest to say, "See for yourself."

If you were trying to tell someone about your congregation and its relationship to Jesus, and you invited that person to "come and see," what would the person see? Would the spirit of your congregation reveal the presence of the Christ? Would God's compassion, love, and understanding be seen in the actions of you and others in your congregation?

Jesus said, "You shall see greater things than that." The church is the body of Christ, as Paul says in Colossians 3:12-16. Let us eagerly and joyfully invite others to come and see the compassion, kindness, courage, patience, strength, and forgiveness all bound together in perfect harmony, to be found in Jesus' presence.

MARY BRAUCH

Dear God, may we abide in your love always, and willingly invite others to come and see. Amen

Prayer concern: Those who have lost a relative

Daily Reflections_____
_____
_____
_____

Let us be trumpets

Let them praise the name of the LORD, for his
name alone is exalted. ❖ Psalm 148:13

Our whole life can speak of our thankfulness. Every condition
and place in which we find ourselves can be a witness to our
gratitude. The time and places in which we live can be better
for our having been there.

The shattered monuments of our human landscape remind
us that misdirected honor is a waste of energy and a mis-
reading of the real purpose of life. Life is given to us for
something more than "mere living." Our lives are not ends in
themselves but rather are intended for the praise of the Giver.
The greatest monument we can build on earth is a simple,
thankful life of service to God.

Let us be trumpets of God's praise. Not that our puny
praise can add to God's glory (nor any blasphemy detract
from it). The blessing tongue cannot make God better, nor a
can a cursing tongue make God worse—any more than the
sun is *bettered* by birds singing or *battered* by dogs barking.

NANCY S. WILLIAMSON

*Praise to you, Lord God, for your infinite greatness and
constant goodness. Accept the shabby gifts of praise we
bring. Amen*

Prayer concern: College students

Daily Reflections

Why God gives

And receive from [God] anything we ask, because
we obey his commands and do what pleases him.
❖ 1 John 3:22

Does God answer our prayers because we keep all of
God's commands to us? If so, we all might as well stop
praying; none of us keeps God's laws perfectly. But verse 22
obviously means to encourage us to pray. It also encourages
us to obey.

Verse 23 says that God's command is to believe in Jesus,
which will lead to loving others. We believe Jesus when he
says we can come to God through him in spite of our sin.
Because of him we dare to pray, and we receive.

Verse 21 tells us that we may confidently come to God
because our hearts do not condemn us. Why not? Because
God is greater than our sins. Through Christ, God has forgiven our sin and erased our guilt.

John encourages us to pray, not because our good deeds
influence God to answer, but because God's love is greater
than our sin. The proof of this is Jesus. We come to God
through Christ. In love, God gives us what we need.

ROLF E. AASENG

*Lord, you have promised to give. For the sake of Jesus,
we come asking for what we need. Amen*

Prayer concern: People on dialysis

Daily Reflections

The down-to-earth God

> That evening quail came and covered the
> camp, and in the morning there was a layer of
> dew around the camp. ❖ Exodus 16:13

"Head in the clouds." We use that expression to describe someone who is impractical—someone who is not really concerned with the harsh realities of life. For many people, that expression seems to describe God. *God is over there in heaven, far removed from human problems. God is uninterested or even impractical when it comes to our daily living.*

But God is really not like that at all. For Israel, God was concerned about quail and manna and the water supply. Jesus said not even a sparrow falls without God's noting it. That means we also are to be concerned about the things of life. We are not to live with our head in the clouds. We, too, are to be concerned that people have enough to eat, that the old have someone to care for them, that children are given guidance and education. We are to show love for others as God shows love and concern for us—feet on the ground, not head in the clouds.

W. A. POOVEY

Lord, help us to be down-to-earth Christians. Amen

Prayer concern: Children in poverty

Daily Reflections

Listen

Hear, O Israel, and be careful to obey.
❖ Deuteronomy 6:3

When I was 18, I left home and went away to college. The entire month of August was spent making preparations for my departure. Part of the preparation included talks with my parents about the responsibilities and the do's and don'ts of college life. Their instruction showed their genuine love for me and their desire for my happiness. They were speaking out of their own experience and wisdom. I can still hear my father saying, "Just listen to your Dad; I won't steer you wrong."

That's the way it was with God and his children, Israel. In preparation for their entry into the promised land, God gave them the Ten Commandments. Moses exhorted the children of Israel to listen and to follow the Creator's instructions so that all would go well with them. Today, we can do no better than to listen and God's instructions for our lives. In Christ, God is our Father.

SALLY T. GENTRY

O Lord, teach us to hear your voice and follow you. Amen

Prayer concern: Young people moving out on their own

Daily Reflections_____

_____

_____

_____

New experiences

> There is the sea, vast and spacious, teeming with creatures beyond number—living things both large and small. ❖ Psalm 104:25

Having been raised on the prairies of Canada, I never saw the ocean until I boarded a ship to sail to Japan as a missionary. Although the trip was exciting and enjoyable, the vastness of the Pacific, the thought of its depths, the huge waves that tossed the big liner when we were near a typhoon—all this made me fearful. I've never overcome that fear.

Perhaps it is because I only see the surface, and I don't know enough about the sea, the "living things both large and small" that teem in its depths, as well as the treasures, beauties, and mysteries that lie beneath the waves.

The Lord was leading me to serve in Japan. I went, but not without fear. How much I would have missed had I looked at that great and wide sea and opted for the security of my home on the prairies. God's creation, vast and various, is but a symbol, a token of God's greatness and goodness. Because of God, we can venture at God's call.

GRACE L. INGULSRUD

Lord, help me to trust you in new experiences. Amen

Prayer concern: Ranchers

Daily Reflections_____

Chosen children

*Because those who are led by the Spirit of God
are sons of God. ❖ Romans 8:14*

Finding a child to adopt is very difficult these days. My husband, an obstetrician, tells me that he receives letters from married couples all over the nation who are eagerly searching for a child.

In the book of Romans, Paul refers to God "adopting" us. What does this phrase tell us about God? For me, it pictures a God eagerly seeking us, searching everywhere, like caring couples who would like to become parents.

Furthermore, when God finds us, God brings us into a parent-child relationship, with all the love and status that implies. Our Creator loves us as much as his only-begotten Son. Through Holy Baptism, the Word, and the Lord's Supper, God draws us in, guides us, and helps us to obey and live up to the family name.

Do we take our adoption by God for granted? Are we living joyfully as God's special chosen children?

INEZ C. SCHNEIDER

Help us, Lord, to remember that we belong to a royal family. Amen

Prayer concern: Couples who would like to be parents

Daily Reflections_____
_____
_____
_____

An about-face

> And so John came, baptizing in the desert
> region and preaching a baptism of repentance
> for the forgiveness of sins. ❖ Mark 1:4

Repentance is not synonymous with feeling bad, with sadness, or with shame. It certainly may contain those feelings, but it is far more than an emotional upheaval. In repentance, the heart is not just broken *for* its sins, it is also broken *from* its sins. The bottom line of repentance is very clear. It means being so sorry for your sins that you want to quit sinning.

Dante said it well: "He who repents not, cannot be resolved. Nor is it possible to repent and at the same time to will to sin, the contradiction not permitting it." Therefore, we cannot decide to sow our wild oats on Saturday evening and then go to church on Sunday and pray for a crop failure.

Repentance involves turning from the sin that binds and blinds. Repentance is action-related. If the boat is sinking, rather than continue to bail it out, plug the leak!

JAMES R. BJORGE

Lord, help me to turn from my sin to my Savior. Amen

Prayer concern: Someone you just met

Daily Reflections_____

_____

_____

_____

Out of Nazareth

Nazareth! Can anything good come from there?
❖ John 1:46

Some of our great leaders have come from undistinguished, even uninviting backgrounds. Sometimes they came from homes with meager funds or with little love. And yet they rose above their adversities.

Today's Bible passage tells us that Nathaniel did not readily accept Philip's news of the new Messiah. Rather sarcastically, he questioned the likelihood of God's own Son coming from a Galilean hamlet like Nazareth. And yet, incredulous as it may sound, Jesus, humankind's Savior, was a product of this obscure village.

God wants all of us to reach everlasting glory. We may not become world figures, but we are guaranteed a place in God's kingdom if we believe in the Lord Jesus Christ. Yes, something good can come out of Nazareth.

JEAN R. SWEIGERT

Dear God, thank you for giving each of us the hope of everlasting glory in your kingdom. Help us to believe in Jesus so that we do not perish. Amen

Prayer concern: People in your neighborhood

Daily Reflections

The lavish giver

You open your hand and satisfy the desires of
every living thing. ❖ Psalm 145:16

Do you know what a cornucopia is? It is a curved goat's horn
overflowing with fruit and ears of corn, often used at
Thanksgiving time as a symbol of the lavish provisions of
God's earth. It is a reminder of God's concern for the
everyday needs of all living creatures on earth.

Many religions picture God as concerned only about the
human spirit or soul. The God we know in Jesus Christ is
quite different. Jesus had an ear for every cry of pain and
hunger. We know God as Father—one who desires to provide
for the health and well-being of all God's children. While we
know that our eternal souls are more important than everything else, we have boldness to call on God for every need in
life. Sometimes we exaggerate our needs, to be sure, but the
elemental needs of food and shelter are on God's agenda.

ALVIN N. ROGNESS

*Let us never forget to thank you, O God, for all the
blessings of life—food, clothing, shelter, family, friends,
governments, and everything else necessary for our lives.
Amen*

Prayer concern: Churches

Daily Reflections

Tests

The spirit is willing, but the body is weak.
❖ Mark 14:38b

There were two tests of purpose and character in the Garden of Gethsemane on the night that Jesus was betrayed. Jesus was tested. His cup of suffering was fast filling to the brim as he faced the cross. He was greatly distressed and yet he was obedient. Jesus prayed, "not what I will, but what you will."

Three of the disciples were tested: Peter, James and John. They might have added their prayers to his, but three times Jesus came back to find them sleeping. It was for our sake that Jesus endured suffering and death. In this testing he gave full obedience to God.

We know by experience the failure of the disciples. In those moments we too have learned what Jesus meant by his gentle words, "the spirit is willing, but the body is weak." Our intentions are not always translated into action, or words matched by deeds.

CHESTER M. PATTEN

Lord, we think about your patience, forgiveness, and understanding when we remember how far short we fall in our discipleship. Deal with us in love and mercy. Amen

Prayer concern: Christians in Cuba

Daily Reflections_____

_____

_____

_____

Are you able to hear?

> There some people brought to him a man who
> was deaf and could hardly talk, and they begged
> him to place his hand on the man. ❖ Mark 7:32

When I was a boy, one of my uncles lived in our home with us.
He was a bachelor and a hard worker. He also had a hearing
impariment and could hear only when we put our lips to his
ear and shouted. Because of this difficulty, there was not
much conversation that could be carried on. He would come
home from work, sit about in the living room, read the newspaper, and then retire to his room. Because of his limited
hearing and consequent isolation, friction sometimes arose in
our household. When my uncle noticed that we were talking
all around him, he would feel uneasy. At times he thought we
were talking about him, even though that was not true.

Is it not the same when we allow ourselves to become
spiritually deaf? God must shout in our ear. God must do
something drastic to be heard. Rare are the times that we
allow God to speak to us or that we converse with God.
Because of this we soon begin to resent God. We think God is
working against us because we have failed to keep in touch
with God. Our conversation with God becomes abrupt, and
soon we feel like strangers. Are we spiritually deaf?

ROBERT W. LUTNES

Open our ears, O Lord, to hear clearly your Word. Amen

Prayer concern: All hearers of the Word

Daily Reflections

God acts

> But during the night an angel of the Lord opened the
> doors of the jail and brought them out. ❖ Acts 5:19

Another miracle! The book of Acts is full of them. The flock
then was very small. Mighty deeds were needed to help
spread the gospel. Does God still act mightily to spread the
Word? I believe so.

Miraculous things happen every day that we take for
granted. Do I doubt that the light will come on if I flip the
switch? Do I doubt that the phone across the country will
ring when I call? No. But do I listen to the still, small voice
within me when doubts arise? Do I appreciate the comfort
and support of Christian friends in a free society? Do I thank
God that I can freely partake in worship and the sacraments
whenever I choose?

Yes, God acts today. God opens the door on which I would
never think to knock. Sometimes God closes doors, and only
in hindsight do I see the reason and the miracle.

MARLYS A. KORMAN

*Dear Lord, strengthen my faith so I might see your hand
in everything. Amen*

Prayer concern: Those in need of friends

Daily Reflections_____

_____

_____

_____

Give glory to God

I will glorify your name forever. ❖ Psalm 86:12b

"ANTIQUES FOR SALE." We often see this sign along the highway as we travel. Such signs lure us in to browse, and sometimes to buy. We look with a discerning eye, comparing what we see with what we might have already at home. We often come away convinced that we are rich with those possessions we already have.

We easily can be carried away with things—we even can worship them. We always must be aware that every *thing* we have that is good was given us by God. God gave us life. All our earthly goods are ours on loan. This includes our property, our time, and our energy. And, as this psalm reminds us, we are given our security and rescue from the Lord as well.

There is one thing that we can give God. In light of all that we receive. We can give our praise! In all we do, we need to give God glory.

ALICE HEIL

Precious Lord, help us to know that everything we have is yours. We give you but your own, O Lord. Amen

Prayer concern: People who are financially wealthy

Daily Reflections_____

Build upon the Lord

As you come to him, the living Stone—rejected
by men but chosen by God and precious to him.
❖ 1 Peter 2:4

As we are welcomed to join with Jesus in his glory and resurrection, it also means being united to him in difficult times and circumstances. The First Letter of Peter was written to remind persecuted Christians of their abundant blessings and kinship with Christ in their suffering.

Early Christians knew that their faith might cost them their earthly lives. When they bound themselves to Jesus "the living Stone," they connected with what was eternal and perfect. While few of us today will be physically threatened because of our faith, our values often are mocked by contemporary culture. We can look to our Christian ancestors for inspiration as our priorities and sense of commitment are tested.

MARY BRAUCH

*Lord, fill my heart with devotion like that of the earliest
Christians. Remind me daily that you are the only true
God. Amen*

Prayer concern: Grandparents

Daily Reflections

God's love is always available

For I am convinced that neither death nor life ...
neither height nor depth, nor anything else in all
creation, will be able to separate us from the love of
God that is in Christ Jesus our Lord. ❖ Romans 8:38-39

I have read these words standing at graveside services. I have
seen them bring strength and comfort to families struggling
with grief, fear and loss. God's word reaches across the pit
of despair and takes our hand. "Lo, I am with you always," said
Jesus. We don't walk through the valleys alone.

I have seen these words bring peace to those who fear that
they have lived so far away from God's intentions that God has
given up on them. The words assure us that nothing we can
do can break God's promise to be with us.

I have looked back over my life and realized that no matter
how tortuous the path, how painful the valleys, or how exalted
the mountains, God has been there. We can't run or hide from
God's love, but we can reject it. Yet even then, God waits
respectfully for our repentant prayers.

CAROLYN MOWCHAN

*Merciful God, thank you for never letting us go beyond
your reach. Amen*

Prayer concern: Those needing a deeper awareness of
God's presence

Daily Reflections_____

Don't put out the fire

Do not put out the Spirit's fire. ❖ 1 Thessalonians 5:19

"Someone lit a fire under them," exclaimed a fan. As a team, they were expected to win the game easily. But in the first half, they were almost totally ineffective and went to the locker room trailing by a touchdown.

The second half was a different story. They scored, seemingly at will, and held their opponents scoreless. They were on fire, and the fire wasn't going out.

In today's reading, Paul admonished his readers not to quench the fire of the Spirit. The Spirit empowers life that reflects a right relationship with God. Elsewhere in his writing, Paul says that such a life is characterized by constant rejoicing, ceaseless prayer, thanksgiving in all circumstances, holding fast to what is good, and abstaining from every form of evil.

Frequently, fans will shout to their team, engaged in competition, "Fire up out there!" In our efforts to rejoice regularly, to resist evil, and to give thanks perpetually, it is the Spirit who can "fire us up" and on to victory.

ROBERT L. ANDERSON

Spirit of God, fire us up to victorious living. Amen

Prayer concern: Those who face defeat

Daily Reflections_____
_____
_____
_____

In Jesus' name

> Salvation is found in no one else, for there is no other name under heaven given to men by which we must be saved. ❖ Acts 4:12

Peter and John met a lame man at the temple gate. The beggar stretched out his hand and asked for money. Money seemed to him, as it does to us, the answer to so many needs.

Is it possible the beggar did not really understand what it was he needed most? And did many people who gave coins to him not think deeply enough to know he needed money all right, but he needed something else even more? But Peter and John did not respond as other people. They neither gave him money nor did they pass by unconcerned. They gave instead, in the name of Jesus, the power for the beggar to stand on his own two feet.

There is salvation in no one else, for here is the whole gospel given to the whole person. Two needs were met, one physical and one more primary. And the man walked out of an old, miserable existence into a new life of self-respect and dignity. So can we. And so can our world, in his name.

JAMES A. BERQUIST

Help us to see what we need, Giver of Life, and let us receive salvation in Jesus' name. Amen

Prayer concern: The Red Cross

Daily Reflections_____

_____

_____

_____

Hope through a victorious king

Rejoice greatly, O Daughter of Zion! ... See, your king comes to you, righteous and having salvation, gentle and riding on a donkey, on a colt, the foal of a donkey. ❖ Zechariah 9:9

When my grandparents came to America, they knew life would not be easy or without risk. Draining and clearing the Black Swamp area of northwestern Ohio demanded long hours of backbreaking labor. The church cemetery tells the sad story that many infants and young mothers did not survive those early days. They came, they labored, and they endured—not for immediate gratification but for hope for a better future—at least for their children.

Zechariah prophesied during hard and difficult times too. Many people were discouraged. He, too, offered hope. He spoke much about the Messiah. He held on to an almost idealized picture of the messianic age to come. He called the people to faithfulness and endurance by offering them a vision of God's better future.

Our kind, Jesus the Messiah, comes to us triumphant and victorious. When times are bleak and difficult, he calls us to hang on for the glorious future that will be ours. This is the hope that Jesus offers us.

LOWELL HESTERMAN

God and Lord, help us to fix our eyes upon the future that awaits us so that we will remain steadfast. Amen

Prayer concern: Those who are discouraged

Daily Reflections

Freedom from the law

> We may be justified by faith in Christ and not by observing the law, because by observing the law no one will be justified.... I have been crucified with Christ and I no longer live, but Christ lives in me. ❖ Galatians 2:16, 20

It is probably a natural human tendency to set up rules and regulations. Then we can watch to see who obeys the rules and we can distinguish between "us" and "them." But rules can get so complicated. And when we're looking out to observe all the rules, we easily can get misled from the original reason the rules were established.

Christ freed us from our bondage to law. Law is what crucified Christ—and we died in Christ, so we are already dead as far as law is concerned, Paul says in his letter to the Galatian Christians. Instead of law, Christians concentrate on Christ, who frees us from the world and all the laws that people make.

We are dead—it is Christ who is living in us. We must allow him to use our minds and muscles to do his work. The good that results is not done by ourselves in order to get to heaven, because we already belong to his kingdom. The good that we do is done by Christ when we permit ourselves completely to be obedient to his will.

RON MORTENSON

Dear God, help us to bring good to others. Amen

Prayer concern: Christians in the Middle East

Daily Reflections

Behold

He will turn the hearts of the fathers to their children, and the hearts of the children to their fathers. ❖ Malachi 4:6

This prophecy brings a message of harmony. It suggests that when everything is right, families are blessed. The name Malachi means "messenger." Some authorities think Ezra might have been the author of this book. It is the last book of the Old Testament and several hundred years stand between this book and New Testament times.

Not too much is known about Malachi. His message is brief and to the point. He deals with Israel's sins, especially those of the priesthood. Malachi warns them of the consequences of their sins. On the other hand, he holds out the eternal hope of salvation for the righteous. God would give the people hope.

Why not get better acquainted with Malachi, the last prophet to speak in the Old Testament?

MILDRED BRENDEN

Lord God, show us the way that we may fully comprehend your message. Bring new joy and hope to families everywhere. Where there is trouble, let your message of healing be heard. Amen

Prayer concern: People who fear

Daily Reflections_____

_____

_____

_____

We're new!

Therefore, if anyone is in Christ, he is a new
creation; the old has gone, the new has come!
❖ 2 Corinthians 5:17

When a baby is born, it is new, not something made over. Being
brought into God's family is the same. We are not *recycled*,
but *reborn*.

This transformation is most apparent to someone who has
lived part of her life outside the circle of Christ's love. When
she accepts that love into her life, she changes and so does
the way she looks at everything around her. Like the baby
leaving the darkness of the womb, the new Christian is
brought into a whole new world. Nothing is the same because
it has all been touched by the marvelous love of the Savior.

Only God can accomplish such a miracle. There is no way
we can generate such a change on our own. Trying harder
may make us over into better people, but we will still only
be recycled, not reborn. Paul says, "All this is from God." It is
a gift.

LOREN SPAULDING

We praise you, Lord, for the gift of grace and new life.
We celebrate this gift in your honor and to your glory.
Alleluia!

Prayer concern: New Christians

Daily Reflections_____

_____

_____

_____

A new song

Sing to the LORD a new song; sing to the LORD,
all the earth. ❖ Psalm 96:1

All of us have said at one time, "I wish that I could put into words how thankful I am." Perhaps the psalmist felt like that. God had intervened in the life of Israel in such a marvelous way that the old songs were no longer adequate. The psalmist called for a new song, one that would reach beyond all previous words of praise to honor God's love in action.

When words fail us in our own prayer and praise life, it's good to turn to songs and hymns that have stood the test of time. The psalms, written centuries before Christ, still speak to our inmost needs.

Pause to thank God for those in every age who have written a new song to stir our hearts and move our lips in deepest praise.

LOWELL HESTERMAN

Thank you, Lord, for hymns that express our yearnings and glorify your name. Amen

Prayer concern: Church musicians

Daily Reflections_____

_____

_____

_____

Comfort and joy

Those who sow in tears will reap with songs of joy.
❖ Psalm 126:5

The psalmist begins by reminding the people of Israel of a time when they were in need and were redeemed by the Lord. The verse for today carries a word of comfort that the Lord will cause joy where now there is sorrow. This verse also brings a word of promise, for the Lord assures us that hard times and arduous effort often end in times of joy.

I am reminded of the verse given to me at my confirmation: "Never will I leave you; never will I forsake you" (Hebrews 13:5). This promise from God has been a source of comfort and hope to me in my times of tears. As Christians, when frustration, sorrow, or regret overwhelm us, we look to the cross and remember the tears of Good Friday and the joy of Easter. Above all, the day will come when God "will wipe every tear from their eyes. There will be no more death or mourning or crying or pain" (Revelation 21:4).

SALLY J. GENTRY

Jesus, thank you for your presence in our lives. Amen

Prayer concern: Someone who is very ill

Daily Reflections_____

God's dwelling place

The LORD is my light and my salvation—whom shall I fear? ❖ Psalm 27:1

The world can be an intimidating place. An anxious woman awaits a report from a pathologist as a tumor tries to steal away her hopes and dreams. Hardworking farmers have worked hard to harvest an abundant crop, yet they worry through the winter months because there still is not enough money to pay the bills and feed their families. For any of us, it can seem as if a host of enemies have encamped around us.

The psalmist knew this feeling well. Yet he also knew of God's presence and promise in the midst of great adversity. Our God does not allow disease or economic uncertainty to have the final word. The Lord hears our cries and will not abandon us, even when all seems futile and lost. God makes a dwelling place with us, right in the thick of our problems, even though we might not feel God's presence. God has promised to be with us. We can trust that promise.

W. BRUCE WILDER

Lord God, you know our fears and worries. Help us to turn to you for comfort and peace. Amen

Prayer concern: Christians in Palestine

Daily Reflections_____

Day 251 ❖ John 9:18-41

Spiritual blindness

> Jesus said, "For judgment I have come into this world, so that the blind will see and those who see will become blind." ❖ John 9:39

Spiritual blindness is a common theme in the Gospel of John, which often refers to Jesus as the "light of the world." In many places, the "blindness" of religious insiders (the Pharisees, temple leaders, and even Jesus' own followers at times) is contrasted with the "enlightenment" of society's outsiders.

John often describes religious insiders as blind to the real presence of God in the person of Jesus. Rather, that welcoming Jesus, they are suspicious and hostile. When we read about these religious leaders, it is easy to overlook that we probably have much in common with them. Aren't most of us religious insiders—members in good standing in our congregations? Aren't we tempted at times to look down on others whose faith or theology doesn't seem as sophisticated or genuine as our own?

When has spiritual pride blinded you to the presence of God in Christ? When have you been tempted to be proud of your faith or to look down on the faith of others? Pray that God will restore your ability to behold the miracles of the Light of the World.

MARK A. HINTON

God of mercy, forgive my pride and open my eyes to see your presence in the lives of others. Amen

Prayer concern: Humility in the lives of Christians

Daily Reflections

Discipline means success

Continue in your faith, established and firm,
not moved from the hope held out in the gospel.
❖ Colossians 1:23

If you begin a formal exercise or diet program to improve your health, you will probably soon hear the word *discipline*. Discipline is taking the skills you learn at the beginning of a program and then using them on a daily basis—maybe even for the rest of your life. Trainers and health educators, knowing that discipline will be the key to your success, actually study ways to help you become more disciplined.

Spiritual well-being also requires discipline. Paul talked about the importance of being steadfast or disciplined in faith. For Christians, discipline is a fruit of faith, something that grows out of our relationship with God. Christian discipline also needs to be connected to God's forgiveness because we will fail in our efforts.

Recently, I rejoined our church choir after a long absence. I am intrigued by the discipline involved: It takes discipline to attend every rehearsal, to warm up before singing, and even to sing with the same rhythm and notes as other members of the choir. Being a Christian requires discipline—a discipline that creates in us a joyful sense of spiritual well-being.

MARY NIXON

Give us the discipline to nurture our relationship with you, dear Lord. Amen

Prayer concern: Christians in Swaziland

Daily Reflections_____

_____

_____

_____

Our one master

No servant can serve two masters. ❖ Luke 16:13

During World War II, a number of Japanese Christians were imprisoned by their government because their beliefs prevented them from serving and worshiping the emperor, who was traditionally revered as a god. They persevered in their faith, refusing to follow the dictates of a patriotism they believed to be misguided—and were punished as a result.

Patriotism is a way of life for some people. But when patriotism replaces or runs counter to our confession of faith, we face the danger of serving two masters. Jesus Christ is the light of the world, and only through him are we saved. We are not saved by military force, or by worshiping objects, other people, or slogans. And when we are invited to split our loyalties, we can remain confident and hopeful in the salvation only Christ can bring. It is to that light we must turn.

EMILY DEMUTH ISHIDA

Help us to focus only on you, God, looking to you only for the promise of eternal life that you give through your Son, Jesus Christ. Amen

Prayer concern: Prisoners of conscience

Daily Reflections_____

Signs

> "Teacher," they asked, "when will these things happen? And what will be the sign that they are about to take place?" ❖ Luke 21:7

How alike we are to those people of Jesus' time! When? What are the signs? We wonder the same things.

We spend much of our lives anticipating, wanting to know what will happen. We have set up meteorological bureaus so we know what weather to expect. Seismologists monitor changes in the earth to warn us of potential earthquakes. Books are written to help us recognize the signs of true love, real men, and a bullish stock market. We read faces to determine love, pain, and prognosis. The defense department is constantly searching for signs of unrest or attack.

It is in our nature to want signs. In the Old Testament, God was revealed through signs; soon we will be reminded that a star was given as a sign of Jesus' birth. Signs are not God's way of making life more secure, however; they are given to us to increase our faith in God.

ALFREDA H. EBELING

Lord, keep us alert to your signs. Amen

Prayer concern: Meteorologists and seismologists

Daily Reflections_____

God's Nobel Prize

> Blessed are the peacemakers, for they will be called sons of God. ❖ Matthew 5:9

Of the five Nobel Prizes, the one for peace has been reserved most frequently; special Nobel institutes have been created from the surplus funds. The world has an abundance of scientists and writers, but where are the peacemakers? Even with the lure of a cash award, few qualify.

The Prince of Peace, Jesus, in speaking to us about life in the kingdom, declares that peacemaking carries the greatest award of all—to be called the children of God. Peacemaking is a disciple's Christlike influence, calming the storms of life in a home, in a congregation, or in whatever place a disciple may be found. The disciple of Christ promotes peace.

Strife has no place among those in the kingdom, which contains the "righteousness, peace and joy in the Holy Spirit" (Romans 14:17). As Paul tells young Timothy, "The Lord's servant must not quarrel; but be kind" (2 Timothy 2:24).

HILDEGARDE KAMPFE

Lord, teach us to follow after the things that make for peace, for we want to be your children. Amen

Prayer concern: Those considering new vocations

Daily Reflections

Angry love

So [Jesus] made a whip out of cords, and
drove all from the temple area, both sheep and
cattle. ❖ John 2:15

The right kind of anger has its place in personal life, in
church, and in society. Our Lord became angry when others
were hurt or when God was dishonored. He even used force.
Jesus berated the traders who had turned worship and prayer
into a business venture. People were being exploited in the
name of religion.

Like a coin, love has two sides: compassion and anger.
Righteous anger leads us to correct those influences and
injustices in society that degrade people, twist the message of
the Scriptures, or place other loyalties above the commitment
we owe to God alone.

Spouses of alcoholics are counseled to have "tough love"—
the ability to speak the truth and to maintain personal worth
and integrity in times of family crisis. That love is something
we can all practice toward others.

LYLE RICH

*Correct us, O Lord, with your discipline when we wander
from justice, love, and truth. By your Spirit help us to
shine as light in the darkness. Amen*

Prayer concern: People struggling with business ethics

Daily Reflections_____
_____
_____
_____

No more tears

And God will wipe away every tear from their
eyes. ❖ Revelation: 7:17

How often I remember wiping the tears from our children's
faces. When they were young, the tears could be wiped away
and the hurt seemed to go quickly. As they grew into adulthood, the tears could be wiped, but the hurts were deeper and
stayed a lot longer.

Once, when our daughter was home from college, I heard
her crying. I went into her room and held her. I wiped some
tears away. She said, "Mom, I can remember you wiping my
tears away before and everything was OK. This time you've
wiped my tears, but the hurt is still there. Why is that?"

"I don't know, honey, I don't know," I replied. "But if I'm
helping to ease the hurt, even a little, then I'll always be here
to wipe them away."

How comforting is it to know that our God will take away
all the hurt, to know that there will be a time with the Lord
when, if there are still tears, they will be tears of joy, not of
sadness.

MARLYS A. KORMAN

*Dear God, we have so many hurts. Help us to remember
the day is coming when they will all be wiped away.
Amen*

Prayer concern: Preschoolers

Daily Reflections

The spirit of truth

> So give your servant a discerning heart to govern
> your people and to distinguish between right and
> wrong. ❖ 1 Kings 3:9

Solomon was young and he knew it. When God asked what gift Solomon wanted, his answer was faithful and humble. He asked for wisdom. This pleased God.

When God bestows the Holy Spirit, it is a spirit of truth and wisdom. This same gift was given to Solomon. We pray for the Holy Spirit at baptism: "The spirit of wisdom and understanding, the spirit of counsel and might, the spirit of knowledge and the fear of the Lord, the spirit of joy in your presence" (*Lutheran Book of Worship*, p. 124).

Even with this resource available to us, life remains complicated. God gave Solomon a great gift. Solomon, in his limited human way, did not use the gift faithfully and then lost its benefit. When we lose sight of God's gift, the reality of our baptism calls us back again. We believe that when we pray "thy will, not mine, be done," we can be assured that God will hear and answer our prayers.

CAROLYN MOWCHAN

Gracious God, teach us how to rely on your Holy Spirit for guidance in our lives. Amen

Prayer concern: That leaders earnestly seek the wisdom of God

Daily Reflections_____
_____
_____
_____

Strong words

> When the chief priests and the Pharisees heard
> Jesus' parables, they knew he was talking about
> them. ❖ Matthew 21:45

Was Jesus speaking about us too? What does Jesus' parable
about the landowner and the tenants say about our culture
today? Perhaps it comments on the way many people view
their own church membership? The tenants in the parable
wanted it all, and they stopped at nothing to get it. They even
murdered the owner's son.

Don't misunderstand me. I am not saying we would even
dream of going as far as those tenants did. But see how often
and how easily we put our wants before God's desires. We
tend to our own comforts ahead of another's needs. We sometimes put the beauty of our church buildings ahead of the
effectiveness of the church's mission and ministry. Some
people are so committed to their own satisfaction that they
would even see the church stagnate rather than grow vigor-
ously, because growth means change, sometimes disturbing
change.

Jesus spoke strong words. Are they words for us? Do we
want it all? Do we put ourselves first?

HAROLD PENNINGTON

*God, fill us and use us, so that the church may be ready
for the coming of your Son. Amen*

Prayer concern: Church growth

Daily Reflections_____

_____

_____

_____

The supreme compassion

When the Lord saw her, his heart went out to her
and he said, "Don't cry." ❖ Luke 7:13

I think that God grieves when we grieve. What father wouldn't
be sad if one of his children experiences grief? This inter-
change of feelings is in any bond of love, and sorrow draws
compassion to it.

Christ was filled with compassion for the widow whose
only son had died. No doubt the people of the crowd were
filled with compassion too. But the depth of human sorrow
far exceeds the uplifting capacity of human pity or sympathy.
In the darkness of death and in inevitable sorrow that it pro-
duces, only the certainty of eternal life with God sheds true
light into our grief.

Jesus Christ can create life in the midst of death. God was
in him, and the son was restored to the widow of Nain. The
compassion of God for us is a measure beyond pity or sympathy. God's compassion is laced with power, and God's
supreme compassion was expressed in a cross of forgiveness
and a resurrection of victory. And it's all ours; it's for everyone of faith.

JOHN W. COFFEY

Almighty God, hold us always in your resurrection power.
Amen

Prayer concern: Those feeling sorrow

Daily Reflections_____

Suffering

> I consider that our present sufferings are not worth comparing with the glory that will be revealed in us. ❖ Romans 8:18

We probably should know something about real suffering before we talk about it. But Paul did understand suffering—firsthand. He knew what it was like to be persecuted, to suffer physically and mentally. Paul suffered so intensely that at one time he wished he were dead. Paul's experiences could probably rival those in a prison camp.

When someone like that talks about suffering, he is worth listening to, even by people who may not know suffering at all. Troubled people who ask why God permits suffering should listen too. Although Paul does not give an answer to their question, he shows them a more important place to focus their attention. Don't dwell on the suffering, he says, but dwell on the victory that will come from God.

If you are one of those who truly suffer, you can find hope in Paul's words. Your suffering is not negligible, but God's future holds something that will make your suffering be forgotten. In that promise, we look forward to what God has in store.

FREDERICK W. BALTZ

Lord, teach us that our suffering is not worth comparing to the joy that awaits the faithful. Amen

Prayer concern: Patience in suffering

Daily Reflections

The best is yet to come

Then I saw a new heaven and a new earth.
❖ Revelation 21:1

King Tut's tomb in Egypt was completely furnished so that his future in the afterlife might be happy. There were wagons, beds, chairs, art pieces, and good clothing—as if in death the young king could enjoy what he enjoyed in life.

In contrast, John envisioned a new heaven and a new earth. His vision was not a new physical universe with material things but a new, better, and more glorious age in heaven. The Greek word for *new* means "a fresh start." The earth as we know it will pass away. The new creation that John writes of will be a place where the Lord will dwell with the people of God. This is a fresh start for all who live in Christ.

Paul said, "If only for this life we have hope in Christ, we are to be pitied more than all men" (1 Corinthians 15:19). The Christian lives happily and courageously in this life, but knows the best is yet to come.

CONRAD M. THOMPSON

Dear God, each day is a day you have made; help me treasure it. Amen

Prayer concern: A fresh start each day

Daily Reflections_____

_____

_____

_____

Delighted

> Blessed is the man who fears the LORD, who finds
> great delight in his commands. ❖ Psalm 112:1

Who could ever "delight" in God's commands? Aren't they so difficult to keep that we usually end up feeling frustrated and guilty? Yes—if we are trying to keep them in order to win God's favor. But that's an impossibility.

However, Christ has fulfilled the law for us. This means that we are free to try keeping the Ten Commandments as a way of showing our gratitude for the One who died because of all the times we have broken them. It sounds strange, doesn't it? But if we live God's law out of gratitude instead of out of obligation, it changes our whole attitude toward God's law.

The Commandments are no longer a ladder by which we climb into God's grace. They are ways to show our love for God and for one another. Still, their greatest value is that they point out our constant need for the Savior. Yes, we can delight in the Ten Commandments!

CHARLES KNORR

*Dear God, help us to live your law out of love for you
and for one another. Amen*

Prayer concern: Waitstaff

Daily Reflections

God's way

> The landowner asked, "Don't I have the right to do what I want with my own money? Or are you envious because I am so generous?" ❖ Matthew 20:15

God's labor policies would not fit well in today's workplace, where equal work commands equal pay. That is not the policy in the realm where God rules. The parable of the laborers in the vineyard speaks of God's astonishing generosity and mercy. The laborers who were hired later in the day were paid the same wage as those who were hired early in the day, and this did not sit well with the early morning work force.

This may not sit too well with us, either. The breadth and depth of God's mercy clearly surpasses our understanding. That the last can be first is an indication that God does not seem interested in keeping score. For God, what matters is not how long we have believed, but in whom we believe.

As Christ captures our faith, as we trust and obey him, as we focus on his cross, the whole matter of wages and rewards becomes irrelevant. We are all beggars at the foot of the cross. But through the extravagant goodness of God, we will hold first place in his love.

JOHN W. COFFEY

Dear Lord, include us in the extravagant goodness of your grace. Amen

Prayer concern: Those who perform dangerous labor

Daily Reflections_____

_____

_____

_____

Wisdom for the asking

> You have known the holy Scriptures, which are
> able to make you wise for salvation through faith
> in Christ Jesus. ❖ 2 Timothy 3:15

Television and magazine ads promise many things, including riches, popularity, and success. But did you ever see an ad that promised to make you wise? That's the promise of this verse in an older translation: "to make you wise for salvation." The apostle Paul isn't the only one to make such a claim for God's word. The psalms say the same: "The statutes of the LORD are trustworthy, making wise the simple" (Psalm 19:7); "Open my eyes that I may see wonderful things in your law" (Psalm 119:18). These writers probably had in mind the insight God's word gives in how to lead a satisfying life. If we live according to God's will, we're likely to get along better with others. Our lives come to have a purpose.

But Paul is writing about a particular kind of wisdom: for salvation, that is, living with God forever. There are many ideas about how to get salvation, such as keeping rules, sacrificing, learning a lot. Paul says wisdom unto salvation is found only through faith in Christ Jesus. And the Bible helps make this possible. The fear of the Lord is the beginning of wisdom, the Bible says. But the Bible doesn't just get us started. It carries the job through—to salvation.

ROLF E. AASENG

God, make us wise unto salvation. Amen

Prayer concern: Christians in Sudan

Daily Reflections

God cares for you

> When I consider your heavens, the work of your
> fingers, the moon and the stars, which you have set
> in place, what is man that you are mindful of him,
> the son of man that you care for him? ❖ Psalm 8:3-4

Creation can't teach you everything about God. But when you know the Creator, creation reveals a lot. The moon and stars in the sky show us the vastness of creation and the vastness of the creator. A bluebird singing, deer playing, a gentle breeze blowing show us the beauty within God. The mighty power of storms, earthquakes, and hurricanes show us the great power of the one who shaped all this with his fingers. God is awesome in power and beauty and height and depth.

And yet, God cares for you and for me. This mighty God considers you worthy of attention. This God of all places considers you of great importance. This beautiful God is willing to face an ugly death on the cross for your sake. What love! What marvelous, powerful, and beautiful love. That love is for you.

JOHN GERIKE

God, you have all power and yet you care for me. Thank you for your wondrous love. Amen

Prayer concern: Our earth

Daily Reflections

One for all

> My prayer is not for them alone. I pray also for those who will believe in me through their message, that all of them my be one, Father, just as you are in me and I am in you. May they also be in us so that the world may believe that you have sent me. ❖ John 17:20-21

I recall reading one of the all-time classics novels, *The Three Musketeers*. The musketeers' devotion to doing good and their bond of friendship seemed to reflect their motto: "One for all, and all for one."

But oneness that we have in Jesus goes much deeper even than that. The prayer for oneness that we read in John's Gospel is also meant for us. The spirit of oneness that Jesus is praying for is a total oneness that can only come as a gift of the Holy Spirit.

Jesus brought a message of oneness to all people. The barriers of race, color, creed, or ethnic background can never destroy this oneness. All of us share in the one family of God. Jesus is the Lord and Savior for us all. He died so we could live.

JAMES E. LESCHENSKY

We pray for peace and oneness between all people of all nations. Help us, O Lord, to work together with others to bring your message of unity to all the world. Amen

Prayer concern: For the one church

Daily Reflections

The first message

Repent and believe the good news! ❖ Mark 1:15b

Parents listen eagerly for the first word their child speaks. Friends wait for the first news from another on a journey. A pastor's first sermon, a president's first speech, a loved one's first letter—all of these are full of meaning to us.

Mark records these words of Jesus from the early part of his ministry. The temptation of Jesus in the wilderness was over. He came back to Galilee and heard that John the Baptist had been thrown into prison by Herod. So Jesus began to preach. And what did he say? "The kingdom of God is near." The time of waiting for God's Messiah had been fulfilled. All the hopes of God's people could now come true. Here was Jesus' first message, the first words of God's new prophet.

As we look at the words we remember that they were meant not only for people of Jesus' time but for us. No matter how often we have heard the story of Jesus, there are times when these words are addressed to us. Faith does grow dim, and doubts do take over. We get careless. Jesus' words are meant for these moments: "Repent and believe."

GARLAND E. GOROSKI

Let me hear your words in faith, Lord. Amen

Prayer concern: Parents

Daily Reflections_____
_____
_____
_____

Fortitude

> But the people there did not welcome him, because
> he was heading for Jerusalem. ❖ Luke 9:53

One of the most heartrending scenes of the Summer Olympics of 1984 was that of the determined young woman who struggled to finish the marathon race in spite of her body's obvious weakness. With legs bending in every direction and arms flapping at her sides, she neared the finish line. Crawling at last, she fell across the line to the cheers of the crowd. Amazingly, we remember her and not the actual winner of the race. She was a winner, in an extraordinary sense.

Determination to follow God is what motivated Jesus as he set his face toward Jerusalem. The race was not finished, he knew. His destiny, by God's plan, awaited him, and he was determined to face it. His strength of purpose and obedience to God's will was enough to see him across the finish line. And we are the winners—in an extraordinary way!

JUDY CHRISTIAN

Lord, keep us steadfast in the faith. Receive us into your glorious home when our race is done. Amen

Prayer concern: Someone who does not attend church

Daily Reflections

A chosen child

Everyone who heard this wondered about it,
asking, "What then is this child going to be?"
❖ Luke 1:66

Joyful parents cradling a newborn child often wonder, "What will this child become?" The family and neighbors of Zechariah had good reasons to wonder about John. Zechariah had emerged from his temple assignment speechless. Elizabeth at an advanced age had conceived and now, when they went against tradition and named the child "John," Zechariah regained his speech.

In their wildest imaginings, they could not have anticipated that God would use them as participants in plans for the redemption of the world. God had chosen this child to prepare the way for the Messiah by preaching a message of repentance and restoration.

Joyful parents cradle an infant at the baptismal font, not knowing what their child will become, but they do know what is important. God receives their child as an heir and as a member of Christ's church.

LOWELL L. HESTERMAN

Thank you, Lord Jesus, for the promise of salvation to us and to our children. Amen

Prayer concern: Christian leaders

Daily Reflections_____

_____

_____

_____

The moment

Seek the LORD while he may be found; call on him while he is near. ❖ Isaiah 55:6

Every life has moments that are like a meteor that streaks across the sky. For an instant there is light, a sharp insight, an impelling thought, a striking experience. These may be times that God is breaking through. God has something very important to say.

We should be tuned to God at all times. But we are busy with work or with play. We don't deliberately tune God out, but God gets pushed to the sidelines and forgotten. Then comes the moment. A great joy floods our souls, a great sorrow almost crushes us, and a great fear paralyzes us. And God is near. We listen and hear God. But when the moment is gone, we may forget.

The moment may not be a crisis. It may come in the quiet of a Sunday worship, or as we walk alone in the woods. But it is God's moment.

ALVIN N. ROGNESS

We are too preoccupied to hear, O Lord. You are nearby, we know. Open our ears, and let us never forget your word to us. Amen

Prayer concern: Those experiencing a crisis

Daily Reflections_____

_____

_____

_____

Have no fear

But Jesus immediately said to them: "Take
courage! It is I. Don't be afraid." ❖ Matthew 14:27

Fear can be a very good and normal reaction. If we were not
somewhat afraid, we might do irresponsible things such as
climbing a tree with an old ladder or driving too fast on a
highway. We might choose to be reckless or daring, perhaps
even showing off when danger lurks around the corner.

However, too much fear can also be a bad thing in one's
life. Some people can never reach their goal because they are
afraid. Others may need professional help. They need such
help because they have a fear that cripples them. They might
be afraid of cats, closed spaces, high places, or other situations or things.

During the storm, Jesus told his disciples not to be afraid.
That is what Jesus would say to us as well. Faith is the answer
to fear. A child who has faith in his parents will jump into the
parent's arms with a laugh for joy! When we give our fears to
God and ask for help, it becomes possible for us to set fear
aside. Give God your fears—and you will have no fear!

ANNE JORDHEIM

*Dear God, we ask you to give us the kind of faith needed
to take away our fears. Amen*

Prayer concern: Those needing courage

Daily Reflections_____

Crucified Christians

> I have been crucified with Christ and I no longer
> live, but Christ lives in me. The life I live in the
> body, I live by faith in the Son of God, who loved
> me and gave himself for me. ❖ Galatians 2:20

Since I became a Christian, many verses have been helpful to
me in guiding my Christian life. The verse that has been the
most helpful is Galatians 2:20. According to this verse, I have
been crucified *with* Christ. When I first read this, a more personal feeling towards Christ came to me. It made my life seem
more important and worthwhile. I felt closer to Christ.

The verse goes on to say that Christ now lives in me. This
scared me. I'm doing so many things that Christ wouldn't
do. This part has been a guide for me during the day.
Sometimes I'll be doing something I know isn't right, and
then this verse comes to me. I can then acknowledge my sin
and ask for forgiveness.

The last part tells me of Christ's love for me. This gave me
the assurance of being a child of God. I no longer have to
worry about sin. With Christ I have forgiveness and because
of God's love I am a saved creature. Through this verse,
I have found a personal Lord and Savior who lives in my heart
and gave himself for me because he loves me.

ANONYMOUS

*Dear God, we thank you for your love and for your Son,
who died for us. Amen*

Prayer concern: Scholars

Daily Reflections_____

We seek freedom

To the Jews who had believed him, Jesus said,
"If you hold to my teaching, you are really my
disciples. Then you will know the truth, and the
truth will set you free." ❖ John 8:31-32

Freedom is an important word for people living today. It is
almost overused in the advertising media that promises to
free us from pain, drudgery, boredom, and discomfort by
buying something we may not even need.

But the freedom that Christ offers is something different
from the superficial appeal of advertising. Freedom is also the
goal of people who feel that they are not getting their fair
share of what society has to offer—freedom from discrimination,
poverty, exploitation, violence, and fear.

Even these more worthy aspirations fall short of the kind
of freedom that Jesus offers. Note that he associates freedom
with truth, saying that the truth shall make you free. The
truth to which he refers is the gospel, and the kind of freedom
that he describes is almost beyond our comprehension.
Freedom from guilt, freedom from uncertainty, freedom from
death—these unbelievable gifts are ours now and forever as
we accept his magnificent offer.

JESSE E. AIKEN

*Eternal God, lift us above the problems and tensions of
our time, as we claim your gift of life and freedom forever.
In Jesus' name. Amen*

Prayer concern: Those longing for freedom

Daily Reflections_____

_____

_____

_____

Look and wonder

> There is the sea, vast and spacious, teeming with creatures beyond number—living things both large and small. ❖ Psalm 104:25

Not many years back, I lived on the prairie of central Nebraska. The land is largely flat and uninteresting, but oh, the sunsets! Each evening I watched the final glory of daylight played out in an orange glow so beautiful it made one weep. No sunset was quite like any other, but each proclaimed the power of God in creation.

The psalmist struggles to express the glory of God that each of us is privileged to experience. He does not merely describe the experience of wonder but also blesses God for the majesty revealed in creation. When God seems too small to help you, look at a sunset and wonder.

DAVID L. MILLER

Wonderful Creator, help us see your hand revealed in the greatness of the sea and in the tender beauty of a flower. Amen

Prayer concern: Someone facing depression

Daily Reflections_____

An antidote for despair

> [God] redeems your life from the pit and crowns
> you with love and compassion. ❖ Psalm 103:4

How does one respond to the suicide of a friend or loved one? The pastor struggles for the right words in comforting the family and conducting the funeral. Friends and relatives are caught in a turmoil of difficult questions, many of which begin with "why?" We look to our loving Lord who died for each of us on the cross, and ask more questions.

There is something we can do. It's a little like preventative medicine. The psalmist seems to suggest that we can be saved from the pit by remembering the Lord's benefits: love, mercy, satisfaction, forgiveness, and healing. This remembering will focus our eyes on Jesus and give us joy even in the midst of pain.

There can never be enough thankful joy among Christians. Maybe through contagious joy God can save us, or someone around us, from the pit.

STEVE SWANSON

Lord, deliver us from despair, from the pit, and make us agents of joy in all your benefits. Amen

Prayer concern: To have a spirit of joy

Daily Reflections_____

_____

_____

_____

A promise of peace

You will keep in perfect peace him whose mind
is steadfast, because he trusts in you. ❖ Isaiah 26:3

Even though conferences are held to promote peace and
awards are given to those who propagate peace, it continues
to be an elusive condition. Throughout all of history, there
have been but a few short periods of time when there was
peace the world over. Yet even in these interim times there
has not really been peace, for there have always been struggling and strife, anger and mistrust, and selfishness and hate
within communities and institutions—or even more sadly,
within families and relationships.

The peace promised in Isaiah is peace within, trusting that
God forgives and loves. It is the peace that holds one up even
when circumstances may seem impossible. But peace can be
obtained only by focusing (staying the mind) on God rather
than on self. It is the peace that comes by clinging to Jesus,
the rock of ages. And it is this *internal* peace that can teach us
how to promote *external* peace everywhere.

NANCY LEE SASSER

Lord, give us the peace that passes all understanding.
Amen

Prayer concern: Nations at war

Daily Reflections_____

The once and future king

> They will look on me, the one they have
> pierced, and they will mourn for him as one
> mourns an only child. ❖ Zechariah 12:10

In this ancient prophecy of Zechariah, spoken to the people of Israel who lived in the fifth century B.C., God promised a day yet to come when Jerusalem would be washed from her sin, and God's reign would once again be as broad as the whole earth.

God promised that the future king would reign in justice and would come from the house of David. God also indicated that there would come a time when that king would be martyred and that God would give a spirit of compassion to those of the house of David.

For us who live 25 centuries later, on this side of Easter, it is not difficult to read these verses and see Christ reflected in them. We belong to Christ crucified, the firstborn child of Mary and Joseph, who were of the house and lineage of David. Jesus' death was grieved by many and remains the center point of our history down to this very day, even as we also rejoice at his resurrection.

STEPHANIE FREY

Lord Jesus Christ, you were pierced and put to death by your enemies for our sake. We thank you for the costly gift of your life, which in turn gave us new life. Amen

Prayer concern: Leaders

Daily Reflections

Delightful growth

All over the world this gospel is bearing fruit and growing, just as it has been doing among you since the day you heard it and understood God's grace in all its truth. ❖ Colossians 1:6

There is delight in watching something or someone grow. The apostle Paul congratulated the Colossians in their growth. He celebrated with them the strength they were finding in their faith in Jesus Christ. What was exciting to Paul was that these people were growing in their faith, which showed itself in their love for others (v. 4).

Their growth in faith is like the beautiful fuchsia plant growing on our porch. Two months ago this plant was three spindly vines, very homely to look at. Its nurture has come from soil, sunlight, and water, under God's blessing. The plant simply sits in the dirt, enjoying the warmth and food. We celebrate its beauty, not the work that has been going on.

Paul encourages us through the Colossians to grow in God's grace and to bear fruit in response to the gospel.

JANEVA STROMBERG

Creator God, continue to grow strong in us, that we may flourish in grace and knowledge of your love. Amen

Prayer concern: All who teach God's word

Daily Reflections_____

Shadows

Even though I walk through the valley of the
shadow of death, I will fear no evil. ❖ Psalm 23:4

Shadows can be unnerving. They seem to hold some sort of
mystery and threat. Possible dangers can hide in the shadows,
ready to leap out. Darkness holds the unknown, the danger
that we cannot see. Is it any wonder, then, that children are
frightened of the dark?

Death often is pictured as a shadow, watching and waiting.
We fear death, not only because of what perils or promises
lie beyond it, but because we do not understand death itself.
Our culture attempts to deny the reality of death. People don't
die, they "pass away," as though we can escape the fear of
death by changing the words. In our modern sophistication,
we tend to ignore what we can't control.

For believers, Christ's triumph over death by his resurrection changes the meaning of death. How we will die naturally
concerns us, but to those who believe in him, the peril of
death is taken away. We know we will be with Christ forever in
a place where there is no danger, only beauty and joy.

MARLYS A. KORMAN

*Dear Lord, thank you for your triumph over the grave
and your victory over death. Amen*

Prayer concern: Those who are suffering emotionally

Daily Reflections_____

_____

_____

_____

Fire on the mountain

> To the Israelites the glory of the LORD looked
> like a consuming fire on top of the mountain.
> ❖ Exodus 24:17

A forest fire is hot, noisy, and terrifying close up. Yet at a distance, it has a singular beauty as flames leap and smoke billows, turning the sun and moon to an eerie red.

The Israelites experienced this beauty day after day as the glory of God accompanied their journey—guiding, protecting, lighting their way. Now it covered the mountaintop as Moses disappeared into its fiery light.

It seems impossible, yet could they have become so accustomed to God's protecting presence that they began to stop noticing it? Is that why only 40 days later they designed a golden calf to worship?

Do we become too accustomed to the blessings of God that we begin to take them for granted? Is that why we sometimes forget God's will and choose to go our own way? If that is true, we need a vibrant sense of God's presence.

EILEEN POLLINGER

Thank you, Lord, for your glory within us. Amen

Prayer concern: Christians in Nigeria

Daily Reflections

Moments of truth

"Who do you say that I am?" Simon Peter
answered, "You are the Christ, the Son of the
living God." ❖ Matthew 16:15-16

For Peter, it was the moment of truth. He spoke from his
heart and said, "You are the Christ." Do we know the feeling
of facing the moment of truth? We learn to avoid giving direct
answers. We protect ourselves, or others, in glossing over the
truth. There is a fine line between being honest and tactful,
a line we may not always be able to see.

It is difficult to be honest with God, with others, with ourselves. How can we learn to be honest with ourselves? The
moment of truth comes when we listen to the silence, alone
with God, and write our inner thoughts or breathe them to
God. "You are the Christ, and I open my heart to you." Make
this your moment of truth. Now.

ROLAND SEBOLDT

*Lord God, grant me grace to pour out my thoughts and
feelings to you, and to accept your love. Amen*

Prayer concern: Honesty

Daily Reflections_____

Willing workers

> Is not this the kind of fasting I have chosen:
> to loose the chains of injustice and untie the
> cords of the yoke, to set the oppressed free
> and break every yoke? ❖ Isaiah 58:6

A nearby shelter for people who are homeless opens its doors each October and remains open through the middle of April, housing 60 to 80 men seven nights a week. The shelter was established after a man froze to death on the church steps nearly 10 years ago. The guests arrive around 7 P.M. each night and are served a hot meal by community volunteers.

One night, while helping serve supper, I met another volunteer named Roland. I was surprised when Roland told me he had spent many months sleeping at the shelter while spending his days looking for work. Not long before, someone had offered him a place to live and meals, which allowed Roland to establish a legal residence. Now he was attending a local technical school.

If it had not been for the Christlike action of a kind benefactor, Roland might still be hoping to have a warm, dry place to spend the night. Isaiah calls all of us to look out for the Rolands of this world.

SUE WOLF

Lord God, we are willing workers, but sometimes there seems to be too much for us to do. Give us your strength today and every day. Amen

Prayer concern: People who are homeless

Daily Reflections_____

_____

_____

_____

Fools for Christ

> But we preach Christ crucified: a stumbling
> block to Jews and foolishness to Gentiles.
> ❖ 1 Corinthians 1:23

He was a brilliant organist and we spent many delightful
evenings listening to Paul play as we relaxed in his living
room. Our children were especially intrigued when Paul
would ask for a phone number or the numbers on a driver's
license or Social Security card. With middle C as number one,
Paul would then blend those notes, no matter how bizarre
their progression, into the theme for a beautiful melody,
building harmonies until it all made musical sense.

Just so, God brings power and wisdom, and miracle and
salvation, out of foolishness. Christ's crucifixion may appear
to be nothing short of foolishness and weakness. Yet through
the strength of God, the cross has been made the world's
supreme symbol of wisdom and power.

HAROLD W. PENNINGTON

*Lord God, if depending on Christ's cross is folly, then I
gladly claim to be a fool. Amen*

Prayer concern: Nursing home residents

Daily Reflections_____

_____

_____

_____

The power of God

A bruised reed he will not break, and a smoldering
wick he will not snuff out. ❖ Isaiah 42:3

Power politics, *power hungry*, and *power plays* all are familiar
concepts to us. No matter what our position in life, we don't
like to be powerless. We would prefer the upper hand rather
than have to answer to someone whom we may not trust.
Some people want the power to control people, but most of us
simply want enough power that we don't feel threatened.

Out of necessity, human power often is big and loud. What
is God's power like? We know that it looks like a baby—in
Christ. We know that the most powerful thing Christ did was
to obey his heavenly Father.

God's power is not spent to protect God but to restore and
to build God's kingdom on earth. God's power is exercised in
tenderness to do this without breaking what is already battered, without blowing out a flame that is barely lit. We need
not fear God's power. We rejoice in it.

DEBRA R. GRANT

*Lord, please care for us, your frail children, and show us
your kingdom. Amen*

Prayer concern: A neighbor

Daily Reflections

Seek not human acclaim

Whoever serves me must follow me; and where I
am, my servant also will be. My Father will honor
the one who serves me. ❖ John 12:26

A friend's little boy died. Knowing the child's birthday a few
months later would be especially hard, I made a point to
spend that day with her. And yet, what a horrible thing I did—
or neglected to do. I told no one else what day it was. Others
who shared the grief could have been recruited, but I wanted
to be the one who remembered.

Good works can be dangerous. They can make us feel
prideful, self-righteous, and puffed up. The hazard lies in
seeking human affirmation instead of being content to be
honored by God.

Mother Teresa of India was effective in serving the poor
and dying because she never sought human acclaim. She
focused on the knowledge that she was serving Jesus by rec-
ognizing him in every soul she met. Jesus says, "Those who
honor me I will honor" (1 Samuel 2:30). For those of us who
want to serve Jesus, let that be the only reward we seek.

NANCY LEE SASSER

*Almighty God, I praise you for those you have sent to
serve. Empower me not to seek human acclaim. Amen*

Prayer concern: Those who have lost a child

Daily Reflections

Teaching our children

> Impress them on your children. Talk about them
> when you sit at home and when you walk along
> the road, when you lie down and when you get up.
> ❖ Deuteronomy 6:7

Probably the hardest time to parent is when children are teenagers. Parents may expect things to be the way they were when the teenagers were children. And teenagers have to deal with peer pressure as well as increasing responsibilities. Sometimes teenagers react by fighting against structure and routine. And one area of conflict may be church attendance.

Today's passage from Deuteronomy urges parents to teach their children about God's love daily and not give up. Although this book of the Bible contains many laws, it is also God's good news for us, life-giving gospel. When our lives express God's love, we teach God's love to our children. And with God's help, we can ourselves learn, bit by bit, how to speak to our children about our own faith. We can tell them what it means to us that God loves us. We can forgive them. We can tell them why we worship. We can take them to worship with us. We can teach with love and grace, the same love and grace we have received from God.

PETUNIA SEGRE

O God, help us exercise your grace and teach your ways to our children. Amen

Prayer concern: Parents

Daily Reflections_____

_____

_____

_____

Doing or being?

> Then, because so many people were coming and
> going that they did not even have a chance to eat,
> he said to them, "Come with me by yourselves to
> a quiet place and get some rest." ❖ Mark 6:31

Many people experience a great shortage of rest. We live in a
always-on-the-go age, always trying to get more done in less
time so there will be time to rest. But if we have the chance to
rest do we take it? Can we really relax? Or are we so geared
for *doing* that we can't stop and take time for *being*?

Yet real life is rooted in *being*, not in *doing*. We do what we
do *because* of who we are. We do not become who we are
because of what we do. To *do* on the basis of what others do is
at best to ignore who we are and at worst to reject who we are.
Our rootedness is in Christ, who dwells in us through the
Sacrament of Baptism. He is the source of our being. Our
identity is rooted in him. Our doing is an outpouring of his
presence in our lives.

RICHARD J. SMITH

*Holy God, in Christ we are new creatures. Let us find rest
and inner composure by focusing our eyes on the source of
our being, who is none other than Jesus Christ, our Lord.
Amen*

Prayer concern: A close friend

Daily Reflections_____

_____
_____
_____

Religion and politics

Hate evil, love good; maintain justice in the
courts. ❖ Amos 5:15

It is still debated today whether faith is only a private matter
or whether it has public implications. We often hear people
say, "Don't mix religion and politics." Such a thought would
be very foreign to the prophet Amos. In ancient Israel, the
legal assemblies were supposed to reflect the faith of the
people. Faithful obedience to God had everything to do with
the political and legal activities of God's people.

Although we live in very different times from the prophet
Amos, his words still hold for us as God's people. God's will is
that our legal assemblies work for truth and justice for all.
The poor are to be protected against such exploitation by the
rich and powerful (v. 11). This is God's will, which leads to
life. God blesses justice and uses it to bind humans in harmo-
nious communities.

JEANETTE STRANDJORD

*O God of truth, bless those who work for legal justice for
all people. Prosper this work so there may be life and
harmony. Amen*

Prayer concern: Politicians

Daily Reflections_____
_____
_____
_____

Daily repentance

Repent and believe the good news! ❖ Mark 1:15

Jesus' opening sermon was not simply, "Believe!" He also said, "Repent!" The Greek word for "repent" suggests a transformation, a redirection, a turning around or inside out.

Jesus comes to us as one who has shown immeasurable love for us, one in whom we can place our hope and trust. But he expects more than a shift of allegiance. He wants to see our lives turned around, with him at the center. The Holy Spirit starts this transformation through our baptism. Paul has said that we die daily to sin, meaning that our transformation is renewed on a daily basis.

We do not merely confess with our lips, "I believe in …," but we are reborn daily through the renewal of our baptism. Such renewal enables us to become more Christlike in acts of loving service to others. The Bible is God's message of assurance that in Christ we can turn from evil ways and live.

KURT T. MEYERS

Dear God, take my life and reshape it after that of Jesus. Amen

Prayer concern: New church members

Daily Reflections_____

_____
_____
_____

A new dimension

> But God demonstrates his own love for us in
> this: While we were still sinners, Christ died
> for us. ❖ Romans 5:8

On the way to Damascus, a new dimension of life suddenly dawned upon the apostle Paul. He was confronted by the immeasurable love of God in the call of Jesus to him. The apostle Paul writes these verses to the Romans with a song in his heart.

We might say that *love* is spelled S-A-C-R-I-F-I-C-E. In marriage, in the family, and in society love works out its way in acts of mercy, care, and kindness. God spelled out compassion for us in the life and death of Jesus. The action of Christ on the cross underlines for us that we are loved in a new dimension—an eternal dimension—not only 2,000 years ago, but now. Rejoice! We can journey through life with a skip in our step and a song in our heart because our God has covered us with a love so deep.

LYLE RICH

O God of boundless love, you have shown your mercy to us in your beloved Son. Draw our hearts to you and make us yours forever. Amen

Prayer concern: People facing rejection

Daily Reflections_____

_____

_____

_____

Do it now

Why shouldn't I be baptized? ❖ Acts 8:36

The Ethiopian from the book of Acts didn't wait. When he heard the gospel and saw that God was giving him a chance to enter the kingdom, even providing water for baptism, he acted immediately.

Many of us, in contrast, put off doing what we know is right. We agree that Bible-reading, tithing, and helping others are good ideas and promise to begin next year. Why are we like this? Sometimes we worry about what people think; we're afraid to be different. Or we have a false sense of humility that persuades us we aren't important enough to take a controversial stand.

Athanasius was only a deacon when he spoke up against church leaders who were denying biblical truth about Christ. Doing so helped preserve gospel. Perhaps we don't want to give up a sin. We admit racial discrimination is wrong, but we'll allow it to stop gradually. Or we admit adultery is sin, but we make excuses for "this one time." When Christ has offered his grace, nothing need prevent us from following his guidance—immediately.

ROLF E. AASENG

Lord, keep us from postponing right action. Amen

Prayer concern: Christians in Ethiopia

Daily Reflections_____

_____

_____

_____

Time to remember

This is my blood of the covenant, which is
poured out for many for the forgiveness of
sins. ❖ Matthew 26:28

On the way to Jerusalem for the last time, Jesus and his disciples paused to share a last meal and to remember Israel's deliverance from Egypt. Roots do matter. But as followers of Christ we have more than roots; we have the presence of our Lord. When we receive and remember him in the Holy Communion we "re-call" him to our side, to our pain, and to our journey.

Whenever I preside at Holy Communion I picture our Lord blessing each person—forgiving, restoring, healing. What remembrances do you carry with you to the sacrament? Every time we take part in Holy Communion, we celebrate our Lord's great deliverance, which he bestowed upon us fully and freely. In our busy, hectic lives, we need a time to remember.

LYLE RICH

*O God, touch us with your presence, help us to remember,
to obey, to follow. Amen*

Prayer concern: People who are divorced

Daily Reflections_____

_____

_____

_____

Faithfulness

> I will bow down … and will praise your name for
> your love and your faithfulness. ❖ Psalm 138:2

Carolyn and I had become good friends. We were both students far from home, and we also shared a love of travel. Happily we planned an outing together for Saturday. "Why don't I meet you here at nine, and we'll tour the old walled city," I suggested.

"That would be great," she agreed.

As planned, I went to meet Carolyn the next morning. But her landlady answered the door. "Oh, she left with Jane around eight," said the landlady. "Carolyn's been talking about their trip to the coast since last week."

I was hurt. "That is no way to treat a friend," I thought. "She just plain lied to me." Sadder, but wiser, I left to make other plans for the day.

Acquaintances, good friends, sometimes even members of our own family can let us down with a broken promise, a lie, or a refusal to help when we need it most. There is only One who is always loyal; only One keeps every promise; only One surrounds us with faithful love at all times. Yes, countless voices down through the centuries echo the psalmist's words to praise God's name.

DARLENE BOWDEN MUSCHETT

Faithful God, help us to be loyal to others, as you are to us; in Jesus' name. Amen

Prayer concern: Children of divorced parents

Daily Reflections

_____
_____
_____

God's assistants

Men ate the bread of angels; he sent them all the
food they could eat. ❖ Psalm 78:25

God fed the Israelites in the wilderness. The psalmist calls the
manna they received "the bread of angels." How does this
relate to the millions of malnourished people in the world
today who receive no heavenly bread? Doesn't God love
people today as in the past? Has God forgotten this world?

A simple story will answer these questions. A young farm
boy overheard his pious father praying for the hungry people
of the world. The boy piped up, "Father, if I had as much grain
as you have in the barn, I'd feed the hungry myself."

Exactly! God has the resources and the personnel to do
God's work. We are God's assistants, able to provide for those
in need. We have the money and the food. It is not a burden
but an honor to be allowed to assist others. God has turned
the work over to us. Let's pray. Let's act. But let's not wait.

W. A. POOVEY

*Lord, I thank you for my daily bread. Help me to share
my blessings with others. Amen*

Prayer concern: Medical researchers

Daily Reflections_____

I know how you feel

> So that we can comfort those in any trouble with
> the comfort we ourselves have received from God.
> ❖ 2 Corinthians 1:4

We have often heard people say, "I know how you feel." And often we were sure that they had no idea at all how we felt! But when one went through the same experience we suffered, then the words had a note of understanding.

How much that means when we have had an operation or serious illness, or when death has taken a dear one from us! Then few words, perhaps only a handclasp or even a sympathetic smile, can comfort us greatly. Read again Paul's kind words to his friends at Corinth. Think of what these words meant when Paul's letter was read to the congregation there.

What a blessed privilege! We share with others the precious comfort God has given us in our afflictions! In our letters, our greetings, our conversations with those who know sickness, sorrow and grief, we can invest our inadequate words with such love that they do comfort.

HAROLD YOCHUM

Lord, we thank you for the comfort you give us; help us to share it with others. Amen

Prayer concern: Those in need of comfort

Daily Reflections_____

Fighting fire with fire

> Are not all angels ministering spirits sent to serve
> those who will inherit salvation? ❖ Hebrews 1:14

Forest firefighters know that one of the best ways to fight fire is with fire. Smaller, controlled fires are set deliberately in advance of an approaching forest fire. When the larger fire reaches the area already burned, there is no fuel to keep the fire burning. So "fire, the adversary," becomes "fire, the friend"—indeed, the conqueror—when used wisely.

So it is that God used death to conquer death. Jesus was Immanuel—God with us—in our humanity, including death. And it was by death on the cross that Jesus met sin and death "eyeball-to-eyeball" to declare the truth that God's love is stronger than death.

In the same way, we are invited to enter the journeys and struggles of others, even to be willing to die for others so that life and love might prevail. Does that sound crazy? Well, not if you can fight fire with fire. Like Jesus, we can fight a death to sin with death in Jesus' name.

JON TEMME

Give us courage, Lord of Life, that trusting in your promises we might live and die and live again daily in Jesus' name and power. Amen

Prayer concern: Firefighters

Daily Reflections

Good soldiers

Endure hardship with us like a good soldier of
Christ Jesus. ❖ 2 Timothy 2:3

Paul was a simple, faithful witness to God's great love in Jesus
Christ. He wanted Christ, not himself, to be central in his
ministry. On his journeys, Paul encountered great difficulties
and often suffered.

Paul was not alone on his travels. In his letters we are
introduced to people like Timothy, Titus, Aquila, and
Priscilla—along with many others. We'd like to know more
about them, but the details of their lives are sketchy. Perhaps
this is a needed reminder for us to focus on the gospel and not
on the person. But we all can imagine the price these early
Christians paid as they struggled to bring the good news of
Jesus Christ to the world.

You and I are called to share in suffering too. The challenges from within and without are many and sometimes
overwhelming. There is suffering, but Paul challenges us
to straighten our shoulders, stick out our chins, and move
ahead "like good soldiers," trusting in God's faithfulness and
steadfast love.

TED VINGER

*Thank you, Lord, for Timothy, Titus, Aquila, and
Priscilla, and all the others who faithfully have witnessed
to you. May our names be included in the list of good
soldiers. Amen*

Prayer concern: Those who suffer for their faith

Daily Reflections

Witnessing power

> But you will receive power when the Holy Spirit comes on you; and you will be my witnesses in Jerusalem, and in all Judea and Samaria, and to the ends of the earth. ❖ Acts 1:8

It always has amazed me how some people do not speak about what God has done, not only for humankind but also within their own personal lives. "My religious life is private. I don't know what to say," many Christians may claim.

To get people to share their journeys, one pastor asked her congregation on Sunday morning for members to say one thing God had done for them in the past week. The first few weeks no one said anything, but by the third week people began to witness about what God was doing for them.

The truth is, the Holy Spirit helps us to bear witness to the acts of God in our lives on a daily basis. Jesus' disciples were told to wait until they received power from the Holy Spirit. After the power came, they could be witnesses empowered by God to testify. The Christian life cannot be lived without the Holy Spirit. It is God's Spirit who empowers us to live the Christian life.

MICHELLE ELLISON

Lord God, empower us by your Holy Spirit to be witnesses for your kingdom in word and deed. Amen

Prayer concern: Strength for witnesses

Daily Reflections

Compassion

Jesus ... had compassion on them and healed
their sick. ❖ Matthew 14:14

This account from Jesus' ministry comes from a time of great
sorrow for him. John had just been beheaded in prison. The
disciples had brought the sad news to him. Jesus was weary;
he needed to get away by himself to think, to pray, to rest. But
when he arrived at the place where he was to rest, the people
had gotten there first and were waiting.

When we are experiencing sorrow, it's hard to face other
people. We want to shut out the world and nurse our grief by
ourselves. Jesus, being truly human, was tempted to do this,
but when the people came to him, he responded with compassion—a compassion that was deeper because he had himself
experienced the loss of a loved one.

Jim and Helen suffered deeply as they cared for two devel-
opmentally disabled sons. But through that experience, they
were given such love for other such children that many
people marveled. Jesus understands our suffering—and he
has compassion.

GRACE L. INGULSRUD

*Lord, help us to be neither too busy nor too weary nor too
sorrowful to share the load that others have. Amen*

Prayer concern: Parents of children with disabilities

Daily Reflections_____
_____
_____
_____

Jesus' compassion

> When [Jesus] saw the crowds, he had compassion
> on them. ❖ Matthew 9:36

Experts who study social trends in the United States say that many people today seem to care only for themselves. People seem to have lost concern for the common good. Most advertising promotes self-indulgence. The political slogans of congressional candidates usually emphasize a very localized advantage they want to achieve. "Vote for me," they say, "because of what I can do for you."

Jesus saw the crowds and felt for their obvious needs. They were harassed, helpless, and like sheep without a shepherd. Jesus wanted to help them all, and he could. Jesus urged his disciples to pray that many of the people would show compassion.

We who have been called through our baptism to follow Jesus are empowered by the Holy Spirit to seek spiritual, physical, and social good for all people. What the Bible tells us is still true today: "The harvest is plentiful but the workers are few" (Matthew 9:37).

OMAR STUENKEL

Lord, help us to show compassion to others. Amen

Prayer concern: All who seek help

Daily Reflections

Who cares about me?

What is man that you are mindful of him, the son
of man that you care for him? ❖ Psalm 8:4

Step outside some autumn evening and, for a change, look at
the stars rather than the sidewalk, at the heavens rather than
your fields and buildings. We look at the heavens. There are
millions of stars, and we know that beyond them there are
galaxies larger than our own in the black and infinite reaches
of space. The Bible says that God created everything and
rules over everything. We look at this earth where we live.
It is a speck of dust in the vastness of the universe, and we see
now it is covered with infinite variety and order.

The question presses in upon us: God rules all this—why
should God be concerned about me? The psalmist asked
the same question. We have been created only a little less
that God, crowned with glory, and given dominion over the
creation. And there is the more amazing word. For God's
revelation in nature is not the final word—this comes in Jesus
Christ. Here we see not only a place of honor and dominion in
creation, but here we have been given life and the power to
love, serve, and care for creation and each other.

CHARLES ANDERSON

*Dear God, we thank you for caring for your creation.
Help us to do the same. Amen*

Prayer concern: People who work with animals

Daily Reflections_____
_____
_____
_____

Surprise!

Surely the LORD is in this place, and I was not aware of it. ❖ Genesis 28:16b

Jacob was wide-awake now. I can imagine that he was trembling from more than the cold night air. He had been so careful. He had run a long way from an angry brother and a hurt father. He had chosen his rocky place carefully so he might sleep safely. But there was this strange dream to think about as he awoke. It was comforting to know that the angels were close by. And God was there too!

Jacob could not run from the presence of God. He could escape neither God's judgment nor God's mercy. God was not limited to the place where Jacob's family lived. He was not the God of a family alone, or a tribe alone, or a nation alone. God was not one of the gods that Jacob's neighbor's worshiped. Jacob was surprised and shocked. God had found him in his safe hiding place.

There are times when we want to run too. We wish we could get away from people we've hurt. We'd like to crawl into a hiding place. And when we do, we find that God is there. Surprise!

GARLAND E. GOTOSKI

Lord God, may we be surprised by joy. Amen

Prayer concern: Safe places

Daily Reflections

A new power

You are witnesses of these things. ❖ Luke 44:48

The resurrection of Jesus brought new life for the world. The church has one task: to be a witness to the resurrection message of hope for a world held captive by injustice, oppression, and sin.

We live in a tragically unbalanced world. Many nations in North America, Europe, and a few pockets elsewhere are wealthy, well fed, and generally free and secure. But much of the world's population lives in poverty, without adequate food, shelter, and medical care. A world so drastically unbalanced cannot endure. It is offensive in the eyes of God, whose love seeks justice for all.

And what about us? We are called to be witnesses of the resurrection, to enter the struggle, to seek change, and to live in the certainty of hope.

JAMES A. BERQUIST

In thanks for the new life we share, let us announce Christ's victory over all our captivities. Amen

Prayer concern: A new life

Daily Reflections_____

_____

_____

_____

Stand tall

Brace yourself.... I will question you, and you
shall answer me. ❖ Job 38:3

This order from God out of the whirlwind was the voice of
authority in the midst of chaos. God was finished with empty
speculations and tedious arguments. God wanted Job to look
squarely at his situation and listen.

The afflictions of Satan and the accusations of his friends
had not destroyed Job, but they must have planted some
seeds of doubt. Now God is ready to show the truth. God wants
Job to face the truth with all the intelligent understanding
he has received.

God doesn't want us to come cowering in fear like beaten
dogs. We are created in God's image. In the light of truth,
we are driven to our knees in repentance. We do so in honest
confession, in a recognition of our need and God's grace. Job
was tired by suffering, but he was not humiliated.

RENEE HERMANSON

*God, help us to stand before you to hear the truth clearly,
not in a spirit of timidity, but as those you have created.
Amen*

Prayer concern: Repentant hearts

Daily Reflections_____

Love levels

For you know the grace of our Lord Jesus Christ,
that though he was rich, yet for your sakes he
became poor, so that you through his poverty
might become rich. ❖ 2 Corinthians 8:9

Trouble often brings people together. Older people who remember the Great Depression will tell you: "We were all in the same boat. We were all poor. And we all tried to help one another." And people who have suffered loss from fire or storm, or who have lost a loved one, will tell you: "I didn't think so many people cared." Love levels life.

The Son of God came into our lives to share our needs. Out of love for us, Jesus left the riches of heaven to share our life. He was born in a stable, was carried to a strange land as a refugee, and during his ministry he sometimes had no place to lay his head. He did this so we might have all the riches of his kingdom.

Such love from God is intended to be shared. The Lord gives us more than enough grace to cover our sins. God expects us to share such forgiveness with others. By the mercy of God, we share daily bread. By the way our care is demonstrated, we show our block the levels of God's love in other people's lives.

LOREN SPAULDING

*Lord, teach us to love so that all people are raised to the
level of richness in you. Amen*

Prayer concern: Communities of love

Daily Reflections

It's good to be used

Here am I. Send me! ❖ Isaiah 8:8c

I had just explained to the ninth-grade class the fact that God knows every detail about our lives, including our thoughts. The full impact came home to one class member who exclaimed, "Oh, my God!" That's how Isaiah felt in the presence of the Almighty. He felt uncovered.

In an act of grace, God released Isaiah from the burden of his guilt. God not only offered Isaiah forgiveness but also a new opportunity too. By that invitation, God let Isaiah know that forgiveness was real. Isaiah accepted the offer. "Here am I! Send me."

If a child is wiping dishes and breaks one, he feels guilty. When his mother tells him that he is forgiven and that she trusts him to go on doing the dishes, the child is certain that he has been forgiven and accepted. That is why it is so precious to be asked to do something for God. Then we know that we have been accepted.

DWAIN OLSON

Thank you, God, for asking me to work in your kingdom for Jesus' sake. Amen

Prayer concern: Congregational leaders

Daily Reflections_____

Serve

Here is my servant. ❖ Isaiah 42:1

Jesus was very familiar with the writings of the prophet Isaiah. At the beginning of his ministry, when Jesus returned to Nazareth, he read from Isaiah in the synagogue on the Sabbath. His words were brief and unforgettable. He told the people that on this day the Scriptures had been fulfilled.

The book of Isaiah says much about the coming Messiah. Here is the revelation that the Messiah would suffer and that he would be the servant of all. Throughout his ministry, Jesus lived under the command of God, doing God's will, being a servant to all people, and finally suffering for our sake.

In his parables, Jesus taught his followers to serve and to be servants. He taught his disciples by example and his words to live a life of service. As followers of Christ, we are servants of God. We are dedicated to God's kingdom. We are called to do the will of God. We serve by serving others in Jesus' name.

GERTRUDE VOGELY

Master of us all, help us to serve. Help us to give our time, to share our talents, and to devote our wealth and ourselves to those in need. Amen

Prayer concern: Those who serve

Daily Reflections_____

_____

_____

_____

I don't mean to brag, but ...

> An argument started among the disciples as to
> which of them would be the greatest. ❖ Luke 9:46

"You're the greatest." We love to hear those words spoken to
us. But somehow the compliment seems wrong if we refer to it
ourselves. So we rarely use those exact words. Instead we say
them in other ways: "I feel I have a knack for ..." or "I don't
mean to toot my own horn ..."

Pride can sneak up on us. We catch ourselves in the
middle of a sentence and realize that we're really saying, "I'm
better than a lot of other people." Self-confidence is important
and good. But pride causes us to look down on others. An
evangelist once said, "Pride is the only disease known that
makes everyone sick except the one who has it."

Jesus showed us a better way. In God's kingdom, the last
would be the first and the first would be last. When we
struggle to be at the head of the line, we need to remember
that Jesus will be found with those on the other end. His
words to the disciples are also meant for us: "For he who is
least among you all—he is the greatest" (Luke 9:48b).

DAVID SATRE

*Keep me from looking down on my neighbor, O Lord, and
keep me looking up to you. Amen*

Prayer concern: True humility

Daily Reflections_____
_____
_____
_____

The goals of life

One thing I ask of the LORD, this is what I seek:
that I may dwell in the house of the LORD all the
days of my life, to gaze upon the beauty of the LORD
and to seek him in his temple. ❖ Psalm 27:4

We are often asked about our goals in life. It is commonly
understood that goals motivate us and give direction to our
lives. There are many goals that we may have. Some people
want to be thought well of by their peers. Others have the goal
of becoming affluent, or of rising through the ranks at their
company, or of putting their children through college.

We must be careful, though. Some goals are empty. We
reach them only to find ourselves unsatisfied. The psalmist
shares this goal; to live life in God's presence, aware of God's
power and glory, full of God's wisdom and understanding.
This does not need to be only the psalmist's goal. We are
challenged to make it the central goal in our lives too.

KEVIN E. RUFFCORN

Lord, help us to seek the important things in life. Amen

Prayer concern: Church organists

Daily Reflections_____

_____

_____

_____

Our God of everything

From everlasting to everlasting you are God.
❖ Psalm 90:2b

We cannot understand *eternity*. We count the days of our lives in a world that began and will end. The idea of a God who always has been, now is, and forever will be, is beyond our grasp.

We cannot understand *omnipotence*. There are individuals who direct huge corporations and rule nations. But no human has ever managed everything and everyone, even for a short time. The idea of a God who forever controls the universe from its greatest part to its least is beyond our grasp.

We cannot understand *omniscience*. Each generation has had intelligent people, but none pretend to have perfect knowledge of the past, present, and future.

Yet this eternal, omnipotent, and omniscient God came to us in the form of a man named Jesus. And when we see our God in the person of our Savior, we know that God is love.

ANONYMOUS

Thank you, God of time and eternity, for making yourself known to us. Amen

Prayer concern: Human leaders

Daily Reflections_____
_____
_____
_____

One gospel

> I am astonished that you are so quickly deserting
> the one who called you by the grace of Christ and
> are turning to a different gospel. ❖ Galatians 1:6

Are there different "gospels"? Can I pick and choose a "gospel" as I would a suit? If it fits and it's stylish, buy it. Certainly good news comes to us with different content and in different ways. Wedding announcements, graduation announcements, and a raise are all good news. But there is only one gospel of God, and that is the good news of Jesus. A living Christ is both the heart of the good news and the bearer of God's captivating message, and that truth is made new and good and real to us each day by the Holy Spirit.

The gospel of Jesus Christ is not the creation of human minds; it does not change with the styles of the times. We do not "buy" the gospel of Jesus Christ; it captures us. The great creative power of God is prolonged and extended in the one gospel of an eternal Savior, and that gospel creates in us the power to believe it.

JOHN W. COFFEY

Lord, keep us ever focused on the one gospel and the one Savior, Jesus Christ. Amen

Prayer concern: Proclaimers of the gospel

Daily Reflections_____

_____

_____

_____

As one who is sent

When Jesus had called the Twelve together,
he gave them power and authority to drive out
all demons and to cure diseases. ❖ Luke 9:1

First days are always exciting. Remember the first day of school, or the first day on the job, or the birth of your first child. Inside, there's a little bit of fear and a lot of excitement.

Today's Bible passage tells of such a first day experience: the disciples were being sent to witness to surrounding towns and villages. In the past, Jesus had always done the speaking. Now it was their turn. And soon even Herod got word of the excitement that was running through the region of Galilee.

For some time now our church has been reminding us of mission outreach. Today's passage is a good reminder that the work of the church is exciting. Our task is to care for both body and spirit.

As those who are sent, we have an exciting mission. It begins with our story—how God has made a difference in our lives. But it also includes our efforts on behalf of justice and mercy for all who are in need. Jesus, the sender, provides all authority. Go in peace.

J. E. JANKE

Lord of power and authority, help me to be faithful in serving you. Overcome my doubts with confidence. Amen

Prayer concern: Missionaries

Daily Reflections

What does this mean?

Amazed and perplexed, they asked one another,
"What does this mean?" ❖ Acts 2:12

Luke reports that the Pentecost event perplexed the people
who gathered to hear the disciples. He specifies that all were
amazed and perplexed. After the initial confusion, they
reacted. Their response was similar to what I suspect ours
might have been. Some asked, "What does this mean?"
Others felt no need to investigate. With nervous embarrass-
ment they brushed it all aside with a quip that the disciples
had drunk too much wine.

Confusion is relieved by honest searching. A question is
often the beginning of enlightenment. Jesus identified the
Spirit as a counselor who will teach us all things.

Saul was exposed to an experience in the tutorial school of
the Holy Spirit. On the road to Damascus he was intercepted
by a great light and a voice, "Why do you persecute me?" Out
of this confusion he called out seekingly, "Who are you,
Lord?" Step by step, Saul received the Lord's answer, was
baptized, and became Paul the apostle.

FREDRIK A. SCHIOTZ

*Giving God, help us to wait upon you for answers to our
questions. Amen*

Prayer concern: Understanding

Daily Reflections_____

_____

_____

_____

Where were you when I needed you?

> When Mary reached the place where Jesus
> was and saw him, she fell at his feet and said,
> "Lord, if you had been here, my brother would
> not have died." ❖ John 11:32

Most of us probably know someone who has just finished a difficult task. If we have come on the scene too late to be of any help our friend may well have asked, "Where were you when I needed you?" Sometimes it may happen that we plan our absences.

The story of Jesus and Lazarus seems to indicate that Jesus intentionally delayed his arrival at the home of Martha and Mary. Mary's comment is a combination of confidence and despair. "If you had been here" indicates confidence that Jesus really could have done something about the illness of Lazarus. But this confidence is combined with the certainty that it is now too late.

We are reminded here that God is with us even in life's most difficult situations. There is a recurring theme here—in Christ, the final word about death is life.

PHILIP QUANBECK

Help us to be aware and to believe that you are present as the Lord of life, even when it seems like you are absent. Amen

Prayer concern: Those who mourn

Daily Reflections_____

_____

_____

_____

One thing I do

"My food," said Jesus, "is to do the will of him who
sent me and to finish his work." ❖ John 4:34

Jesus came to the world for one thing. He came to seek and
to save those who were lost—and that includes you and me.
It took his death on a cross to accomplish it, and as he died he
said, "It is finished."

You and I may think we have been born for many things—
to eat, to have friends, to be successful, to live a long life. But
on a deeper level, we too have been created for one supreme
thing. We are to glorify God these few swift years we have. We
serve God by serving one another. And we enjoy God by
enjoying others. Each of us serves as a kind of representative
for God, so we find God in one another.

ALVIN ROGNESS

*Help me, O Lord, to glorify you and your kingdom by
turning from myself to find a fullness of life in serving
others. Amen*

Prayer concern: To follow God's will

Daily Reflections_____

_____

_____

_____

On what can we stand?

When the foundations are being destroyed,
what can the righteous do? ❖ Psalm 11:3

Many people today share in the question posed by the psalmist in today's text. Everything that was tied down seems to be coming loose. The seemingly firm supports of society appear to be cracking. The sources of our security are drying up. What can we do in the face of uncertainty in nation and government, energy resources and food supplies? Evil seems to be on the rise, if not triumphant. "When the foundations are being destroyed, what can the righteous do?"

The psalmist answers on two levels. First, he notes that it is in the Lord that refuge is to be found (v. 1). The Lord at times sends tests, even to his own (v. 5), but also provides for them. Second, this same Lord loves justice (v. 7). Those people who follow God are urged and expected to be upright —yes righteous—by God's power. They are to act, to correct, and to control the evil around. Take refuge and take action in the person and the power of God.

CHARLES ANDERSON

Dear God, give us power that we may believe your promise and obey your commands. Amen

Prayer concern: Our one foundation

Daily Reflections

The light of the world

For God, who said, "Let light shine out of darkness,"
made his light shine in our hearts to give us the light
of knowledge of the glory of God in the face of Christ.
❖ 2 Corinthians 4:6

I remember once as a child waking up from a very bad dream.
My room was dark, and somewhere in the darkness lurked a
nameless horror. My bedside lamp was close, but I was afraid
to reach out into the darkness to turn it on. I don't know how
long I lay there in growing agony; it seemed like an eternity.
Finally, in sheer panic, I reached out and turned on the light.

Then the panic subsided. My body relaxed. I almost
laughed aloud in relief. I was in my room. There was my
dresser; there were yesterday's rumpled clothes. Everything
looked so ordinary. There was nothing to be afraid of. All
I needed was the light.

God makes it even simpler and offers Christ as the light
for our darkened lives. We have no need to live in fear of the
unknown; there is no reason to panic. With Christ's light in
our lives, there is nothing to fear.

EDITH A. REUSS

*Dear Lord, thank you for bringing us out of the darkness
into the light of your love. Amen*

Prayer concern: Courage

Daily Reflections_____

_____

_____

_____

A song of confidence

The LORD is my light and my salvation—whom shall
I fear? The LORD is the stronghold of my life—of
whom shall I be afraid? ❖ Psalm 27:1

Joe was self-confident to the point of being arrogant. He did
a lot of bragging and talking about always being a winner.
His associates were tired of his success stories. When Joe fell
on his face, many people secretly were glad.

We are encouraged to be self-confident, but there is a difference between self-confidence because of the trust we have
in God and in being over-confident because we believe solely
in ourselves.

Psalm 27 is referred to as a triumphant song of confidence.
One senses the struggle. There is fear and anxiety in the
psalmist's life, but the psalmist's confidence comes through
loud and clear.

We can learn from the psalmist whose confidence was not
in self but in God. "The LORD is my light and my salvation—
whom shall I fear?" That's a crucial emphasis for our daily
walk. Let us look to the one who is our light, salvation, and
stronghold. With such resources on our side, what do we
have to fear?

TED VINGER

*Lord, I can't but you can and you have. Help me to
remember this today. Amen*

Prayer concern: Those who lack confidence

Daily Reflections_____

_____

_____

_____

Tears for fears

Then you will call, and the LORD will answer;
you will cry for help, and he will say: Here am I.
❖ Isaiah 58:9

There were times during my father-in-law's illness and death
that I cried. I cried with my wife. I cried with her family. And
I cried with my own father, thinking of what it would be like
to lose him.

As I cried, I experienced healing. Tears began to wash
away my hurt, anger, and frustration. Tears were able to
renew me and open my eyes to see God's love in the midst of
the dark wilderness of death.

I was glad I was able to cry. Tears serve as a tremendous
relief when something emotional has happened. Sometimes
the emotions are wonderful; sometimes the emotions are
wrenching.

Most importantly, tears can feel almost baptismal, because
tears can deliver us into God's loving arms. There, God cra-
dles us and holds us. God says, "Here am I. You are my child
and I love you."

Thank God for tears.

ERIC BURTNESS

*Thank you, God, for letting us cry, and thank you even
more for being with us in our tears. Amen*

Prayer concern: Those who are crying

Daily Reflections_____

_____

_____

_____

So that you may believe

Thomas said to him, "My Lord and my God!"
  ❖ John 20:28

Have you ever been called a "doubting Thomas"? Usually it is meant to be negative, suggesting that questions or doubts are somehow wrong or that one's faith is weak. But doubt is not necessarily the absence of faith.

Questions and doubts are a part of human existence. They serve a purpose. Just as our knowledge grows when we ask questions, so our spiritual life grows. To question or doubt is to look for something more than we now know. In our search, what we believe becomes clearer to us, our faith increases, our relationship to God deepens.

Jesus doesn't condemn Thomas for having doubts, nor does he condemn us. Rather, he says in effect, "Come to me. Touch me. Let me show you that I am real and alive, so that you may believe." Jesus invites us to look to him for new growth. Our searching provides an opportunity for the Holy Spirit to speak and work in us, and our faith increases. Then we can say in confidence along with Thomas, "My Lord and my God!"

LINDA HOXTELL

Lord God, strengthen our faith and help us look to you for answers to our questions. Amen

Prayer concern: Those with doubts

Daily Reflections_____

_____

_____

_____

Cup of water

I tell you the truth, anyone who gives you a cup of
water in my name because you belong to Christ
will certainly not lose his reward. ❖ Mark 9:41

A famous actor gives his wife one of the largest cut diamonds
in the world. An eccentric businessman hires a helicopter to
fly over a golf course and parachute a huge bouquet of roses
to his wife on the green below. Both are examples of people
seeking unusual ways to show their admiration.

Over the centuries, people have created huge cathedrals,
elaborate monuments, and masterpieces of art in honor of
Christ. A cup of water seems insignificant by comparison—
until we read these words of Jesus.

The motive for the cup of water is not common courtesy.
The motive for the providing is the name of Christ. The cup of
water is given out of respect for the One whose life and death
reveal total commitment to the twin commands: Love God and
love your neighbor.

MILAN C. INGMAN

*Lord, may every act of kindness bring honor to your name.
Amen*

Prayer concern: Church unity

Daily Reflections

Inhibitions

> I love the LORD, for he heard my voice; he heard
> my cry for mercy. ❖ Psalm 116:1

Those of us who are privileged to teach young children are constantly amazed and blessed by their spontaneous and simple expressions of love for Jesus. It shines from their faces and bubbles over in their voices. It shows in their deep concern for Christ's passion and suffering. It is evidenced by their offerings of gratitude to God and their requests that God help those who suffer. Children are not ashamed to show their love for the Lord.

It is often more difficult for adults to proclaim, "I love the Lord!" Ambiguous cultural values, fear of laughter and mockery, personal insecurity, doubts about one's ability to speak, nervousness, and weakness—all these things contribute to their faintness of heart. But that need not be! God hears our prayers. God is forgiving and enables us to proclaim as a child does, "I love the Lord!"

JANET REINHARD

Release my inhibitions, dear Lord. Amen

Prayer concern: Singers

Daily Reflections_____

No one is able

My Father, who has given them to me, is greater
than all; no one can snatch them out of my
Father's hand. ❖ John 10:29

I think we fear the wrong things. When we think of attacks
on our faith, when we worry about spiritual dangers of our
children, we think first of "outside influences." Folk tales and
popular entertainment abound with reports of human souls
spirited away from God by evil beings.

Yet Jesus said that no one—not even the devil—is able to
snatch God's people from the "Father's hand." Does that
mean that once we become God's children, we can never go
astray? Not at all. We can leave God's hand by our own free
will. God has the power to compel us to stay but allows us to
make the decision. What we should fear most is the internal
influence of our own sinful natures.

Even so, we can rest in God's love and might. God is
stronger than all the forces of evil, strong enough to protect
us even from ourselves.

INEZ M. SCHWARZKOPF

God, thank you for your refuge. Amen

Prayer concern: Institutional chaplains

Daily Reflections_____

Accepting undue punishment

> For we are getting what our deeds deserve. But
> this man has done nothing wrong. ❖ Luke 23:41

Three men were crucified that day. One was a criminal whose attitude, even in the face of death, was brash and unrepentant. The second, who was also a criminal, accepted the consequence of his offenses. And then there was Jesus, the innocent one.

Some people refuse to take full responsibility for themselves—like the first criminal. They try to shift the blame or make excuses for their actions. Others are able to accept punishment when it is deserved—like the second criminal. But then there is Jesus, who embraces suffering that is not his due. Jesus did not deserve to die on the cross, but he accepted this supreme injustice anyway.

There are times when we might find ourselves accepting undeserved punishment, as well as times when the power of sin in the world leads to suffering. When we suffer, though, we can be confident that Jesus Christ, through his undeserved death and glorious resurrection, overcame the power of sin and death. Suffering for any reason does not have the last word. God does.

GREG GABRIEL

Thank you, Lord, for taking upon yourself the suffering that should have been ours. Amen

Prayer concern: Victims of serious crimes

Daily Reflections

The importance of being equal

I tell you the truth: Among those born of women
there has not risen anyone greater than John the
Baptist; yet he who is least in the kingdom of
heaven is greater than he. ❖ Matthew 11:11

From what do you draw your importance? Is it money, fame,
accomplishments, or abilities? Does it come through your
spouse, children, parents, or peers? The Scriptures give us
examples of people who gain their sense of importance in all
these ways.

In Matthew 11, Jesus addresses this issue. In the kingdom
of heaven, all believers are invited to be servants of the king.
As we serve, no one is counted greater or lesser than another.
Everyone will be equal in the sight of God. The world, with all
its measures of greatness, will eventually pass away. Then our
eternal importance will rest solely on God's grace and mercy.

Matthew 6:33 tells us to "seek first his kingdom and his
righteousness." What a challenge it is for us to let God and not
the world give us our sense of importance.

SUSAN ANDERSON

*God, we struggle to be important to ourselves and others.
Help us find that importance in you. Amen*

Prayer concern: Those in authority and power

Daily Reflections_____

_____

_____

_____

Plain speaking

> Otherwise they might see with their eyes, hear
> with their ears, understand with their hearts, and
> turn and be healed. ❖ Isaiah 6:10

God spoke plainly to the people of Israel, but in their desire to rely on their own understanding, they completely missed the point. These strange words, given to Isaiah after he responded to God's call to prophesy, are puzzling. It sounds like God does not want the people to hear.

Jesus repeats Isaiah's prophecy when he explains to the disciples his reasons for speaking in parables. Paul quotes these words, in frustration, as he tries to preach to the Jews in Rome. (See Acts 28.)

"You make it too complicated," Jesus says. "Just listen to me. It's really quite simple."

Paul said to the Jews, "If you won't listen to me, I'll take God's word to the Gentiles."

As long as we struggle to hear God's message with our ears and try to comprehend it by human understanding, we will not get it. Give thanks that by God's Spirit, we can see, hear, and understand.

GEORGE MUEDKING

It is when we are unable to rely on our own strengths and abilities, O Lord, that we become open to your words. Help us. Amen

Prayer concern: Openness to hear and see God at work

Daily Reflections_____

_____

_____

_____

Shared revelation

The LORD called Samuel a third time, and Samuel got up and went to Eli and said, "Here I am; you called me." Then Eli realized that the LORD was calling the boy. ❖ 1 Samuel 3:8

After an especially discouraging time in his ministry, a pastor sought professional counseling with plans to pursue another career. At the counselor's request, the pastor jotted down his skills on paper. Together, they walked over career prospects in communications, education, and public relations. After a few visits and much soul searching, the counselor paused, looked deep into the other man's eyes, and said, "Jim, can you see how well your talents and faith suit you to work as a pastor?"

To this day, the pastor maintains that the gentle, well-timed question from another believer renewed his devotion to the ordained ministry. Like Eli to Samuel, the counselor told his friend that the Lord was calling. Modern-day stories like this remind us how God helps believers nurture one another so that faith may grow. Throughout the centuries, the Word of God flows through humanity, one witness at a time.

MARY BRAUCH

Gracious God, let our faithful witness help reveal your power and love to others. Amen

Prayer concern: Counselors

Daily Reflections_____

_____

_____

_____

Jesus loves us

I am the good shepherd. The good shepherd lays
down his life for the sheep. ❖ John 10:11

What a contrast we see in this text! A good shepherd gives his
life for the sheep, while a hired hand flees because he cares
nothing for the sheep.

Why does Jesus care so much for us? Is it because we
attend church regularly or do good deeds or reach out to
others or honor our parents or donate food, clothing, or
money to local charities?

A shepherd does not love the sheep because of what they
do, but because they are the shepherd's own sheep. Likewise,
Jesus loves us because we are his people. Jesus has chosen to
love us and claim us as his people. Thus, we are caught up in
this marvelous encircling grace of Jesus' love, a love so great
that he laid down his life to ransom us from sin and make us
his own.

The marvel of Jesus' love for us is that it isn't caused by
what we do. Jesus loves us always, even enough to lay down
his life for us.

BETTY HEIDEMANN

*Holy Spirit, enable us more fully to comprehend Jesus'
great, unconditional love for us. Amen*

Prayer concern: Nurses

Daily Reflections

Faith and hope

> I have fought the good fight, I have finished the
> race, I have kept the faith. ❖ 2 Timothy 4:7

Nearing the end of his career, the apostle Paul writes to young Timothy with a poignant blend of exaltation and despair. After that fateful day on the road to Damascus, Paul's whole life was transformed. He let the Lord direct his ways, and he worked tirelessly for his new master.

Now in prison in Rome, Paul is awaiting execution. His friends, Demas, Titus, and Crescens, have left him. Without his cloak, he asks Timothy to bring it to him. And that vexing thorn in his flesh, which he three times asked the Lord to remove, persists.

Yet with all this discouragement, there is absolutely no question that Paul remains faithful: "I have finished the race, I have kept the faith. Now there is in store for me the crown of righteousness.... The Lord will rescue me ... and will bring me safely to his heavenly kingdom. To him be glory for ever and ever." Oh, what a testimony Paul leaves us! What faith God works.

O. Henry Hoversten

Dear Lord, despite times of adversity in our lives, keep us, like Paul, faithful to the end. Amen

Prayer concern: Prisoners

Daily Reflections_____

Reach out and love someone

When Jesus saw that [the teacher] had answered wisely, he said to him, "You are not far from the kingdom of God." And from then on no one dared ask him any more questions. ❖ Mark 12:34

The man in dialogue with Jesus was aware that the basic characteristic of God's kingdom is love. In the book *The Road Less Traveled*, Dr. M. Scott Peck defines *love* as the will to extend one's self for the purpose of nurturing one's own or another's spiritual growth. That is at least one aspect of Christian love.

Jesus reached beyond friends and social barriers to nurture the leper, the foreigner, the woman, the child, the tax collector, the thief, and people with physical disabilities. Even now he reaches through the barrier of time to enfold us in his saving love.

Dare we extend ourselves by reaching beyond our inner circle of friends, beyond our own comfort, to find ourselves nearer the kingdom of God?

ANONYMOUS

Dear God, help us to grow in our ability to reach out in love to others. Amen

Prayer concern: Someone who is sick

Daily Reflections_____

Not our type

> A Canaanite woman from that vicinity came to
> him, crying out, "Lord, Son of David, have mercy
> on me! My daughter is suffering terribly from
> demon-possession." ❖ Matthew 15:22

After ministering in Jerusalem, Jesus and his disciples trekked northward. There, alongside the Mediterranean seacoast near Tyre and Sidon, their relaxing time was interrupted by a Canaanite woman of that region.

"Have mercy on me," she pleaded.

"Send her away," the disciples urged Jesus. Their request was legitimate. They needed rest. They didn't want to get involved. Besides, they were Jews, and it was audacious of her, a foreigner, to ask help from *them.*

During the almost 2,000 years since this account was written, times have changed, of course. But human nature has not. It's still easier for each of us to reason, "I'm too tired," and fail to give the time and trouble to help others. And it's still easier for us to say, "They're responsible for themselves. And, doing something once is just asking for more pleas for help." But those excuses are no more valid today than they were in the past.

ISABEL CHAMP WOLSELEY

Have mercy on me, O Lord, whenever I fail to see the need for helping others. Amen

Prayer concern: Christians in India

Daily Reflections

The fountain of youth

"You will not surely die," the serpent said to the woman. ❖ Genesis 3:4

Throughout history, people have searched for a remedy for aging that would keep them young forever. Ponce de León thought he uncovered the Fountain of Youth when he found a spring of water in Florida. In his book *Lost Horizon*, James Hilton weaves a fantasy of perpetual youth in his Shangri-La. And in one of his most famous novels, Oscar Wilde shows us how Dorian Grey was so deceived by a portrait of himself that he actually believed he would have eternal youth.

But let us not laugh at these examples. People continue to find ways to appear younger. What about the miracle lotion that makes a woman look 15 years younger? Or the cream that changes a man's hair color almost overnight? True eternal life, however, is not a commodity we can buy. So rather than search for fountains of youth, would it not be better to seek that eternal life which comes through the source of living water?

NANCY NAU-OLSON

My soul longs for you, O God. Amen

Prayer concern: Your dearest friend

Daily Reflections_____

God's eye is on us

Do not hide your face from your servant; answer
me quickly, for I am in trouble. ❖ Psalm 69:17

The boy was afraid of the dark. As his mother tucked him into
bed, she promised to sit there and look at him in the darkness
until he fell asleep.

There are moments like that in our everyday lives. Our
dearest friends may not know the anxieties and depression we
feel. It may not be easy for us to express them, nor may we
want to let them be known. At such times, there is One who
knows without being told. The Lord's face is soft with compassion and strong with courage. Knowing that the Lord never
leaves us is the ultimate comfort.

ALVIN N. ROGNESS

Thanks, O Lord, for keeping me always in view. Amen

Prayer concern: Broadcasting ministries

Daily Reflections_____
_____
_____
_____

God is good

Give thanks to the LORD, for he is good; his love
endures forever. ❖ Psalm 118:1

Greta and Laura are twins. At one month, they weigh four
pounds. They are healthy but also helpless and totally dependent upon the faithful love and care of their parents. And what
steadfast nurturing they receive! It never ceases. The parents
don't complain, day or night—even when they are awakened
every three hours.

We, too, are dependent upon God's goodness. Luther, in
explaining the First Article of the Apostles' Creed, reminds us
that God not only has given us life, but also sustains and
preserves our need for family and friends and meaningful
work. God protects us from danger and guards us from evil.
These gifts God continues to give, not because we deserve
them, but because God is so good.

CORINNE CHILSTROM

*God, we praise and thank you for your love that created
and sustains us. Help us show our thanks by giving our
lives wholly to your service. Amen*

Prayer concern: Newborn infants

Daily Reflections

That which lasts

> The world and its desires pass away, but the man
> who does the will of God lives forever. ❖ 1 John 2:17

A young girl, lost in the downtown section of a large city, said to the police officer, "If I could find the church, I could find my way home."

The church's business is to point people to God, whose holy kingdom lasts forever. Through Holy Baptism, it grafts us into Christ. Through the Word and the sacraments it releases the Holy Spirit into our lives, to assure us of forgiveness and love, and to guide us to find the will of God. It does even more; it inspires us to want to do the will of God.

When at last we come to die, it may not seem very important that we had a good salary, that we amassed some property, or that we were elected to some office. That which will give us deep satisfaction is that we do try to do God's will, that we befriended people in need, and that we gave hope to people who were discouraged.

ALVIN ROGNESS

We thank you for many things, God, but most of all for claiming us and for honoring us with tasks in your kingdom. Amen

Prayer concern: Those who are dying

Daily Reflections_____

_____

_____

_____

Peter's conversion

John preached how God anointed Jesus of
Nazareth with the Holy Spirit and power, and how
he went around doing good and healing all who
were under the power of the devil, because God
was with him. ❖ Acts 10:38

This is the account of Peter's conversion—not Paul's, but
Peter's. Most of us recall how Paul was converted from one
who persecuted to one who proclaimed Christ as Lord. But
Peter also needed conversion from a myopic belief that Jesus
came for a chosen few. That misconception was blasted away
by the wonderful display of the fullness of God's creation and
love (vv. 10-16).

Grasping God's infinite love is a challenge set before each
believer. Living that truth is an invitation that stretches our
faith and sets us amid places and people never before experienced. The converted Peter rightly preached the truth of how
Jesus did good and healed those who were oppressed. To live
in the wideness of that love means we will, like Peter, require
ongoing conversion from our narrow concerns. This question
is simple, yet lifelong: "What conversions do I need in order
to love as Jesus did?"

JON TEMME

*Convert us daily, Jesus, from our petty prejudices to the
truth that you came for all. Amen*

Prayer concern: People with racist beliefs

Daily Reflections_____

How can I live in the world?

> For if you live according to the sinful nature, you
> will die; but if by the Spirit you put to death the
> misdeeds of the body, you will live. ❖ Romans 8:13

"How can I live in the world as a faithful follower of Jesus?"
This is a question Christians have asked themselves again and
again throughout the history of the Christian church. And it is
a question they have answered in a variety of ways. Some have
thought that Christians must have as little to do with the
world as possible. Some became hermits. Some became
monks or nuns. Others have identified certain activities as
"worldly" and therefore prohibited.

Paul says that death and resurrection have to do not only
with the end of life but also with the way life is lived. Putting to
death the deeds of the body is not the abandonment of the
world as the place where we live. It means instead that we do
not depend on being recognized by others. Status, hard work,
position, craftsmanship, wealth, education do not bring life.
Life comes from God. And the cross teaches us that life comes
through Christ.

PHILIP QUANBECK

*Lord our God, though we are much inclined to justify
ourselves, help us to learn how to live in the world as
disciples of Jesus. Amen*

Prayer concern: The needs of this world

Daily Reflections

The relationship is key

Blessed are those who have learned to acclaim
you, who walk in the light of your presence,
O LORD. ❖ Psalm 89:15

For the past 16 years, our daughter has brought her children
to the lake to spend a few days with us. We wondered this
year if her oldest son would come along. He had summer
jobs and, well, he was 17. In her words, "Tim said that he
wants to come so that he can fish with his grandfather," I felt
a rush of joy.

Is this what faith is like—to find joy in God's presence, to
delight in being together, to rejoice in a close relationship?
Why do I praise God? God has given me family, health, comfort, home, and blessings too numerous to count. I ask myself,
"Would it be enough for me simply to know that God has
embraced me through Jesus and has forgiven me all my sins?"
Do I praise God for the showering of gifts, or do I praise God
for the delight of being in fellowship? In a materialistic
society, we need to be reminded that our greatest gift is to
know that, through Jesus, we have fellowship with God and
walk in the light of God's countenance.

LOWELL HESTERMAN

Thank you for the joy of living in your presence. Amen

Prayer concern: Joy in worship

Daily Reflections

Living masterpieces

Just as Christ was raised from the dead through
the glory of the Father, we too may live a new life.
❖ Romans 6:4b

British Prime Minister Winston Churchill was fond of
painting, but he kept it in perspective. Churchill realized
that he was a statesman first and after that an amateur painter.
He said, "An amateur does not aspire to masterpieces; rather
he contents himself with the pleasure his hobby gives him."

That's a fine attitude about a hobby, but too many of us feel
that way of living. We tend to leave the masterpieces of living
to the so-called saints and be content with the little pleasure
our own crude sketches give us. But that is not walking in the
newness of life in Christ. We must dare to aim for a masterpiece, for the great joy and promise of the gospel is the
knowledge that we *can* care and grow and change. In Christ
our lives *can* become masterpieces.

HAROLD PENNINGTON

*Lord, grant that I may become a masterpiece as I renew
my life in your name. Amen*

Prayer concern: Artists

Daily Reflections_____

The touch of Jesus

And laying his hands on each one, [Jesus] healed them. ❖ Luke 4:40b

Tired and scared, with stomach hurting, our eight-year-old faced an emergency appendectomy very late one evening. Much of his fear faded when our family doctor arrived on the scene. The familiar voice brought comfort.

The touch of Jesus brought comfort and healing to the many sick people that were brought to him. These people were undoubtedly tired and fearful. They had no miracles of modern medicine to turn to. Their only home for life rested in a miracle by this man named Jesus. Their fear left when he touched them.

As we read God's Word, and join in worship, we can also feel the touch of Jesus. Because he died, and then rose from death, we can confidently look forward to a time when we will have a new body, be completely healed, and be a whole person.

His touch in our lives can heal us. It isn't always a physical healing. He can touch us and bring us peace of heart and mind. He can help us to accept our life as it is. His touch does change our lives.

KATHRYN EHLEN

O Lord, touch us and make us whole. Take away our fear and fill us with your peace. Amen

Prayer concern: Health-care professionals

Daily Reflections

Faith does not equal fact

> Philip said, "Lord, show us the Father and that
> will be enough for us." ❖ John 14:8

How frustrated Jesus must have felt when Philip asked to see the Father! Philip had witnessed so many miracles in his walk with the Savior—the dead raised, sight restored, twisted bodies made whole—and yet he still craved proof.

What did Philip expect Jesus to do? Call forth a display of heavenly fireworks? That could be a magician's trickery. Send Philip on a quick trip to heaven and back? It could be rejected as a hallucination. Nothing tangible could give Philip faith. God gives many signs to believers; all can be explained away by those who refuse to believe.

We have been brought up in a scientific age. We tend to act when we are supported by facts. Faith goes beyond the boundaries of science; it forces us to go beyond facts. It rests on trust in God. Paul lists faith as one of the gifts of the Spirit (1 Corinthians 12:9). Let that be our clue. Faith cannot be earned by our own reasoning; we receive it only by the grace of God in Christ.

EDITH A. REUSS

God, help me to always recognize the fact that faith is a gift from you. Amen

Prayer concern: Faith

Daily Reflections

Good-bye

> Aim for perfection, listen to my appeal, be of one
> mind, live in peace. And the God of love and peace
> will be with you. ❖ 2 Corinthians 13:11

A daughter leaves for college and you say good-bye. Good
friends move to another city and you say good-bye. A loved
one is dying and you say good-bye. What words can you use to
share your feelings at such times? How can you convey your
deepest hopes and concerns? This time of farewell allows you
to share what is closest to your heart and dearest to your soul.
What will you say?

As Paul finishes his Second Letter to the Corinthians, he
says farewell. He says good-bye. Paul leaves us with his final
assurance: "And the God of love and peace will be with you."

No matter what else happens, God will be with you.
God is with the daughter heading to college and with the
friends moving to another city. And when we say farewell for
the last time here on earth, the God of love and peace is still
there. Just as God dwells with you now, God remains with
you forever.

JOHN GERIKE

*Loving God, be with us in all our good-byes and fill us
with your love and peace. Amen*

Prayer concern: Those who feel alone

Daily Reflections_____

_____

_____

_____

Vanities

Turn my eyes away from worthless things; preserve
my life according to your word. ❖ Psalm 119:37

There was a time when looking into a mirror was considered
sinful, a sign of pride and self-centeredness. Indeed, it can be.
If we spend our precious moments preening—more than
giving, learning, and considering others—we risk losing
touch with God.

There may be other vanities with which we attempt to fill
our human emptiness. People may vainly seek a sense of satisfaction by accomplishing tasks. An achiever has peace only as
long as one is fully able and successful. But success evades
everyone at some time, and the vanity of personal success
rises before us.

God watches us seeking and grasping at vanities—the
so-called security of financial gain, our ever-changing appearance, the fleeting attention of others, and the illusion that
life is forever. All our temporal and temporary pursuits are
vanities and, in the end, only God remains. No wonder we
pray to God to turn our eyes from looking at vanities.

JUDITH MATTISON

*Loving God, remind us that in a world of change and
imperfection, only you are the one who is steadfast in love
and ready to forgive. Amen*

Prayer concern: Humility and contentment

Daily Reflections

What's there to tell?

For one of these must become a witness with us
of his resurrection. ❖ Acts 1:22b

The disciples went into hiding after Jesus' crucifixion. But
something happened—Jesus rose from the dead! Suddenly
his words were remembered with fresh force. His power
became unstoppable. He was the Messiah, the promised One,
and the Lord. All that he had done or said hung on this event.
Is it any wonder that the disciples from that time on would be
sure to tell about Jesus' resurrection?

We have inherited that mission of witness. And the heart
of the message is the same. "I am the resurrection and the
life," Jesus said. "He who believes in me will live, even though
he dies" (John 11:25).

What does the resurrection mean for us? We have the
sign of God's power over death as well as over life. We have,
in the resurrection, God's approval of Jesus' ministry. We are
witnesses to the miracle by which God turned the world
around. That's what there is to tell.

DAVID SATRE

*Thank you, Lord Jesus, for the victory of your resurrection.
Amen*

Prayer concern: Christian witness

Daily Reflections

Trust from God

I will give you and your descendants the land on which you are lying. ❖ Genesis 28:13b

Not every dream comes true. We're usually happy for that because even nice dreams sometimes ask the impossible of us. Jacob's dream was used by God to convey a gift and to remind Jacob of his responsibility for it.

Think about it for a moment. Jacob was in a strange country, far from his father's home. He was running from an angry brother, and he still had miles to go before he felt safe. Yet God promised him this land, and promised it to his descendants. He had to believe that God would let Jacob's children and grandchildren live there. He had to be ready to care for God's gift. His father, Isaac, and his grandfather, Abraham, had learned to believe God. They had learned to care about God's gifts.

So we have a trust from God. We call this trust the days of our life. Someday we will give an accounting of this trust to God. If God called for an accounting today, what would be found? What have we done with the gif of life that God has entrusted to each of us?

GARLAND E. GOLOSKI

Lord, help us to be faithful in all that you have entrusted to us, in Jesus' name. Amen

Prayer concern: Trusting hearts

Daily Reflections_____
_____
_____
_____

A new environment

The desert and the parched land will be glad; the
wilderness will rejoice and blossom. ❖ Isaiah 35:1

One of the first names for Easter Sunday was the "eighth day."
This term comes because the early Christians remembered
the seven-day creation story from Genesis. God made the
world in six days and rested on the seventh. The "eighth day,"
Easter, was thus seen as the start of a new creation. Here was
the kind of new life Isaiah expected in his vision of a renewed
wilderness in the Day of the Lord.

Easter faith, like Isaiah's prophetic faith, touches all of
life. Jesus' resurrection signaled the possibility of new life
even for the broken world of nature. People have exploited,
despoiled, and misused the good gifts of God's earth. Such
acts are the result of human sinfulness and greed, and we are
held accountable.

The debate about our environment has meaning for
Christians. We know that one part of responsible stewardship
involves using God's gifts for the welfare of all.

JAMES A. BERQUIST

*Make us sensitive, Creator Lord, to your gracious gifts of
sun, air, water, and land. Amen*

Prayer concern: Our environment

Daily Reflections

Kindness happens

> What does the LORD require of you? To act justly
> and to love mercy and to walk humbly with your
> God. ❖ Micah 6:8

I saw a bumper sticker the other day that said, "KINDNESS HAPPENS." It brought a smile to my face. Right away, I found my thoughts wandering to different acts of kindness that had been directed toward me during the past few days. My husband had brought me flowers for no special reason. My neighbor, with whom I share a washer and dryer, had taken my clothes from the dryer and folded them neatly. Someone held the elevator door open for me at the office, knowing that 9:00 A.M. was fast approaching. So many acts of kindness!

The prophet Micah makes it clear that the appropriate response to God's love toward us is to live in ways that *act justly*, *love mercy*, and *walk humbly with God*. Micah's words were for the Hebrew people, and I think they are for us too. What we do as individuals shapes what we do as communities. So that day I thought, had my actions been reciprocal? Had I responded with kindness toward those who crossed my path? I'd like to think so—and I will keep working on it. I'll never forget that bumper sticker!

DENISE STRADLING

Dear God, thank you for all who are earthly examples of your loving-kindness. Amen

Prayer concern: Those who spread kindness all around

Daily Reflections

Ready to work

> Jesus was troubled in spirit and testified, "I tell
> you the truth, one of you is going to betray me."
> ❖ John 13:21

Many of us feel unprepared for the tasks God lays before us.
We feel we need more knowledge, greater eloquence, or a
deeper sense of spirituality. We want more experience, more
time to prepare, and more confidence. But all we need to do is
look at the disciples to know that God meets us and uses us
as we are right now.

In this passage, it's tempting to cluck our tongues at Judas.
But while he acted decisively to betray Jesus, the other disciples just "looked at one another," completely unaware that
there was a traitor in their midst, oblivious to what Judas was
about to do, and clueless as to the significance of any of it.
Their ignorance of all this shows how little they understood,
but even more important, how little they really knew each
other—and the Lord. Still, Jesus loved them, forgave them,
and sent them to do God's work.

So it is with us. We may lack knowledge, eloquence, and
spirituality. We may need more confidence and experience,
but God chooses us anyway. God loves us, forgives us, and
sends us. Let's go to work.

MARCIA ERICKSON BATES

Here I am, Lord. Send me. Amen

Prayer concern: Sunday school teachers

Daily Reflections

Seek my face

My heart says of you, "Seek his face!" Your face, LORD, I will seek. ❖ Psalm 27:8

Two young Lutheran missionaries, along with 30 other people, were stranded on Ali Shan Mountain in central Taiwan during a typhoon. The typhoon brought horrendously strong winds and dropped more than 40 inches of rain in 24 hours.

On the third day, word came that there was insufficient food and all guests must leave. The only conveyance down the peak was the railroad, but the tracks were washed out or buried in 14 different places. A train would meet the guests, however, just below the wrecked railroad track. To get there, everyone was to walk several hours in the rain. The greatest danger was crawling down a muddy 60-degree slope (with a pregnant woman in the group) and crossing a railroad bridge where one misstep would lead to death up to 70 feet below. Yet all arrived safely. I know, because my pregnant wife and I were there.

ROGER A. DOMYAHN

Lord, continue to lead us through life's events, that we may always seek your face. Amen

Prayer concern: Someone who is hospitalized

Daily Reflections_____

_____

_____

_____

The coming kingdom

But the way of the wicked will perish. ❖ Psalm 1:6b

As a pastor, I am often asked, "How can you believe in a loving God when there is so much evil in the world?" The question is sincere and springs from human observation and experience. Unlike the claim of the psalmist, it often appears that the wicked are not perishing at all. Rather, they seem to be prospering. How could the psalmist believe in the goodness and promise of God? How can we believe in a gracious and powerful Lord while the world suffers from so much human strife and environmental decay?

Part of any response must include the reality of sin. As God's stewards, we must confess that much pain and destruction come from our hands, not the Lord's. But this is only a part of the answer. We believe because of faith, not mere observation and transient conclusion. Our God has promised that no matter how things appear to be, the kingdom is secure and creation will be restored. This is God's promise in Jesus Christ. This is all that we have. This is all that we need.

W. BRUCE WILDER

Give us a sure and certain faith that we and all creation are in your hands, O Lord. Amen

Prayer concern: The worldwide family of faith

Daily Reflections

Have no other gods before me

Their mind is on earthly things. ❖ Philippians 3:19

There is much to love on this earth. We need not be ashamed to say it. For God even loved the world and sent Jesus to us to restore the relationship between God and the world. Yet there are words of caution in texts like the one we read today about *our* loving the world. We are not to replace God by loving the world too much, by letting the reality of our bellies, our homes, our jobs, or our finances consume us.

At the same time, we are not to despise the world. If we were to despise earthly things, we would not care enough about the world to work to preserve God's garden and love God's people. Finding the balance between caring and idolatry is the task for God's people. Only with the help of God through the discipline of prayer and the guidance of other Christians can we care for the world without setting our minds on earthly things.

CAROLYN MOWCHAN

Dear Lord, there are many ways in which our loyalty can be divided and our choices difficult. Help us live as you would have us live, lovingly and generously. Amen

Prayer concern: Those who farm the land

Daily Reflections

Time

This will result in your being witnesses to them.
❖ Luke 21:13

The concept of time means so many different things to us, relative to the various points in our lives. When we're very young, time means nothing. When we're busy or happy, time often flies. When we're ill or lonely, time hangs heavy on our hands. For many of us, time is how we keep a record of our lives. When we lose our sense of time, we lose touch with who we are and become disoriented. But time can be very specific, too, as anyone who has chased after a bus or train knows. This narrow sense of time is what Luke is speaking of in the verse quoted above.

The New Testament writers had two words for time. They referred to a length of time as *chronos*. To designate an appointed time, they used the word *kairos*, a special moment determined by God, for bearing witness to Christ. When that time comes we must follow Christ in the way of the cross, knowing that he goes with us.

ALFREDA H. EBELING

Lord, our times are in your hands. Amen

Prayer concern: Someone who has suffered a stroke

Daily Reflections

From the depths

Out of the depths I cry to you, O LORD.
❖ Psalm 130:1

In sincere sorrow for his own sins, the psalmist cries out to God. It is from the depths of faith, as well as of guilt, however, that the psalmist calls out. And it is from a sense of failure, his self-confident pride is gone, that he now humbly pleads to be heard.

We are reminded of Job, who also cried out to God. Even as Job sits on the dung heap of his former life, his trust in God makes a marvelous faith statement. Furthermore, we are often amazed by the early believers in the New Testament. They were people just like you and me, who rejoiced under the most dire circumstances. Paul, for example, wrote some of his most soaring words while he was in prison.

This level of faith may seem impossible to us. But by the amazing grace of God, we too can find the faith to praise God's mercy, even among our ashes.

NANCY NAU-OLSON

Dear Lord, grant us the faith to proclaim your mercies, even in the deepest valleys of our lives. Amen

Prayer concern: Christians in South Africa

Daily Reflections

Praise for the past

You showed favor to your land, O LORD; you restored
the fortunes of Jacob. ❖ Psalm 85:1

Sometimes the joy of anticipation is flawed in the process of
fulfillment. A long-planned trip can be marred by the fact that
the luggage gets lost at the first stop. A happy wedding is
forgotten in the hard work of making a marriage.

The people of God know of such experiences. We don't
know just what prompted the psalmist to pray the prayer that
is Psalm 85. But something seems to have happened that
caused distress. How can we face the hard facts of life when
things do not turn out the way we anticipated?

One way is to recall the past with its blessings and
to praise God. "You showed favor ... restored the fortunes ...
forgave the iniquity ... covered all their sins ... set aside all
your wrath and turned from your fierce anger." All that and
more God has done in the past.

STANLEY D. SCHNEIDER

*Lord, help us to remember your goodness. Accept our
praise for that. Amen*

Prayer concern: People facing hardships

Daily Reflections

The way of the righteous

He is like a tree planted by streams of water.
❖ Psalm 1:3

A strong, leafy tree flourishing by the side of a riverbank, roots sunk deep in the earth, can be a symbol of health, vigor, and beauty. Even when rain is scarce, such a tree does not die. Sun and heat do not wither it. The tree bears fruit in season. It is nourished by the flowing water, its constant source.

That tree proves a fitting analogy to the righteous person, one who tries to do right by the measure of God's will. Such a person is fed by spiritual rivers, divine commands, and promises that never fail. And how is the righteous person nourished? "His delight is in the law of the LORD." That person's source of strength is the Word of God. And through this, he or she is fed.

As a result, spiritual health shows. Spiritual people have a serenity of heart, mind, and spirit because they have a right relationship with the Lord. They are righteous people by the forgiving grace of God.

HILDEGARDE KAMPFE

Dear Lord, help us to find time every day to receive our spiritual nourishment from your Word. Amen

Prayer concern: Renewers of the church

Daily Reflections

God's way

> And afterward, I will pour out my Spirit on all
> people. ❖ Joel 2:28

Ancient Hebrew writers described two ages: the corrupted
Present Age and the glorious Age to Come. As God's chosen
people, the Jews eagerly waited for God to break into history
and lift up the nation of Israel. But between the two ages
would come a time of terror and destruction—the Day of the
Lord. Joel predicts this time of judgment in chapter 2.

Centuries later, in his first sermon in Acts, Peter quotes
Joel. Peter is convinced that the Day of the Lord has already
come: the prophecy has been fulfilled—but without the wide-
spread destruction. Instead, God has entered history in the
loving person of Jesus Christ.

Sometimes our expectations of God are like those of the
people of Israel. We too hope God will "save" us from the
tedium or tragedy of our lives. But our ways are not God's.
Once again, God enters into history, not with spectacular
solutions, but with the helping and healing Spirit.

JULIE DENNISON

*God, help us to be surprised and delighted by your way.
Amen*

Prayer concern: Those waiting for good news

Daily Reflections

Strange testimony

> But the Jews were jealous; so they rounded up some
> bad characters from the marketplace, formed a mob
> and started a riot in the city. ❖ Acts 17:5

Sometimes those people who most resent our work for Jesus Christ give strange testimony. By their very opposition, they give witness to the fact that we are not to be ignored.

It is insulting to have an enemy of the gospel ridicule you when you seek to do God's will. Have you ever stopped to think that it could be a greater insult if our enemies thought our message was not worth opposing?

What better compliment could Paul have received than that which came from his opponents when they basically said, "These men ... have turned the world upside down!" What an exciting accusation to have hurled at you! Even though they were nearly blind with jealousy, the bullies of Thessalonica knew there was dynamite in the message Paul and Silas preached.

We'd rather have peaceful times. We'd rather have our neighbors agree with us. But if and when they don't, we take courage. What we're doing matters. That's worth a lot.

DAWN M. PROUX

Embolden us, Lord, to live the truth. Amen

Prayer concern: Those who suffer

Daily Reflections

Stronger than superglue

Who shall separate us from the love of Christ?
❖ Romans 8:35

A feeling of panic swept over me. The superglue held my thumb and one finger captive. How could something that looked so harmless have such power? I frantically read the label. Superglue is an instant adhesive and has a tensile strength up to 5,000 pounds per square inch. Excessive force may tear skin. How could I hope to free my finger?

Tears stung my eyes, what could I do? I called the emergency number and a calming voice informed me that, if I put my hands in water, eventually the glue would release its hold. I put my hand in water and eventually my finger and thumb came unglued. As strong as superglue holds some things, it still can be detached.

How fortunate we are that nothing can separate us from the love of Christ. No matter what type of personal tragedy strikes, God is there with us, upholding us through difficult times.

VICKY LEE HOFFMAN

Thank you, Lord, that nothing can ever separate us from your love. Amen

Prayer concern: Emergency workers

Daily Reflections

Remember the Sabbath

When will the New Moon be over that we may sell grain, and the Sabbath be ended that we may market wheat? ❖ Amos 8:5

When I spent a school semester in Germany, our advisor told us to be sure to get enough food on Friday for the weekend— stores were closed Saturday afternoon and all day Sunday. That is a concept foreign to most of us in the United States, who are used to shopping at almost any hour.

Amos talked about people who anxiously waited for the Sabbath to be over so they could get back to business. How those people would have enjoyed modern America, where much of society revolves around making money. Some big businesses trample their employees, manufacture goods in parts of the world where labor is exploited, or ignore the way their industry might damage the environment.

Are we so caught up in the quest to obtain wealth that we ignore our Lord, our families, our other obligations to God's world? Do we forget to honor the Sabbath?

EMILY DEMUTH ISHIDA

Lord, help us to slow the pace of our lives and always to put you first. Amen

Prayer concern: The environment

Daily Reflections

Losing our lives

For whoever wants to save his life will lose it,
but whoever loses his life for me will save it.
❖ Luke 9:24

The Bible often seems to show us an upside-down world when compared with the world we live in today. In today's reading, Jesus speaks a word that flies in the face of our own nature, and of the high achievement, me-first orientation of our time.

This talk of denying ourselves and losing our lives to be followers of Jesus sounds gloomy at best. How can we really be who we are if we do not develop and progress in keeping with our potential? The important point in this verse is that in Christ we deny ourselves and lose our lives for something else—something far richer and brighter than we can even imagine. The life of faith always frees us *for* something else. It does not just free us *from* something. So also our lives are lost for the new life in Christ. When we know what it means to lose our lives for Christ, there is no true loss—only gain.

STEPHANIE FREY

Gracious Lord, fill our lives with the unsearchable riches of your grace. Help us see that losing life in you is only gain. Amen

Prayer concern: Those who resist God's gifts

Daily Reflections

Good stewardship

I tell you, use worldly wealth to gain friends for
yourselves, so that when it is gone, you will be
welcomed into eternal dwellings. ❖ Luke 16:9

I never understood the parable of the dishonest manager until
I learned that the debts the manager forgave provided the
money from which the manager would have been paid. So the
manager was praised, not for giving away his master's money
but for shrewdly giving away his own to win friends in the
long run.

Even when we understand that the steward was not giving
away his master's money, however, it strikes us as strange
that Jesus would advise us to make friends through dishon-
esty. If we set aside our confusion about this story, though, we
find an important message about our stewardship of the
gospel, God's creation, our money, possessions, relationships,
and ourselves. We are to use wisely everything God has given
us in order to serve our true master in heaven.

In creating the world, God put an enormous amount of
wealth before us. We are called to use the wealth in such a
way that our use will benefit others and in a way that will be
pleasing to God.

EMILY DEMUTH ISHIDA

*Lord God, you have given us so much. Help us return it
to your glory. Amen*

Prayer concern: Business people

Daily Reflections

Sometimes we need help

> I pour out my complaint before [the LORD]; before
> him I tell my trouble. ❖ Psalm 142:2

Young Andrea was moving her dollhouse down the steps from her bedroom to the family room. The load was too big for her. She needed help, but Andrea was determined to do it herself. As she neared the bottom step, she stumbled, and the dollhouse crashed to the floor. The chimney broke off the house.

Andrea burst into tears. Her parents, who had been watching close by with bated breath, rushed to her aid. Her dad assessed the damage and assured her that he was able to fix the chimney. But Andrea's tears quickly turned to anger. "You should have helped me," she said. "Then this wouldn't have happened."

"But you never asked us to help," her parents responded.

We often try to tackle life on our own. Meanwhile, God waits by our side until we discover our weakness, admit our need, and ask for help.

KEVIN E. RUFFCORN

Stand by us, Lord, for we cannot live life alone. Amen

Prayer concern: Children

Daily Reflections

Keeping love alive

For God so loved the world that he gave his one
and only Son, that whoever believes in him shall
not perish but have eternal life. ❖ John 3:16

Most healthy relationships have their bitter-sweet elements
where love and hate come together. But apathy partakes of
neither love nor hate. Apathy is a cruel lack of interest.

We are in danger of falling into a gray pool of apathy concerning things of God. The organized church is not often
attacked by hate-filled opponents. Yet the church often fails to
reach its goals due to inner stagnation.

Our most beloved rallying points have taken direct hits.
The Lord's Prayer is rattled off without thought, the depths of
wisdom in our liturgy are yawned at, and one of the most
beloved verses of all time, John 3:16, is in danger of becoming
a cliché. We must constantly struggle to find fresh new ways
of reading and studying the Bible. Keep love alive!

DAVID A. SORENSEN

*Lord, continue to call us back to your ever-creative love.
Forgive us our apathy and restore us to your fresh love.
Amen*

Prayer concern: A school bus driver

Daily Reflections_____

_____

_____

_____

Give glorious praise

Shout with joy to God, all the earth! Sing the
glory of his name. ❖ Psalm 66:1-2

God is worthy of praise and thanksgiving. The Lord's name is
glorious in and of itself. God's power is awesome and without
comparison. All the earth worships and sings praises to God.
When Christians gather on the Lord's Day, they gather first
and foremost to worship God. We call our liturgy a service
of worship in praise and adoration of God. We do not come to
the sanctuary preoccupied with our own individual needs,
however we may perceive them. Instead, we come as a fellowship of believers mindful of our greatest common need—
to worship and praise our great God for all we have received
through unearned, divine mercy.

Our brothers and sisters in the Orthodox Church can
teach us much about doxology as the center of Christian
worship. Believers do not come to the Lord's house to be
entertained or cajoled. They come as creatures in pure,
unashamed adoration of the Creator; to praise God in one
doxological voice of thanksgiving.

BRUCE WILDER

*Lord God, we add our voices to those of believers every-
where who praise and glorify your holy name. Amen*

Prayer concern: Our life of worship

Daily Reflections

_____

_____

_____

Grace

Carrying his own cross, [Jesus] went out to the place of the skull (which in Aramaic is called Golgotha). ❖ John 19:17

The procession moved slowly up the hill. A slight rain had fallen in the night, the birds were circling overhead, and the sun shone on a beautiful, warm spring morning. This should have been a day for joy and hope.

Surely Jesus must have seen all that—the fields ripening, the flowers blooming along the wayside, and the sun shining above the valley. This was the beautiful world that God had made—a beautiful world, so far removed from the tears and hate and pain that brought this procession to the place called Golgotha.

Jesus was there because he wanted to be there. The last thing he saw before his death was the evil of angry faces, cursing and taunting him. The last he felt was pain and loneliness. There they crucified him. It happened because he saw each of us as we were and as we are, and despite it all, he loved us.

LUTHER ABRAHAMSON

Thank you, Jesus. You were willing to go to the cross so that we might always remember your compassion. May we return to be renewed by the assurance of your love. Amen

Prayer concern: The church

Daily Reflections

Believing in the Lord

Mary Magdalene went to the disciples with the news: "I have seen the Lord!" And she told them that he had said these things to her. ❖ John 20:18

"I have seen the Lord!" Mary's words did not bring an immediate end to the despair and hopelessness of the grieving disciples. Only gradually did the darkness of Holy Saturday give way to the glorious light and life of Easter.

It is an ancient custom to respond to the announcement "Christ is risen" with "He is risen, indeed!" This was not, however, the response given on the first Easter. On the evening of Easter, the fearful disciples still kept their doors locked (v. 19). Mary's announcement of the resurrection seemed to fall on deaf ears.

Resurrection, new life, comes to our lives in various ways—sometimes gradually, sometimes suddenly, sometimes after a long wait, sometimes without our expecting it. Since we are not alone, we benefit from one another's experience of resurrection. Even when we are not sure, we can join the chorus of believers. Their faith helps us to say, "Christ is risen, indeed!"

CHERYL MATTHEWS

Lord, I believe. Help my unbelief. Amen

Prayer concern: Those who proclaim the resurrection

Daily Reflections_____

_____

_____

_____

For all believers

> And afterward, I will pour out my spirit on all
> people. ❖ Joel 2:28

The term "all people" used by the prophet Joel refers specifically to the covenant people of Israel. But when Peter recalls
Joel's word in his Pentecost sermon, he expands the application to the New Testament's sweeping everyone (Acts 2:21).

The gift of the Spirit is not limited to the professional
servants in the church. Nor is it limited to those who have
been formally trained in theology. Joel's announcement points
to a sovereign, gracious God who will not allow anyone to
stand in the way of the Holy Spirit.

I have frequently been impressed by the spiritual wisdom
and grace found in some people living in a very primitive
society. I recall a number of such people whom I have met in
different churches in the world. Some of these people were
not able to read, but they would listen and think. Who, other
than the Holy Spirit, could tutor them in their incisive grasp
of the meanings of the gospel?

FREDERICK A. SCHIOTZ

*Lord, help us to govern our actions by the leading of the
Spirit, who comes to us in Holy Baptism. Amen*

Prayer concern: Bible translators

Daily Reflections_____

_____

_____

_____

Jesus is at our table

> May the Lord make your love increase and over-
> flow for each other and for everyone else, just as
> ours does for you. ❖ 1 Thessalonians 3:12

After a trying day working with needy people, Sara, a social
worker, joined her husband and daughter at a fast-food
restaurant. As she was about to bite into her sandwich,
seven-year-old Jessica reminded Sara that they forgot to pray.
Sara hurriedly mumbled, "Come, Lord Jesus, be our guest."

As the family continued their meal, a man in tattered
clothes with a disabled foot walked over and said to Sara's
husband. "Please sir, I haven't eaten all day. Could you buy me
a sandwich?"

"Sure," the husband said. "Let me go with you to pay for it."
Afterward, the stranger whispered his thanks.

When Jessica asked why her father was doing this, Sara
said, "It's because of something Jesus said. When you give a
cup of water or some food to someone in need, it's like giving
it to him."

Then Jessica said, "Mom, your prayer was answered. You
asked Jesus to be our guest, and he really did come!"

WILLIAM LUOMA

Lord, let us never forget those in need. Amen

Prayer concern: Those living in poverty

Daily Reflections_____

The magical gift

Guide me in your truth and teach me, for you are
God my Savior, and my hope is in you all day long.
❖ Psalm 25:5

When author James Michener was 9 years old, he mowed the
lawn for an elderly neighbor, Mrs. Long. She could not afford
to pay him much, but she did promise Jim a Christmas present. Young Jim had visions of a baseball glove, or ice skates,
or perhaps a toy train. But when she handed him his present,
it was definitely not a glove, or skates, or a train. It was a flat
box, about 9 by 12 inches.

When Jim opened it Christmas morning, he found a box
with 10 flimsy sheets of black paper labeled "Carbon Paper
Regal Premium." Aunt Laura, a schoolteacher, was there and
said, "It's magic!" She took some paper and showed him how
it works.

Years later, Michener said, "I was enthralled! I can honestly say that on that Christmas morning I understood as
much about printing and the mystery of disseminating ideas
as I have learned in the remaining half-century of my life."
It was not what he wanted or expected, but something much
better ... just like the surprises the Lord has for us.

WILLIAM H. LUOMA

You surprise us, O Lord, with more kindness than we
deserve. Amen

Prayer concern: Writers

Daily Reflections

Treasures to God

> They saw the child with his mother Mary, and they bowed down and worshiped him. Then they opened their treasures and presented him with gifts of gold and of incense and of myrrh.
> ❖ Matthew 2:11

The precious gifts the magi offered to Mary's child were given in gratitude, a sign that the magi acknowledged that this baby was a king.

Sometimes when we give, we merely are reaching for our purse or billfold. On occasion, we may be tempted to compare our gifts with what others have given. Our gifts to God are so much more than matters of habit or competition. When we give to the church, we are giving to the Lord and to the extension of God's kingdom. Even more important, our giving is an act of worship, a way of acknowledging the one who gives us life.

The incense of a loving heart is fragrant to God, and the gold of good deeds and selfless acts are shining gifts to our Lord. In proportion to the gifts God has given us, ours are small. But they are acceptable because they are given with cheerfulness and love. Like the magi, we too can offer our treasures to God.

NORMA SCHIRCK

Lord Jesus, king of creation, guide us that our gifts may be acceptable in your sight. Amen

Prayer concern: Those traveling

Daily Reflections